LEGAL INSTITUTIONS
IN MANCHU CHINA

LONDON SCHOOL OF ECONOMICS

MONOGRAPHS ON SOCIAL ANTHROPOLOGY

Managing Editor: Ioan Lewis

The Monographs on Social Anthropology were established in 1940 and aim to publish results of modern anthropological research of primary interest to specialists.

The continuation of the series was made possible by a grant in aid from the Wenner-Gren Foundation for Anthropological Research, and more recently by a further grant from the Governors of the London School of Economics and Political Science.

The Monographs are under the direction of an Editorial Board associated with the Department of Anthropology of the London School of Economics and Political Science.

Judicial Process (*see page* 69)

LONDON SCHOOL OF ECONOMICS
MONOGRAPHS ON SOCIAL ANTHROPOLOGY
No. 24

Legal Institutions in Manchu China

A Sociological Analysis

by

SYBILLE VAN DER SPRENKEL

UNIVERSITY OF LONDON
THE ATHLONE PRESS
NEW YORK: HUMANITIES PRESS INC

Published by
THE ATHLONE PRESS
UNIVERSITY OF LONDON
at 4 Gower Street, London WC1
Distributed by Tiptree Book Services Ltd
Tiptree, Essex

First edition, 1962
First paperback edition, with corrections, 1966
Reprinted, 1971; *with new matter*, 1977

U.K. SBN 0 485 19624 7
U.S.A. SBN 0 391 00755 6

First printed by
ROBERT CUNNINGHAM AND SONS LTD
ALVA

Reprinted by photo-litho by
WILLIAM CLOWES & SONS, LIMITED
LONDON, BECCLES AND COLCHESTER

Foreword

As a student of Sociology I had been puzzled before going to China at the fact that westerners should ever have sought extra-territorial rights in a country whose civilization was in so many respects superior to our own.

My husband and I spent the years 1948 and 1949 in North China, where he was visiting Professor at Nankai University, Tientsin, under the auspices of the British Council. I was for a time lecturer in the Modern Languages Department at Nankai and later on the staff of the British Council Centre, Peking. Until the fighting actually reached Tientsin, we lived among our colleagues and students on the university campus, where at the time we were the only foreigners. In Peking after 'Liberation' my work brought me into contact with teachers in schools, and with staff and students in the universities; I conducted English conversation classes through the summer and autumn of 1949 which were attended by Chinese office-workers, and with Chinese friends as guides I visited industrial co-operatives and craftsmen's workshops.

From our students and colleagues at Nankai in 1948 we learned something of police methods, and once as a consequence we encountered a judge sent from Nanking (during the hyper-inflation) to try those suspected of communist sympathies—but with insufficient funds to set up his court. Later our own contacts with officialdom multiplied, as permits were required for journeys outside the city, or to import books and on other occasions; and once our curiosity to see a temple fair, combined with the inefficiency of the permit-issuing office, resulted in our being held under arrest for six hours. We heard about the new People's Courts, but had no experience of them ourselves. Despite the fascination of events and their impact on the lives of our friends and on us, however, these years of upheaval and suspicion, at the climax of a civil war and the inauguration of a new regime, were no time for pursuing dispassionate social enquiry.

When I returned to England in 1950, I decided to make a study of the traditional Chinese legal system, and I eventually submitted a thesis on this as part of the requirement for a Master's degree in the University of London.

At the London School of Economics I received supervision and encouragement from Professor M. Ginsberg and Dr M. Freedman, and the stimulus of fellow-researchers in the Departments of Sociology and Anthropology, while I was able to continue my study of Chinese and learn some Japanese at the School of Oriental and African Studies.

I owe Otto van der Sprenkel a debt of gratitude, first for tolerant encouragement with a subject he thought an unwise choice, and since then for much help at various stages of the work. Among Sinologists from abroad, I should like to thank especially Professor Balazs, Professor Fairbank, Professor Hulsewé and Professor van der Valk for the inspiration derived from their visits.

I am grateful to the Australian National University for the opportunity I have had in the Department of Far Eastern History of studying earlier developments, so as to make better sense of Ch'ing institutions, and of revising, correcting and adding to the original study. Professor FitzGerald has kindly read the typescript.

The text translated in Appendix 4 is not an easy one, and I wish to acknowledge many generous hours of help given, in the earlier stages, by Mr Lo Hsien-hao, Mr Piet van der Loon and Mrs H. M. Wright, and, in correcting the final version of this and Appendix 5, by Dr Wang Ling. Mr S. Yanada helped me with texts in Japanese.

I also wish to thank the Wenner-Gren Foundation for Anthropological Research for permission to quote from Dr Hu Hsien-chin's monograph, 'The Common Descent Group in China and its Functions' and the Geography Department of the London School of Economics for preparing the map and diagrams.

Mrs Ines de Rachewiltz of the School of Oriental Studies in the Australian National University has most kindly undertaken the work of typing the index of Chinese characters, the extra calligraphy required being done by Mrs Wu Huang Chieh.

Publication has been assisted by a grant from the funds administered by the Universities China Committee in London.

Finally, because of the distance between London and Canberra, this book must have involved Dr Stirling in more work than usually falls to the editor.

S. v.d. S.

Canberra,
November 1960

Preface to the 1966 Reprint

IT SEEMS that interest in legal and related institutions in China has grown rapidly since I began my researches, and in the time since I completed my manuscript a number of books and articles have appeared. I am glad of this opportunity to include these and make good a few earlier omissions in a supplementary bibliography.

As it is not possible in this edition to include revised references throughout the text, I should like to draw attention particularly to the additional material on administrative structure and judicial machinery contained in the authoritative books of Professor Hsiao Kung-chuan and Professor Ch'ü T'ung-tsu; to Professor Bodde's scholarly assessment of the Chinese achievement in the field of law; and to the illuminating work of Professor Skinner, which offers a new perspective on the balance between various aspects of social structure—rural-urban relations and the relative significance of official and spontaneous organisation in rural communities. The titles of the other works indicate the points at which they are relevant.

I think that it is true to say that the effect of recent studies is in the main to re-inforce rather than to invalidate one another. Except for a few matters of detail, I should wish to stand by what I wrote, so perhaps a revised edition may wait until it is possible to take account of other work now going on.

I should like to mention two more general books which have appeared since I wrote this. Perhaps others besides myself may be relieved to discover from Professor Hart's *The Concept of Law* that it is not only in the Chinese part of the field that scholars still face problems about the exact content of the term. And finally I should like to thank Professor Sawer of The Australian National University for doing what I hoped would some day be done—namely, including material from recent studies of Chinese law in his comparative survey, *Law in Society*.

S. v.d. S.

Leeds,
February 1966

Preface to the 1977 Reprint

THIS LITTLE BOOK grew out of a thesis, presented in 1956 in the University of London, which I had the opportunity of preparing for publication when I held a research post at the Australian National University, Canberra.

At about that time, and unknown to one another, a number of scholars in different parts of the world were researching in closely related areas and the results of their work appeared in close succession. Reprinting for the paperback edition gave me the chance to mention some of this work.

The eleven years since then have seen an increase beyond all expectation in the amount of scholarly interest directed to both Chinese law and Chinese society, and with the expansion and greater cohesiveness of the profession, standards of scholarship and of the training that young disciples can be given have risen appreciably. The researches of historians and social scientists are steadily making traditional Chinese society less opaque, and some of the gaps in knowledge I referred to when first writing have to some extent been filled. Much more is known for example about secret societies, about servile status and about temple and other organisation in Chinese towns and cities—though each addition opens up more questions. The study of Chinese law itself is finding a place in the curriculum of universities and law schools in many parts of the world and series of specialist publications are already well established.

It is gratifying to know that students have continued to find *Legal Institutions in Manchu China* useful. With so much more now available, it will no doubt be used mainly as an introductory overview, soon to be followed by more detailed recommendations. With this, and the need to keep costs down, in mind, I have not attempted comprehensive revision but have added only a page as postscript to chapter 6, to take account of some objections which have been raised—I think justly, and a short supplement of fairly specialised bibliography.

Leeds,
March, 1977

S. v.d. S.

Contents

Illustrations

Introduction

THE AIMS OF THIS STUDY

ONE of the aims of this book was to find out what has to be studied on the Chinese side before valid comparisons can be made between the Chinese and other systems of law, so that China's place can be assessed in a typology of legal systems. Professor Gluckman has drawn attention to similarities between *adat* law in Indonesia and African customary law,[1] and I think that those who are familiar with the material on these two areas (and, I hope, others) will be struck at some points by parallels in China. The differences may be as instructive as the similarities.

Anyone who sets out to study Chinese law—even supposing that he has a working knowledge of the language—is faced at the outset with a number of problems. He is confronted with a great deal of material of different kinds, all of which appears to have something to do with what is called law in other societies, yet it is difficult to see exactly what in China corresponded to the different branches of law as we know it—a problem familiar to students of pre-[modern]-industrial societies. We owe the earliest known reference to the use of iron in China (in the *Tso Chuan*) to the fact that in 513 B.C. the penal code was inscribed on cast iron *ting*, or tripods, and, we are told,[2] it was the significance attached to the code that made the event and the material worthy of mention. Successive dynasties had their legal codes and fourteen of the twenty-six Standard [dynastic] Histories (*Cheng Shih*) contain monographs on law and punishments. Chinese popular literature abounds in stories of court trials, and yet there did not develop in China either a legal profession or a science of jurisprudence. The Chinese law of contract, it has been said, was a branch of common law resting on the jurisdiction of clans, guilds and headmen of the village,[3] so if one wants to know what the law was, one has to look at other things than legal codes and courts, and customary law has recently claimed the attention of Chinese and Japanese researchers. It appears that much of Chinese social organization had a legal aspect, but it is not clear what relation law had to other institutions, nor what value legal studies have for a knowledge of Chinese society.

Valuable monographs have been written which throw light on the

[1] Gluckman (1949), p. 63. Full references are given in the Bibliography at the end of the book.

[2] Read (1937), p. 403. Characters for Chinese words are given in an index, p. 162.

[3] Escarra (1924), p. 239.

different legal and quasi-legal aspects of Chinese institutions, but it remains difficult to get a conspectus of the legal system as a whole. Recent works which have gone some way to fill the need should be mentioned. Professor Niida's very useful *History of Chinese Legal Institutions*[1] uses both documentary sources and modern research into customary law, and his book brings together a wealth of material, but his method is to follow institutions one by one in their development through the centuries without relating them to one another at successive stages. Dr Ch'ü T'ung-tsu's *Chinese Law and Chinese Society*,[2] on the other hand, is mainly concerned to relate the content of law at different periods, as recorded in codes and decisions, to the contemporary form of certain other institutions—marriage, kinship organization, class structure and religion—but it does not deal with unwritten law or with the agencies of enforcement or adjudication. So, in spite of these substantial contributions, the problems have not entirely disappeared. Professor Hulsewé's magnificent reconstruction of Han dynasty legal institutions will, when it is completed, give us a full picture of their working for Han times, but should we be justified in thinking that this will apply also to later periods?

The present study attempts a preliminary survey of the whole complex of legal and quasi-legal institutions but for a limited period, aiming at finding answers to such questions as the following: Of what did the traditional Chinese legal system consist? Who operated it, and with what objects? How were the different parts related to one another? Was it in fact one system or a plurality? What part did it or they play in the working of Chinese society? How were legal (or quasi-legal) institutions related to other social institutions?

THE CHOICE OF PERIOD

Various reasons suggested that the Ch'ing or Manchu period (1644–1911) would be the best to choose for this purpose. Its institutions deserve interest as being the culmination of the Chinese imperial system. The China of that period was that with which westerners first made large-scale contacts and which therefore they had to observe and describe to their fellow-countrymen in order to come to terms with it. The ruling dynasty, being itself non-Chinese and not able to take Chinese institutions for granted, had an interest in studying them and sponsored various encyclopaedic projects—including the compilation and publication of several collections of recorded law-cases, such as the *Hsing An Hui Lan*, which are fairly easily accessible. Moreover as the Ch'ing legal system was that in operation when the Chinese came into contact with western systems, it was what they had to adapt to meet changed world conditions—consequently the one they studied and criticized themselves. There is, therefore, taken altogether, a great deal of extra material for this period

[1] Niida (1951) [in Japanese].
[2] Ch'ü (1946) [in Chinese; published in English 1961].

to supplement the historical and literary sources available to students of other periods.

SOURCES USED

For a study of this kind there could clearly be no single main source: the information has had to be pieced together from wherever it could be gathered. In outline, my method has been to look first at Chinese official sources—the legal monograph in the dynastic history, the penal and administrative codes and collections of cases—for what they could be made to yield; next, to supplement this by wide reading in western accounts, which, besides helping to husband one's energies for use on the most fruitful Chinese material, have an intrinsic value for this kind of study, since western writers have felt it necessary to describe and explain things that were strange to them but which Chinese writers would regard as too familiar to call for comment. Sometimes I have found confirmation or amplification of matter so collected in specialist studies by modern Chinese and Japanese scholars, such as the study of the *pao-chia* system[1] by Wen Chün-t'ien, and, on a wide range of topics, in Professor Niida's history already referred to. Occasionally it has been possible to find the sort of detail that I was looking for in a general history of the period by a modern Chinese scholar—for example, what Hsiao I-shan writes of village self-government in his history of the Ch'ing period—and I have also found illustrations of particular points in Chinese popular novels and detective stories. Finally, in judging of the spirit in which magistrates and their advisors considered lawsuits and conducted investigations, I have drawn on a short book of advice to magistrates' advisors by Wang Hui-tsu (1731–1807) who, during the course of a long career, acted in this capacity to many magistrates. A translation of the relevant extracts is included as Appendix 4.

The materials in western languages fall into six categories:

(*a*) Contemporary first-hand accounts of China as they found it by western travellers, officials and missionaries—e.g. Barrow's *Travels in China*, Meadows's *Chinese and their Rebellions*, MacGowan's article on Chinese guilds.

(*b*) Translations from the Ch'ing dynasty penal code[2] by Staunton, Boulais, Lind and Jamieson (and, to a lesser extent, of Chinese ethical writings, by Legge, Waley, etc.).

(*c*) Studies of law and procedure, such as those by Alabaster and Jamieson, based on actual recorded cases and on personal observation of the operation of Chinese law from the authors' experience as foreign assessors in the Mixed Court at Shanghai.[3]

[1] See pp. 46–9.

[2] See later, pp. 56 and 58 ff.

[3] Set up 1864—to deal with cases involving foreigners in which the defendants were either Chinese or foreigners who did not enjoy extra-territorial privileges. See Keeton (1928), ch. viii. The story of the origins and development of this court

(*d*) Monographs on particular institutions—e.g. those by Hoang on marriage and property, by Hu Hsien-chin on lineage organization, and many others.

(*e*) Ad hoc reports by commissioners appointed to enquire into Chinese law and custom—by the Chinese Republican Government for all provinces of China (1930)[1]; by the Shanghai Municipal Council on the administration of Shanghai (the Feetham Report, 1931); by the Government of Hong Kong regarding Chinese residents in that colony.

(*f*) Twentieth-century investigations by sociologists or social anthropologists—some Chinese, like Fei Hsiao-t'ung and Lin Yüeh-hwa, and some western, Gamble, Kulp, Fried and so on.

Works in the last two categories, all rich sources, have to be judiciously used as guides to earlier times, but provided that allowance is made for known changes in conditions, much can be inferred from them. For example, while it is likely that the proportions of land held under different types of tenure may have changed quite drastically between 1830 and 1930, it seems less likely that the types of tenure would themselves have changed very much. Again, it may be that in modern conditions there is more possibility than there used to be for an individual to evade lineage or village discipline; however, to the extent that this did still exist in the nineteen-twenties or 'thirties, the methods by which it was then observed to be attained are probably fair indications of part at least of what happened formerly. In general, one knows that innovating policies met with resistance just because of the tenaciousness of custom.

LIMITATIONS

By collecting evidence for the period chosen from as many different parts of the field as possible, I have built up what I hope is a fairly reliable picture of the legal system as a whole and its wider social context. I have treated rural conditions rather more fully than urban because there is more sociological material available for Chinese villages than for Chinese towns. I have not, however, taken into consideration special conditions obtaining in outlying regions like Tibet, Mongolia or Manchuria. While I am aware, as the reader will realize, that it would be incorrect to assume the complete stability of society during a period of more than two centuries, I have not attempted here to relate changes in legal institutions and in other parts of the social system to one another. The sort of modifications

has great interest both from the viewpoint of international relations and that of legal history.

[1] In the event reports were not sent in for five southernmost provinces. For the circumstances of compilation and publication of this survey, see Kroker (1953), pp. 216–9. In this article the material for Shantung only is translated.

this would involve would not, I think, much affect the validity of the main argument.

Finally, I hope that what I have written will be of interest to sinologists, but I must remind them that this is primarily a sociological study and does not pretend to deal fully with all the questions that would occur to sinologists.

Map of China showing provinces in Ch'ing times

I

Some Relevant Aspects of Chinese Social Structure

THE Chinese Empire under the Manchu dynasty consisted of a large, relatively homogeneous central area—the Eighteen Provinces,[1] often referred to as China Proper—in which was contained the greater part of the population of the Empire, and a number of outlying territories: Manchuria, Mongolia, Sinkiang and Tibet. The central area was isolated by natural barriers: impenetrable mountain ranges on the west, deserts to the north-west, tropical swamp to the south and the Pacific Ocean on the east. Only in the semi-arid region to the north (which was unsuited to the characteristically Chinese style of cultivation) were the obstacles to movement and penetration, though still real, less effective. Here, where the sedentary Chinese had to face their barbarian pastoral-nomadic neighbours, they had long ago supplemented nature by building the Great Wall.

The compact area of China Proper thus isolated—and isolation is a factor which helped to produce a sense of cultural identity—is nevertheless characterized by great physical diversity. At its greatest extent, the Empire stretched from eighteen to fifty-seven degrees north, and a roughly similar distance from east to west. Geographers disagree about the number of natural regions into which China should be divided, but all agree on the great range of variations in topography, climate and vegetation to be found there.[2] China, particularly South China, is more mountainous than any comparable area in Europe or America, and the mountain ranges constitute internal barriers enclosing and isolating contiguous areas—hence the great importance of navigable rivers in linking together different regions. In Fukien the mountains also cut off the interior valleys from the sea, thus excluding this as a possible means of communication (facts no doubt related to the existence of 108 separate dialects in this province).[3]

This physical diversity was matched by a wide range of cultural pheno-

[1] Listed on p. 39.

[2] It is impossible to treat the geography of China briefly. For the geographical background see Needham (1954), ch. iv; Cressey (1934) and (1955); Gourou (1953), pp. 91–188; or Ginsburg (1958), pp. 155–238.

[3] Cressey (1934), p. 12.

mena. The civilization which began in the river valleys and plains of the north spread gradually southwards enclosing within its borders people of other cultures, some of whom never became completely assimilated to the Han Chinese. Languages of a number of minority peoples continued beside the numerous dialects of Chinese. In religion, in addition to a wide range of native cults and a sinicized form of Buddhism, Mohammedan communities were to be found in north-west and south-west China. Density of population was also very uneven over the area, there being great concentrations in the fertile riverine and coastal plains while mountainous districts and the interior (Szechwan excepted) were relatively sparsely populated.

Despite her natural barriers, China's isolation was never complete. Increasingly from the Han period onwards, people and ideas, skills and material culture crossed her frontiers in both directions, the outward traffic being perhaps the heavier. Neighbouring peoples borrowed Chinese writing, laws and techniques of manufacture; by land and sea routes her products reached distant places. Moreover, besides giving, the Chinese also gained, both from the missionaries and traders and from the 'conquest dynasties' that at various times ruled in North China. Until the nineteenth century, however, the effect of such contacts was usually to enrich, sometimes to disturb, but never to disrupt, the existing society.[1]

The civilization which flourished for thousands of years in relative isolation from the rest of the world, against the background of physical and cultural variety referred to above, had three broadly unifying features which were themselves interrelated: dependence on irrigated agriculture; a centralized, bureaucratic administration; and a literary tradition, the most important elements in which were ethical philosophy and history. A centralized hierarchical bureaucracy, which identified itself with an ethical and political orthodoxy, was able to impose on the governed a picture of society in which the unity of the whole was exaggerated, its own role was overstressed and the value of Confucian thought was overweighted in relation to that of other schools. (These features will be expanded in succeeding chapters.) Even if one is aware of this, it is often difficult to know how much allowance to make for the known bias and so to distinguish the reality from the deliberately fostered myth.

From the orthodox point of view society consisted of two broad divisions, people of culture and common people. The former were those who

[1] For a general discussion of the movement of ideas, see Needham (1954), section 7. A detailed account of the cultural exchanges between China and Central Asia and Persia will be found in Laufer (1919). The Chinese contribution to Japanese civilization is well described in the early part of Sansom (1946). For a case-history of the transmission of the Chinese inventions of paper and printing, see Carter (1955). On the borrowing of law, see, for example, Aubaret (1865). The best account of China's external trade is by Bonmarchand, in Lacour-Gayet (1953). Two recent studies of the reception of Buddhism in China are Wright (1959) and Zürcher (1959).

devoted themselves to classical learning, educating others and assisting the ruler in governing the mass, while in their leisure they pursued scholarly recreations like poetry and painting. They were supposed in their lives to set a good example to others by putting into practice the ethical teaching—as re-stated by Confucius, Mencius, etc. from the earlier *ching* or classics[1] and developed by their successors and commentators. The core of this was that good was to be promoted by the cultivation of personal virtue, which consisted in defining and conducting personal relationships with propriety, laying particular stress on relationships within the family. One owed respect, obedience and support to family superiors during their lifetime and veneration with prescribed ritual and within prescribed degrees after death. From these obligations there arose other derived obligations: to value one's body as a gift from one's forebears, to add lustre to the family name, to continue the line of descent and to acquire the means to provide fittingly for the departed.

Ordinary people, who performed the drudgery of life, were thought to be incapable of being cultured. We read in Mencius:

> . . . there is a saying, 'Some labour with their minds and some labour with their strength. Those who labour with their minds govern others; those who labour with their strength are governed by others. Those who are governed by others support them; those who govern others are supported by them. This is a principle universally recognized.'[2]

The division however was not rigid: theoretically it was possible to pass into the ranks of the upper class on merit (as will be explained in Chapter 4). Meanwhile the common people were supposed to follow the example set them by their superiors to the best of their ability.

Looked at from the bottom upwards, society must have presented a different picture. The great majority of Chinese people were peasant cultivators or small-scale skilled craftsmen. They were only interested in irrigation so far as it affected their own plots of land. Their experience of the administration was confined to contact, usually indirect, with the District Magistrate's *yamen*, which might be a day's journey away from their homes. Few could read—consequently, so far as the majority were concerned, their knowledge of the ethical teaching was only second-hand, though they did share in some of the beliefs which inspired it (as, for example, in the necessity of rites for departed ancestors) and they did therefore more modestly try to imitate the ritual practices of their 'betters'. The latter were probably defined in peasant eyes as those families which, because they had other sources of income—whether from rents or official salaries—were removed[3] from both the exertions of manual work and the

[1] For a convenient summary of the works constituting the Confucian canon, see Hsü (1935), pp. 14–15.

[2] Legge (1895), vol. ii, pp. 249–50.

[3] In both senses. Sociologists are coming to the view that this class commonly had their residences in towns. See later, pp. 24 f.

risks of trading, yet still lived well and enjoyed official favour. The lives of most peasants and artisans were bounded by the village community, except for occasional visits to neighbouring villages or to a town nearby, beyond which few had travelled. Because of the prestige learning conferred, and because it opened the way to power, influence and what appeared to the peasant as wealth and security, peasants were ready to make considerable sacrifices to obtain a literary education for their sons, who would then be lifted above the common level and be able to help the family in other ways; but only a minority achieved this, and the rest adopted by imitation the way of life of the community in which they grew up.[1]

Orthodox and 'realistic' views are combined more objectively in the observation of one social scientist. Wittfogel has suggested,[2] with acknowledgment to Max Weber, that in studying stratification in Chinese society the key criterion should be that of power, as evidenced by participation in the state apparatus. Those who did were the rulers; the rest were the ruled. Though the exercise of power was unequal at different levels of the bureaucracy, all its members, he claims, shared in the control of the mass of the commoners, who possessed no real independent power. The two 'classes' are to be further distinguished by the different criteria by which they were stratified internally. In the first, position in the hierarchy is the primary determinant, wealth secondary. 'Within the ruled class, types and dimensions of property are the primary determinants of social status, whereas differences in relation to the government tend in this apolitical world to play a minor role or no role at all.' As a first approximation this is an attractive theory, though, as I hope to show, some blurring of its clear-cut lines must be allowed for.

Peasants were constantly engaged in a grim struggle to keep above subsistence level. They cultivated small scattered plots with skill and patience, but on most holdings the ratio of labour to land was above optimum, and, while yields were high in terms of area, they were low per worker. Some extra income was earned from handicrafts carried on through the year by the women in the household and, in the slack farming season, by men. Such crops as cotton were of course sold for cash, but even when the crop grown was rice, most poor peasants would sell that and buy cheaper quality grains to eat themselves. Agriculture had its hazards; there were frequent floods and droughts, bringing bad harvests. Taxes had to be paid, rent too by tenant-farmers, and the expense of these and other social obligations—such as funerals and weddings—led many into debt from which it was difficult to escape. All peasants aimed

[1] This seems to be in accord with the distinction Redfield makes (in an interesting chapter, 'The Social Organization of Tradition') between a great tradition and a little tradition which co-exist in societies based on peasantry, each contributing something to the other. See Redfield (1956), p. 70.

[2] Wittfogel (1957), pp. 303–5.

at increasing their holding of land, but chronic aggregate land shortage was a feature of the rural economy and was exacerbated by unevenness of distribution.

Most villages had a few specialized craftsmen—such as carpenters, masons, brickmakers, papermakers and metalworkers—in addition to the simple handicrafts pursued at home. They were frequently members of poorer farming families and assisted on the family plots in the busy season, while their earnings might be of considerable significance in lifting their families out of the worst poverty. Not all villages were self-sufficient in these skilled crafts and an exchange of services went on between villages.

It was usual for a village to have at least one general shop, while larger villages had several. The margins on which business was conducted were small and retail trade involved much physical labour; the store-keeper had to attend fairs and markets at villages round about, carrying his wares slung on a pole or pushing them on a wheelbarrow. It was not an enviable way of earning a living and those who followed it did not command the respect of their neighbours.

As a way of life the cultivation of crops, even as a tenant, was preferred to trade or crafts, and the possession of land was highly prized. In addition to its intrinsic and practical value, land also conferred prestige, and a plot of land which had been owned by a family for generations acquired a symbolic and ritual significance, being the focus of the family and, part of it, the resting place of revered ancestors. Land was also the preferred form of investment, even though the return on it was less than could be obtained from some other types—large-scale trade or money-lending, for example. Yang Lien-sheng has suggested[1] that the reason for this preference may be found in the significance of land ownership for the obtaining of credit—either as a security to pledge against a loan, or at least to confer an impression of reliability and credit-worthiness, the farmer being considered a person unlikely to abscond.

Under the Manchu dynasty—apart from inalienable grants of land in Manchuria and around Peking to Manchu chiefs at the beginning of the dynasty—the traditional system was followed as regards land ownership in China, i.e. while theoretically all land belonged to the throne, in practice all arable land was privately owned and freely disposable,[2] subject to compliance with tax and corvee demands and regulations for valid sale. Waste land and uncultivable land belonged nominally to the Emperor (though not as a private estate) but grants of such land could be authorized by government officials to those who were prepared to reclaim and cultivate it.

[1] Yang (1952), pp. 1–2.

[2] Private ownership and freedom of sale in land (and a consequent tendency to concentration of ownership) dates back to the fourth century B.C. See Yang Lien-sheng (1946), p. 122.

There were, of course, gradations of wealth and degrees of poverty, but there was not in China a rigid division into landed and landless. To be a 'landlord' did not necessarily imply great wealth—though wealthy landlords did exist. For example, a widow, with young children and her late husband's parents to support, might rent out land until her children were old enough to cultivate it themselves, or a family which owned more than its members could themselves cultivate might rent out the surplus. Others in the same position preferred to hire help from those who possessed too little land or none. Every family would try to keep its holding of land intact (only resorting to sale when prolonged borrowing had failed to solve its problems) and, bearing in mind that there would have to be a division[1] at some date in the future, to buy more, if possible. It would aim at combining its labour-power and management skills—which varied through time according to the stage in life reached by its members—and its land-holding in the most productive proportions. The distribution of land was thus always in flux, some families being forced to mortgage and sell while others were able to buy or rent extra land.

Many different customary forms of tenancy were in force, the rents payable being fixed sometimes in cash, sometimes as a proportion of the crop (in which case the landlord usually supplied the seed) and sometimes in unremunerated labour on the landlord's plot at the busy season. (The negotiation of leases will be considered in Chapter 8.)

Jamieson estimated, on the basis of data collected from different parts of China, that one-half of the soil of China was tilled by peasant owners while the remainder was owned by retired officials and their families, or by corporate bodies like clans and temples which let it out for cultivation.[2]

Professor Tawney has drawn attention to a regional difference in the proportion of owner-cultivators to tenant-cultivators, the former preponderating in the north, the latter in the south.[3] To illustrate from surveys made in the nineteen-thirties: investigators at Ting Hsien in Hopei (North China) found[4] that land was cultivated by owners, part-owners and tenants in the ratio of 70 : 25·2 : 4·8 (=100); while Ch'en Han-seng found in Kuang-tung, in the south, that the percentage of tenants varied from 57 to 90, and he estimated the area owned by clans as collective landlords at one-third of the cultivated land in the province.[5] Between these, Dr L. K. Tao gave figures[6] for Chekiang as: owners 32·9 per cent, part-owners 30·4 per cent and tenants 36·7 per cent. Professor Tawney suggested that higher productivity and consequent investment of commercial capital in land explain the higher tenancy ratio in the south.[7] So far as this is due to higher productivity, it may have existed also in earlier

[1] See later, p. 16.
[2] Jamieson (1888), pp. 76–77.
[3] Tawney (1932), pp. 37–38.
[4] Gamble (1954), p. 64.
[5] Chen (1936), p. 3.
[6] Quoted in Tawney (1932), p. 35.
[7] Freedman (1958) also examines this in a detailed discussion on lineage landlordism at pp. 126–30.

periods of history, but in so far as growing commercialization is the reason, it may be dangerous to build too much on the figures quoted above for the period of our study.

Besides the form of tenure and the usual co-efficient of skill, peasant incomes depended on quantity and quality of land cultivated. Again, if we look at the evidence brought forward by twentieth-century investigations, great disparity is revealed in the size of holdings. For example, the Ting Hsien survey (of 400 farms in 62 villages, all of course in one area of North China) showed that per capita holdings ranged from 1·8 *mu*[1] on the smallest to 9·1 *mu* on the largest farms, while the averages were, for owners 5·2 *mu*, part-owners 4·2 and tenants 3·5 *mu*. After payment of rent, this must have meant a considerable range in income. Though the recent redistribution of land in China may be the most effective ever carried out, the idea has deep roots in China[2] and the importance attached to this part of their policy[3] by the *T'ai P'ing* leaders suggests that the problem was urgent in Ch'ing times.

In local society, ownership of property and size of income were important ingredients but they were not the sole determinants of status. Material success within the limits of opportunity was one criterion, but the way one used such success to behave according to socially approved standards also counted. One was expected to provide suitably for a parent's funeral, to make generous gifts when marriages or births occurred in nearby families, and to avoid being connected with anything shameful, like quarrels or divorce.[4] Age, experience and a reputation for wisdom all conferred prestige. Having the leisure to be seen often in the neighbouring town and to take part in discussions at tea-shops there was another asset. Further, where so many were completely illiterate, to have had any education gave disproportionate distinction, and, if it resulted in passing official examinations, with consequent privileges, so much the greater. Most important of all, probably, was having a past or present connection with someone in authority—a relative or perhaps a *t'ung hsüeh* (fellow-student) who held a post, preferably a high-ranking post, elsewhere,[5] but spent time at home between assignments. This would greatly affect the attitude of the authorities to his village or town and consequently enhance the prestige of the particular family which could claim ties with the in-

[1] The *mu* was a measure of area, not standard for all regions of China, but usually converted at the rate of 6 *mu* to one acre.

[2] As can be seen from the discussions on land policy and attempts at agrarian reform, often associated with fiscal policy, as early as the dynasties between Han and T'ang (third to seventh centuries A.D.). Yang (1946) describes the system of official land allotments known as the *chün t'ien* (equal field) system (pp. 127–8), and Balazs (1953) quotes a contemporary document on the agrarian situation c. A.D. 577 (pp. 276–81).

[3] Set out in *T'ien Ch'ao T'ien-mu Chih-tu* (Land System of the Heavenly Kingdom) in *T'ai-p'ing T'ien-kuo*, pp. 319–26. (See Bibliography, Official Compilations.)

[4] See later, pp. 82 f.

[5] See later, pp. 53 f.

fluential person.[1] In almost every neighbourhood there would be a number of persons who were respected by the rest, on account of their possession of a combination of some of these qualities, and who were extremely influential in local affairs—whether they exercised this influence directly or indirectly. The Chinese use the expression *shen shih* to describe them: this term is frequently translated as 'gentry', but its exact connotation is still a matter of controversy.

At the other end of the scale there were a number of occupations, the followers of which were universally despised—barbers, actors, musicians, prostitutes, etc—and in some areas there were people of officially servile status.[2] The remaining families fitted in somewhere along the line that joined the most respected and the most despised: this was not something fixed and immutable, but there was constant movement back and forth along it, as family fortunes (in the widest sense) ebbed and flowed.

In China the primary economic and social group for many purposes was the household, *hu*, which consisted of the elementary family, the *chia* (or those of its members who were, at any given time, living at home), plus domestic servants, labourers, or apprentices who lived with them. The Chinese family is in itself a subject on which volumes can be written. Suffice it here to say that it is a co-residential kinship group of varying composition, sharing in certain ritual practices and having a common budget—that is, dividing productive tasks among its members, pooling income and sharing its consumption. It might include any of the following: a married couple, their sons (or adopted sons), unmarried daughters and the wives of married sons, and it might extend to generations lower or higher to include children of married sons and the parents of the male member of the married couple who formed its core. The fact that it *could* include all these relatives led to exaggeration in the supposed size of the Chinese family[3]: recent studies have all shown an average of between four and six persons. Other members of the household shared the tasks with the family, on the principle of an agreed return being made to them, but they were not the equals of the family either in responsibilities or rights. The head of the family, *chia chang*, managed the business affairs of the household, exercised authority over its members and was its representative to the outside world. The *chia chang* was usually the eldest male member, most frequently the father of the family, but the eldest

[1] There is a saying: 'When our neighbour takes office we all rejoice.' See Scarborough-Allen (1926), p. 63.

[2] See later, p. 27.

[3] By westerners—who made the mistake of supposing that the upper-class families described in novels were typical of the whole population. The regular publication in China of population figures, by households and individuals, could have left the Chinese themselves in little doubt as to the reality, though the expression '*pa k'ou chih chia*' (a family of eight mouths) for an average family suggests that they may have had their own reasons for exaggerating. [This occurs in *Tso-chih yao-yen*, in section 34, which is not included in Appendix 4.]

brother might act as family head on his father's death or retirement, or, exceptionally, the role might be filled by a widow of strong character.[1]

A man was permitted to take more than one wife,[2] the first being considered the pricipal (*ch'i*) and others, who were as a rule her social inferiors also, secondary (*ch'ieh*), though the children of all wives were legitimate and no distinction was made between them in matters of inheritance. If we consider Chinese society as a whole, concubinage was not as common as one would suppose from reading novels and biographies that depict upper-class life. Expense was one obvious deterrent. When the Ting Hsien survey was made, concubines were reported in less than 1 per cent of the families and were significantly more numerous in families which had a land-holding of over 100 *mu* than in those with under 50 *mu*. The reason these people gave for having taken a concubine was the wish to have a son.[3] In earlier times this was the official reason for countenancing the practice: under the Ming dynasty, and the Ch'ing, until the rule was abrogated in 1740, a man of the people was not permitted to take a concubine until he was 40 years of age, and then only if he had not any sons.[4] For Chinese of all classes, the desire to avoid the shame of being without descendants was probably often the true motive,[5] but sometimes there were also other reasons. Besides the possibility of gratifying the desire for pleasure and prestige which the system offered those who had the means, another motive no doubt existed in the dissatisfaction felt by some men with the marriage arranged for them by their families and their wish to exercise personal choice.[6] (For unhappily married women there was no such simple and socially approved solution.[7])

Another method of ensuring the continuance of the family was by the adoption of an heir.[8] That this was done deliberately with a view to providing for the succession to the line of descent is indicated by the term used to describe this type of adoption, *ssu chi*, 'to continue the succession'

[1] Among families surveyed at Ting Hsien, the age of the *chia chang* ranged from 15 to 80, though 86 per cent were between 30 and 69. Of 515 families, six had women as *chia chang*.

[2] The rules applying to marriage, betrothal, adoption, incest, divorce, etc. are very comprehensively set out in *Le mariage chinois au point de vue légal* by P. Pierre Hoang, Shanghai, 1898, revised by the author, 1915. (Cited as 'Hoang 1915', as my page references are to that edition.) Or see Möllendorff (1893).

[3] Gamble (1954), p. 38.

[4] Lingat (1952), p. 23.

[5] See, for example, biographies of Ts'ui Shu and Wu Ju-lun in Hummel (ed. 1943 and 1948). From the information given and the dates, it appears that the need for a male heir was the reason for taking a concubine.

[6] See, for example, Waley (1956), p. 34.

[7] Divorce by mutual consent and under certain other conditions was allowed. A man could re-marry, but not a woman. See Hoang (1915), p. 110; Lang (1946), pp. 40–41.

[8] Martin Yang reports a general prejudice in his Shantung village against plural marriages and preference for adoption as a way of solving the problem of childlessness. See Yang (1945), p. 115.

(which is distinguished from adoption from other motives, e.g. benevolence, from within the lineage, *kuo fang*, or from outside it, *ch'i yang* or *ming ling*). If a man had no son by either wife or concubine he was required by law to adopt an heir,[1] selected according to fairly clear rules from among agnates. In case of difficulty in providing for succession to several branches of the lineage, the senior branch had prior claim over other branches in securing an heir. It was permitted for one man to be heir to two or more lines of descent and in many parts of China[2] it was customary for such a man to take a principal wife and found a family for each line. This practice was explicitly forbidden by edicts of 1755, 1815 and 1820 but the prohibitions were apparently ineffective. Only if there was no suitable lineage-member available for adoption as an heir (and a member of the same generation was not considered suitable) could an heir be taken from outside the lineage, and this would be recorded in the lineage genealogy, so that rules of lineage exogamy would not be infringed. It has been estimated that 5 per cent of Chinese families possessed adopted children.[3]

Sons inherited equally, *per stirpem*, with the exception of a small extra allowance to the eldest son, who had the responsibility of providing for surviving parents and the obligation to carry out sacrifices on behalf of the line of ancestors. There was social approval, however, for families which remained together without dividing the property, but the low average size of the peasant family shows that this was an ideal seldom fulfilled. There were probably more advantages, or fewer disadvantages, in keeping the family property intact when the 'property' was a business concern or land let out to tenants than in cases where it would have meant a larger working team sharing in tasks of cultivation on land held in common. Hard work and a grim struggle against poverty would have given rise to friction on the plot and in the kitchen, and such quarrels were

[1] '. . . un homme n'ayant pas de fils, ou ayant seulement une fille, est obligé par la loi d'adopter, comme héritier nécessaire, un fils d'un frère germain ou, à son défaut, un fils d'un cousin de la même souche paternelle du degré le plus rapproché. Un fils unique peut ainsi etre héritier nécessaire de deux familles, à savoir, de son père et de son oncle paternel privé de fils; autrement dit, il peut succéder à son père et en même temps être adopté légalement par son oncle. Adopté légalement, il jouit des mêmes droits qu'un vrai fils.' (Hoang, 1915, p. 20.)

For other aspects of adoption in China, see the article on this topic by J. J. M. de Groot, and Möllendorff (1893), pp. 182–7.

[2] This was reported (in the nineteen-thirties) from ten provinces. (Van der Valk, 1956, p. 45.)

A case from the *Hsing An Hui Lan* is quoted in Hoang (1915), pp. 104–5. The term used was *chien t'iao* or *ch'eng t'iao*.

[3] Jernigan (1905), p. 124, following Möllendorf and E. H. Parker. This (nineteenth-century) estimate is difficult to check. Twentieth-century village studies, though they all agree on the obligatoriness of adoption, are reticent on the degree to which it actually occurs. The Ting Hsien survey—the only one which attempts to measure it, so far as I know—reports adopted children in less than 1 per cent of the families. See Gamble (1954), p. 29.

avoided by partition.[1] This seems to have been the case particularly among the poorest: surveys have shown increase in family size with increase in income.[2] Whether the division took place at the death of the family head, or earlier or later, depended on the character and circumstances of each family.

Besides the disability of not sharing in the succession to land[3] (except in very rich families), the position of women within the family was influenced by the fact that a woman moved on marriage from her family of birth to live and work among her husband's family.[4] A woman had mourning obligations to her husband's ancestors which he did not reciprocate; at death, her memorial tablet would be placed with that of her husband; her sons would continue his line. Families had the expense of bringing up daughters only to lose them on marriage, whereas sons would continue to work as part of the family team into their maturity and commonly for much of their lives. Thus sons were considered more important than daughters. Moreover a woman suffered the disadvantage of going to work among strangers, sharing domestic duties with the other daughters-in-law of the house and being subject to the discipline of her mother-in-law (though her status did improve after she had borne a son.[5]) At disadvantage *vis-à-vis* her brothers in childhood, and as an adult a stranger in her new home, only in later life did she make up for her disadvantages when it became her turn to exercise authority over her sons' wives.

The *chia* was part of a wider kinship group, the *tsung tsu*, patrilineal clan or lineage, called by Hu Hsien-chin 'the common descent group'. This could vary in size from a few to hundreds of constituent *chia*. It was an exogamous unit: 'the most important function of the *tsu*', writes Fei Hsiao-t'ung,[6] 'is in the regulation of marriage.' It very often owned land,

[1] How friction led to division in one family is described in Lin (1948), pp. 122–3.

[2] See for example Gamble (1954), p. 55, table 3, where the average size of family is shown to range from four or five persons in families with holdings of less than 10 *mu* up to approximately 13 persons for families with holdings of 100 *mu* and over. Lang (1946), p. 136, shows the highest proportion of joint families among rural landlords.

[3] Women had rights over other personal property; for example, a husband might not dispose of his wife's valuable ornaments. At marriage, a daughter was provided with furniture to take to her new home, and some prestige accrued from lavish provision, if that were possible. But these were minor matters compared with land ownership. See Fei and Chang (1945), pp. 109–14; McAleavy (1955), p. 546.

[4] It could happen that, in a family without a surviving son, a man might be taken in as husband for a daughter. There was one case among 515 families at Ting Hsien, see Gamble (1954), p. 29. Such a man was despised, probably without any compensating gain in esteem for his wife. The term used is *chao hsü*, to invite a son-in-law.

[5] That this was crucial for status is demonstrated by the fact that a widow without children had undiminished obligations towards her own parental family. See Hoang (1915), Annotations, p. 30; also later, p. 83.

[6] See Fei (1939), p. 86.

the rent from which was used for ritual purposes or for the benefit of lineage members. In the larger *tsu* there were other groupings between it and the *chia*, namely the *fang* and the *p'ai*, both of which mean subdivision or branch. All had their recognized leaders, *p'ai chang*, *fang chang* and *tsu chang*, who exercised authority over their members in matters which concerned their respective groups. Variations in the intensity of clan ties in different parts of China will be discussed in Chapter 7 when their disciplinary and judicial aspects are considered.

Households clustered together in hamlets and villages (for which various words are used: *li*, *ts'un*, *chuang*, and many others). The Ting Hsien survey showed a variation in village size (within the same *hsien*) of from six to 1,200 families, while 75 per cent of the 443 villages had fewer than 200 families. Hsiao I-shan suggests a range of from three to over 100 families.[1] In areas of dense population one village would have several other villages within a mile radius in different directions. In many villages a mud wall encircled the cluster of houses, and it might appear to an observer that the village ended at the wall, separated from other similar walled villages by the intervening land. In fact, however, the land surrounding the cluster of dwellings was just as much part of the village as they were, and the village boundary was the limit of its land—its frontier, as it were, with the next village. The walled centre served as a natural focus or pivot for the whole, from which the various families went out to cultivate their plots, which were usually scattered over different parts of the village land.

Some villages are named after local geographical features or by reference to some historical association, while the names of others indicate the dominance, or earlier dominance, there of a particular clan, as for example *Shih-chia-chuang*—village of the Shih family. Whatever may have been the earlier situation, by the Ch'ing period a village might be co-terminous with a *tsu*, it might include two or more complete *tsu*, as a rule territorially distinct,[2] or the members of one *tsu* might be scattered between several villages.

In matters of general concern the village acted as a unit. It has been mentioned that some villages were walled, to protect residents and their dwellings against intruders. The building and repair of the village wall, for example, would be a corporate responsibility. With the same aim, a service of watchers was organized to safeguard the ripening crops. Maintaining the water-supply for agriculture, by irrigation or by digging a well, and seeing that no family took more than its fair share of the available water, would be another matter of concern to all. The government had no official representative of its own in the village[3] but left the villagers to

[1] Hsiao (1945), p. 102.

[2] See Freedman (1958), p. 3; Yang (1945), p. 6.

[3] The *ti-pao* (see p. 46) was a villager who acted as recognized agent for the authorities but had low status in the eyes of fellow-villagers.

manage their own affairs as long as its tax and corvee requirements were met and there were no major disturbances. Ceremonies in honour of local deities were performed, markets were held, and theatrical performances by travelling troupes of actors were arranged—by villages. If a dispute arose between Chang of village A and Wang of village B as to where the exact boundary of their holdings (i.e. the village frontier) lay, this would involve not only the two individuals concerned, and their families, but might easily develop into a dispute between their two villages.

All these activities went on under the direction or guidance of recognized leadership. There seems to have been some variation in the form which this leadership took in different villages—possibly a regional difference, but the evidence is insufficient to support or disprove such an hypothesis. D. H. Kulp, writing of Phenix Village (a one-clan village) in South China, speaks of a group of village leaders, apparently equal in rank, composed of family elders and respected scholars.[1] Leong and Tao speak of two distinct elements among village leaders: the first elected on the principle of annually rotating local representation, responsible for routine administration; the second, those who, because of personal prestige, are held to represent the village to the outside world, who are held responsible for its behaviour and consequently exercise authority and jurisdiction over their fellow-villagers.[2] Martin Yang, describing Taitou village in Shantung,[3] speaks of *the* village head, *chwang-chang*. There is an account of a one-lineage village near Canton where the village head was chosen from the most eminent branch of the lineage. In this village—presumably a constellation of hamlets, as it had a population estimated at between six and eight thousand—he exercised a customary authority, having the assistance of fourteen watchmen, and was recognized as responsible for the village by the government authorities, notwithstanding the fact that the government actually had official staff at a customs-house situated in the village.[4]

Yang also mentions an elected *she-chang* at the head of a number of villages,[5] and Hsiao I-shan suggests this as an alternative possibility to there being one or more leaders within the village.[6] If this is put together with what is said above about the distribution of *tsu* over villages, it seems that the type of village leadership and lineage structure may be connected. According to Hsiao, village leaders usually combined such duties with those of lineage leader, *tsu chang*: as there were usually several *tsu* in the village, *tsu* leadership, though it gave a judicial power, would not on its own have conferred any executive authority, he says. In a one-lineage village it is not always clear whether the head was excercising authority by virtue of position in the village or in the kinship group. Yang says of

[1] Kulp (1925), ch. v, 'Village Polity', p. 116.
[2] Leong and Tao (1915), p. 34.
[3] Yang (1945), p. 173.
[4] *Chinese Repository*, vol. iv, p. 414.
[5] Yang (1945), p. 173.
[6] Hsiao (1947), p. 101.

Taitou that at the annual election of the village head, *chwang chang*, 'some representatives of each of the four clans must be present or the election is not considered valid'.[1] The *chwang chang*'s 'constituency' seems to have been the separate lineages of which the village was composed rather than the same people thought of as residents of the locality. Elsewhere village leadership may have had more of the latter character (no doubt in places where *tsu* organization was weaker) and there were no doubt various blends of the two. It could be that where we hear of several villages having one person as leader, the residents of these villages, or the dominant ones, shared common *tsu* membership. (The head, *she-chang*, of the group of villages which included Taitou, though he lived in a neighbouring village, was a member of the lineage which dominated Taitou.) It should be possible to reach firmer conclusions on this question when the evidence in surveys of Chinese rural custom published in recent years in China and Japan has been studied.

Whatever the local variation in numbers and form, it seems clear that leadership and authority were exercised in the village by those who possessed the highest prestige (though they might act through a nominal head), and that the same members of the village acted as leaders in all spheres of activity. It is clear from Lin[2] and Hsiao[3] that village assemblies were formally constituted and met at regular intervals. Leong and Tao have called attention to the wide powers of the village as a corporate body, comparing them with those of an English county council,[4] while Hsiao suggests the comparison with a small state. (Intra-village jurisdiction will be examined in Chapter 8.)

Besides family, lineage and village communities, there were associations of individuals or, more properly as a rule, of family heads, based on shared interests or common needs. It was customary for people to associate together as a quasi-insurance against intolerable financial burdens (to provide for the expense of funerals, for example), and to exchange labour at seasons when a large team working together at the proper moment, e.g. for transplanting rice seedlings, was more efficient than it would have been for each individual family to work steadily through the year on its own plot. Members of different families also co-operated by joining loan-clubs, as a means of accumulating a little money, for whatever purpose it might be needed, and often there were several of these clubs in existence in a village at one time, each with a different membership. Another common motive for co-operation was to share the expense of a tutor to teach the sons of several families. Thus links were forged between people otherwise unrelated.

There are several proverbial sayings which indicate a desire to avoid complete dependence on kin. For example,

[1] Yang (1945), p. 175.
[2] Lin (1936), on the lineage-village.
[3] Hsiao (1945), pp. 102–3.
[4] Leong and Tao (1915), p. 34.

On a journey you need good company, at home you need good neighbours.
To be on good terms with one's neighbour is as good as finding a treasure.
Better good neighbours near than relations at a distance.[1]

It is a common misconception that in China loyalty stopped at the family or the clan. In fact, the Chinese excel at building personal relationships, whatever the bond on which these are based.

The attachment of Chinese people to their village was almost as strong as that to their kin. Even when circumstances forced them to spend much of their time away from their family home, they still felt it to be home. So long as any of their family lived there and owned graveland, it was considered desirable to be buried with the family ancestors, and Chinese would spend large sums to carry the body of a deceased relative home for burial. Pressure of circumstances might force whole families to migrate, but for many generations they would speak of belonging to the old native village.[2] To come from the same village, or at least from the same district, was immediately a common bond when people met elsewhere.

Though there was no formal unit of self-government higher than the village (or, as mentioned above, sometimes a village cluster), there were some informal links between villages. Some *tsu* extended to more than one village, so these villages were linked by kinship. Where a whole village was composed of one *tsu*, the rule of *tsu* exogamy involved relationship with members of other villages through affinal kin. Even where this was not so, there was commonly still a preference for choosing a bride from another village: this facilitated compliance with pre-marital avoidance rules, left greater scope for bargaining than there would be if families were meeting regularly, and then, if marital disharmony developed later, it would not lead to factional dissension within the village. Hsü has drawn attention to preferred marriage patterns as between *tsu*:[3] this must also have meant regular linking between villages. There was a certain amount of specialization in auxiliary occupations as between villages, one specializing in paper-making, another producing roof-tiles, while others made bricks, straw-hats, etc. This led to an exchange of products or skills—at village fairs, or in the course of visits to other villages by the craftsmen

[1] Scarborough-Allen (1926), p. 61.

[2] Nowadays, apparently, for overseas Chinese (drawn mostly from South China) thinking of returning, the pull exercised by the native village is dependent on the continued residence there of members of the particular household in which the emigré was brought up, or of persons closely related to it—not just someone related to him however distantly. See Freedman (1957), pp. 74–75. This may be a modern tendency or we may have here a regional difference in attitude (or a regionally patterned change in attitude). There is a hint that the sentiment of local attachment may have been stronger in North China than in South. See Yang (1945), p. 200. The Southern Chinese all had at least one migration as part of their tradition.

[3] Hsü (1948), p. 80.

concerned, or through the mediation of the local market town.[1] Villages were thought of as grouped according to which route or town-gate was their direct means of access to the town, and presumably people from different villages met on the way there.[2] We hear of certain temples and shrines which were frequented by people from a wide area. In the neighbourhood of T'aitou there were two such temples: the Confucian one was a meeting place for rural scholars, while peasant families visited the Buddhist one when they felt the need of blessing or protection. Significantly, both of these were located in or near the market town. Local leaders combined to manage temple affairs. (Shrines were located on hills on the outskirts of the region, but these were less frequented than the temples.) In strong hands, such an association might have become powerful in other spheres of activity, but this depended on local circumstances. If we except areas where villages combined to elect one head, as Yang reports from Shantung (and I am not sure that this was a pattern of common occurrence), there was no regular organization, other than the administration imposed over all, which subsumed the different villages.

A great deal more work will have to be done before we can write very confidently about the towns of China and the relation between the town and the country around it. It is clear that the terms 'urban' and 'rural' have a different meaning for China from that in which they are generally used.

Towns served as a market for the exchange of produce from surrounding villages; as an entrepôt for forwarding high-value products—like tea, silk and porcelain—to other areas, and for distributing commodities brought in from outside, whether for consumption or as the raw material for local crafts; as a focus of financial transactions, among which the most important was the supply of credit; as the headquarters of the local militia; and one town in each district, the *hsien* city, as the place from which the *hsien* magistrate administered the district. The character of towns varied according to which, or which combination, of these functions they served and which predominated. Crafts and trades grew up (the same person generally combining the roles of craftsman and tradesman) to supply those engaged in these basic activities, each specialized trade usually being

[1] The degree of self-sufficiency of the Chinese peasant economy is a matter on which opinions differ. I think that M. Yang is wrong in claiming that the peasant's dependence on outside supplies is a recent phenomenon (p. 198) though it has no doubt increased and sources of supply may be more distant. Goods have been transported over long distances—by easy stages—for centuries, and even low-value products were exchanged at neighbouring markets. (For a different view, see Wright (1957), p. 150.) On the other hand, it is possible because of this to exaggerate the degree of integration of the total Chinese economy which until recently was a series of small inter-connecting local economies of which some were harnessed to world trade before all had been integrated into a whole. See Adler (1957), pp. 10–11.

[2] See maps showing the relation of *hsien* or market town to surrounding villages in Fried (1953), Appendix; Yang (1945), p. 192; Gamble (1954). p. 5.

concentrated in one street or area of the town. The town was also the place where people from the different outlying villages most conveniently met one another—as well as travellers from more distant parts passing through—and exchanged personal news and information on such vital topics as movements in agricultural prices, climatic and other disturbances in the area around, bureaucratic changes, etc. Martin Yang gives a lively picture[1] of the importance of the market town in the lives of people in the villages around. 'Some member of nearly every household in the village is in the town on market day.'[2] (The various market towns around had 'staggered' market days, so those engaged as whole-time traders could attend them all.) Many informal discussions of village, or inter-village business, took place in the relative detachment of the town tea-house or wine-shop. The town was a centre—for business and recreation—for people from the surrounding villages as well as being home and workplace for those who lived there. It served in fact to integrate the whole area—somewhat loosely, it must be admitted—and to provide a tenuous link with the world outside.

Though there was no standard shape for towns, they were usually arranged on a rectilinear street-plan, with a few main intersecting thoroughfares and lanes of houses, *hutung*, lying between them. Most towns were surrounded by a wall, with gates that shut at night as protection against intruders, and there was included within the enclosed area a certain amount of agricultural land—presumably to enable them to stand a siege.[3] Towns of any size were divided into wards, *fang*, each *fang* managing its own affairs in the same manner as a village, though self-government based on locality was probably more important in the village than the town, where such functions were shared with associations based on craft or trade. (These will be discussed in Chapter 7.) There was no corporate government for the town as such.

Though other business forms did exist—partnership, for example—the most usual was the family concern, sons being trained in the craft by their fathers and in turn inheriting and continuing the family business. Non-kin extensions of the household were, however, more important in the town, both apprentices and trained assistants being employed, with consequent gradations in occupational status.

Apprentices were taken by both merchants and craftsmen and lived during the term of their apprenticeship in their master's household. During this time a craftsman's apprentice received only his board and a fixed amount of clothing: a merchant gave his apprentice pocket-money as well. After training, the apprentice might be given further employment

[1] Yang (1945), pp. 190 ff. [2] ibid., p. 191.

[3] Plans of towns and cities are to be found in modern Chinese atlases and most local gazetteers (compendia of information compiled by local scholars about their province or district—the former usually sponsored by Provincial Governments, the latter privately but with local officials among the sponsors). M. Fried (1953) has a sketch-map of Ch'u-hsien after the Appendix.

by his master, he might be recommended by him to another employer, or he might return to his village as a skilled craftsman. (Apparently apprenticeship provided an outlet for surplus labour from the village, and so served to link town and village.) A merchant's apprentice might be taken on as a shopman. Journeymen were those who had passed their apprenticeship but who, not having the capital necessary to start on their own, were employed either at a fixed wage or on piece rates, usually being given two meals a day with the employing family.[1] Relationships within the work-group tended to be patterned on relationships within the family, even when the work-group outgrew its original form, i.e. an extension of the craftsman's family. Mutual interest and obligation extended to what we in the West would regard as private life.

Some residents in the town owned land outside from which they drew rents, either personally or corporately: many guilds invested funds in land. This was another link connecting town and village—the relationship of landlord and tenant. There was another simple one in family ties: the son who was sent to the town to work when times were hard perhaps made good and stayed there with his wife and children after the old family divided, but he probably returned to visit his kin, and so maintained his ties with the village. It is noticeable that in these relationships between townsman and villager, the former usually has the position of strength. We are told[2] that villagers dealt with tradesmen in the market town who were originally from their own village; with them they deposited surplus money or were allowed credit for periods of up to a year. One guesses that mostly it would be the farmer who owed the townsman, the latter thus being in a position to include an interest charge in his prices to the consumer. However, the paradox of rural indebtedness, as observed in Ireland by Arensberg,[3] applied also to China, i.e. the farmer's debt to the town store was a symbol of lasting mutual social obligations—an assurance to the one of custom and to the other of continuing supplies—which neither would wish to remove altogether. The permanence and the degree of mutuality in such a debtor-creditor relationship gave some protection against exploitation on one side, against loss by default on the other, and so created confidence. While the balance of advantage may have lain one way, both derived some benefit from their mutual dependence.

Towns are to be distinguished from villages for their greater involvement in trade and the consequently greater use made there of money; for their greater range of occupations (within which agriculture would have engaged only a minority) and range of status within occupations, and for the strength of organizations based not on kin or locality but on occupation. (The guild as an agency of control will be discussed in detail in Chapter 7.) Size was not in itself a distinguishing characteristic: the Ting Hsien survey[4] showed that some towns were larger and some smaller

[1] See Fried (1953), pp. 157–8, and Kroker (1957).
[2] Yang (1945), pp. 192–3.
[3] Arensberg (1950), pp. 170–3.
[4] Gamble (1954), p. 21.

than villages around them. One can probably assume that there would have been other differences such as greater wealth in the towns[1] and a higher degree of literacy and sophistication. It seems likely that differences in occupational structure would have been related to differences in family structure: for example, that 'business families' stayed undivided longer than farm families, but I have no evidence on this. Town life would clearly have involved a greater variety of relationships than were experienced in the village—between customers, suppliers, fellow-apprentices, employers, competitors, etc.—and the importance of the kinship bond may well have been less in town than in village. It is significant that in a recent study dealing with urban conditions,[2] great stress is laid on the value in all the vicissitudes of life of friendship and *kan-ch'ing*—a warm personal relationship between two otherwise unrelated individuals of unequal status.

The administrative aspect of the town will be discussed in Chapter 3.

In the attempt to deal with Chinese social structure within the compass of a single chapter, it is inevitable that there should be omissions. I shall conclude therefore by mentioning briefly a few institutions which affected all or most parts of China and might be supposed to have had some connection with legal institutions.

In matters of religion most Chinese were eclectic. In addition to rituals practised in their homes, their villages and their guilds, many attended Taoist and Buddhist temples as suited the occasion, while the Confucian cult was supported by local scholars and officials. The Ting Hsien survey, for example, showed 855 temples in 62 villages (not all villages had a temple), of which 345 were Taoist, 223 Official, 215 Buddhist and 72 individual or miscellaneous cults.[3] There were Mohammedan mosques in the *hsien* city and two villages, adherents of this faith being concentrated in the neighbourhood of the mosques. Figures by themselves give little idea of the richness and variety of religious activities.[4]

Social functions other than religious worship or the propagation of dogma were also associated with these institutions. Temple fairs held to honour the gods offered opportunities also for amusement, recreation, business and sociability. For reasons connected with their religion, it was common for sellers of beef and mutton to be Mohammedan. Buddhist monasteries performed charitable services, such as giving hospitality to travellers, and individual Buddhists undertook as works of piety public-spirited actions, such as the building of bridges. Generally speaking, priests did not rank high on the social scale, they were not influential as a

[1] 'Only two villages reported their largest holding to be over 1,000 *mu*. The largest amount of land owned by one family was 3,950 *mu*. That was a city family. . . .' Gamble (1954), p. 211.

[2] Fried (1953), passim.

[3] Gamble (1954), p. 401.

[4] See, for example, Day (1940), p. 13. It is interesting that lawsuits come high on the list of matters in which the support of supernatural beings was enlisted. This book has a good bibliography.

class, and some had to earn part of their living by other work.[1] Religions other than the official Confucian cult, which was somewhat remote from people's personal lives, were not centrally organized.

I shall have a good deal to say in the next chapter and later on the relation between the Confucian code of morality and ideas of law, since the Confucian teaching remained the ethic of public life. It is not part of my present purpose to examine the influence of Buddhism on law in China, since this had ceased, so far as public life was concerned, long before the period of which I am writing—its impact came much earlier. Those who were drawn to Buddhism or Taoism found in them an orientation to the universe suitable for their private lives, to complement the deficiencies of Confucianism in the spiritual or a-rational areas of existence. If a connection between religion and law is to be sought in the China of these centuries, it must be looked for, I think, in the microcosm of the small group (small, that is, at least in the sense that members knew one another personally).

We shall see later that the internal jurisdiction of groups based on kin, neighbourhood and craft constituted an important extension of the official legal machinery, and I would suggest that the power of such groups to control their members was considerably enhanced by their religious beliefs and practices. Without entering into the detail of these, I think it is clear that participation in ritual observances made individuals conscious of the ties by which they were bound to fellow-members (and at the same time cut off from the rest of the world) and the mutual dependence and responsibility these implied. Moreover, the solemnity of ritual occasions and the dignity acquired by those who took a leading part in them was easily transferred to other occasions. To take an example of the sort of thing that happened in all the groups, *mutatis mutandis*: those present in the ancestral hall when the head of the *tsu* made offerings to the *tsu* ancestors, in an atmosphere of extreme reverence and awe, must have received an intense impression, as the result of which the leading figure and the setting would alike be associated in ther minds afterwards with thoughts of ancestors, solemnity and power. This both facilitated acceptance of the *tsu-chang*'s authority in other matters and inspired respect for rules recited or displayed in the ancestral hall.

The Chinese have for centuries combined in fraternal associations which, because of official discouragement, flourished as a sort of underground movement against authoritarianism.[2] These secret societies provided a focus for feelings of rebelliousness against the established order, often idealistically expressed. Their particular purposes were often merged in a vague hostility, which was capable of flaring up into open rebellion against the authorities, if conditions became intolerable, or of

[1] Gamble, op. cit., p. 403.

[2] See, for example, Favre (1933). For anyone interested to pursue this topic, twelve other sources are listed in Freedman (1958).

being turned against other enemies and oppressors if there seemed to be a chance that action against them could succeed. Sometimes their objects were political—to foment opposition to the dynasty; sometimes religious —to promote specific beliefs which were antagonistic to the orthodoxy of Confucianism; sometimes to protest against features of society which oppressed particular sections, e.g. anti-marriage societies formed by girls; sometimes they had more the character of bands of thieves and robbers. They were as a rule formally organized in branches, and had recognized leadership and adopted formal rules and ceremonial. The number of their adherents and the range of classes involved in them probably increased in bad times. (Hutson describes how in the early years of this century an almost rationalist Confucian society combined with other superstitious and revolutionary societies to oppose the proposed development, by foreign capital, of railways in Szechwan.)[1] In 1896 their members were said to average from 20,000 to 200,000 per province,[2] which, though imprecise, indicates considerable support, and shows that this was one type of organization which spread across village boundaries.

Lastly, a note about slavery, if only to suggest that too great importance should not be attached to it at this period.[3] Slavery existed officially in China until it was abolished by law in 1906, but accounts agree that it was of a mild type. There were two forms, official and private. The former was imposed on those who were transported to the outlying provinces, originally to serve the troops on the frontier, as a punishment for treason and other serious crimes. Private slavery was usually domestic servitude and arose through private sale, particularly of girl children in times of distress. Such slaves were the property of their masters, but the period of servitude ended, for girls, when they married out into another family, or, if a girl bore her master a child, she was treated as a secondary wife. The conditions of such slaves seems to have been bearable, the main objection of the Chinese themselves to the system having been, apparently, that it led to cases of kidnapping and abduction.[4] In law, slaves suffered disabilities,[5] as punishment of crimes against persons varied according to the relationship of the persons concerned, and violence against a superior was punished more severely than violence to an inferior. However, as will be seen later, the provisions of the penal code were not always invoked.

It is hoped that this sketch of the social background will help the reader to visualize the scene in which legal institutions operated.

[1] Hutson (1920), p. 87.
[2] Couling (1917), pp. 501–2.

[3] The terms *liang* and *chien* earlier had the connotation 'free' and 'unfree'. However, by Ch'ing times, while they are still used with these meanings in the headings to sections of the code (e.g. *Liang chien hsiang ou*, Fights between free persons and slaves), in ordinary usage they had come to mean something much more vague, like 'honourable' and 'unworthy'. Usually the words *nu p'u* or *nu pei* (=male or female slave) are used in the body of the text and remove ambiguity. See Boulais (1924), pp. 602–7; Hoang (1915), pp. 225–30.

[4] See Meijer (1949), p. 46.
[5] See Alabaster (1899), pp. 210–5.

2

The Theory and Functions of Government in China

THE UNDERLYING PHILOSOPHY

THE theory on which the edifice of government traditionally rested in China is well stated by Meijer:

> Chinese philosophy started from the idea that heaven and earth were governed by one principle—called *tao*, the way, the creative principle of natural order. Any act contrary to this order in human society resulted in a disruption of the harmony between heaven and earth, and might lead to such calamities as flood, drought, internal disorder. So that the order might be preserved, heaven chose men of outstanding virtue, *te*, and gave them the mandate, *ming*, to rule their fellow creatures.[1]

In an extension of this theory the Emperor, with the title 'Son of Heaven', was seen as poised between heaven and earth and as endowed by heaven[2] with a mandate to rule the earth so long as he was capable of maintaining the harmony undisturbed. This harmonious order, it should be noted, was not man-made, but existed naturally throughout the universe and had merely to be preserved. If the Emperor proved incapable of doing this, he would be responsible to heaven for the disturbance of the natural harmony and the mandate would be transferred to another. This doctrine implied a right of revolution, and if the revolution succeeded in establishing an effective new government, it established at the same time its legitimacy.

This ultimate responsibility for everything that happened in the whole of the Empire the Emperor delegated to his subordinates in the degree that he delegated authority to them; and they in turn delegated it to their subordinates, through all the ranks of officialdom and beyond it. Authority in China was always accompanied by responsibility for ensuring that the natural harmony was preserved within the area of activity over which

[1] Meijer (1949), p. 2.

[2] 'Heaven' translates 't'ien', of which Fung Yu-lan (1948, p. 192) writes:
'My colleague Prof. Y. L. Chin has said: "Perhaps if we mean by *T'ien* both nature and the divinity which presides over nature, with emphasis sometimes on the one and sometimes on the other, we have something approaching the Chinese term" (unpubd. MS).'

that authority was exercised. The Emperor owed responsibility to heaven, under pain of withdrawal of the heavenly mandate if he failed in the duty entrusted to him; lesser people owed responsibility to their immediate superiors—through a chain of delegated authority which reached down to the head of the household.

It was in virtue of this pervasive responsibility that those in authority could lay down precepts to be followed by those in their charge, and require obedience to standards of conduct covering all aspects of life, and take action, both positive and negative, to promote and restore the harmony which it was their responsibility to preserve. The authority of law and government derived directly from the doctrine of responsibility which, as it infiltrated every department of public and private life, provided theoretical justification for law and government to be all-embracing too.

Hence followed also the explicitly ethical character of Chinese society and the intermingling of ethics and administration. To govern, in the Confucian view, was to set a good example and promote good behaviour among people, that is, to create conditions in which people could live without disturbing the natural harmony. Any such disturbance was in itself a sign of the failure of government, and this was an inducement to conceal or play down lesser disturbances and to pretend that all was well. If in practice this was impossible, action had to be taken to fix responsibility somewhere, and due amends had to be made for the disruption in order to prove that government was in capable hands. The belief that disastrous natural phenomena—floods, droughts, tempests, insect pests—were the consequence of human disorder provided further theoretical justification for punishment of wrongdoers: they were a double menace to society. As Meadows puts it: 'Vice is, with the Chinese, nothing but an infringement of the harmonious order of the universe which, being punished by the operation of that order, leads to misery.'[1]

It is doubtful whether Chinese peasants were interested in this theoretical justification. They did, however, have a practical interest both in order being maintained, so that they could labour undisturbed and enjoy the products of their labour, and in the maintenance of public works necessary to the irrigation system. Contemporary observers seem to agree that the need for government was accepted so long as it was efficient and its demands were kept within recognized limits. There is a saying that governing is like cooking a small fish: it should be done just enough and no more.

> Such indeed are the disposition and habits of the people, that so long as the multitude can procure their bowl of rice and a few savoury sauces, that cost only a mere trifle, there will be less danger of a revolt, and the govern-

[1] Meadows (1856), p. 382. Generally similar ideas seem to be found among the communities in the Indonesian archipelago where, in *adat* law, concern for recovery of the cosmic equilibrium is the ground for punishment of delicts. See ter Haar (trans. 1948), pp. 213 f.

ment is so well convinced of this, that one of its first concerns is to lay up in the public magazines erected in every part of the empire, a provision of grain to serve as a supply for the poor in times of famine or scarcity.[1]

Partial insurrections occasionally happen, but they are generally owing to the extreme poverty of the people which in seasons of scarcity and famine, compels them to take the means of subsisting life.[2]

If we may consider Sir George Staunton a reliable observer, acceptance of government included acceptance of the need for punishment:

With all its defects, however, and with all its intricacy this Code of Laws [the penal code] is generally spoken of by the natives with pride and admiration; all they seem in general to desire is its just and impartial execution, independent of caprice, and uninfluenced by corruption.[3]

The fact that, for the son if not for his ambitious father, the way to an official career lay open, via material success and then through scholarship, was no doubt one factor explaining popular acquiescence in the official view of the aims of the government.

Chinese political thinking of later ages reflects the two strands of what was a violently contested philosophical controversy in the fifth to third centuries B.C.—the Warring States period of Chinese history. While Confucian thinkers asserted that the end of all government was to promote wellbeing and preserve social harmony, the Realists (*Fa Chia*, sometimes called School of Law, or Legists) subordinated everything to building up the strength of the state.

The Confucianists taught that if a ruler, basing himself on the sage rulers of antiquity, set his people an example of benevolence and encouraged them to observe the proprieties in personal relationships, the good of the community would automatically follow. The Realists believed that this doctrine, though it may have suited a small community in the past, was inadequate to serve as the basis for a state strong enough to subdue its neighbours—and this, in the troubled period of the Warring States, was the prerequisite of continued existence as well as of internal order and stability. People had to be made to contribute to the strength of the state—even against their natural inclination—by clearly defined and impersonal commands and penalties.

The first side of this controversy can be illustrated from almost any page of the Confucian classics. Here we are inevitably involved in some discussion of the key concept of *li*, for which there is no simple and direct translation. For example:

The Master said: 'If you govern the people by laws, and keep them in order by penalties, they will avoid the penalties, yet lose their sense of shame. But if you govern them by your moral excellence, and keep them in order by your dutiful conduct, they will retain their sense of shame, and also live up to this standard.[4]

[1] Barrow (1804), p. 380. [2] Barrow, p. 396. See also my footnote 2, p. 35.
[3] Staunton (1810), Introduction, p. xxviii. [4] Soothill (1941), pp. 8–9.

The phrase 'by your dutiful conduct' translates '*i li*'. This Waley renders as 'by ritual', but he makes it clear that what is intended are rites practised by the divinely appointed ruler, whose example would, of course, exert an influence on the populace.[1] He stresses the general Chinese belief that there is a proper form for every action.

Of *li*, Hu Hsien-chin writes:

> It is best expressed as approved patterns of behaviour between individuals standing in a definite relationship to each other, and in conformance with a definite system of values relating to such social relationships . . . *li* has a coercive power almost as great as law, but transmitted to the individual by the socialization process of childhood and youth, the personality comes to perform its dictates automatically.[2]

Dr Needham defines *li* as the customs of the society based on ethics and on ancient tabus, including in addition all kinds of ceremonial and sacrificial observances.[3] For another modern Chinese writer, the essential element in *li* is the exercise of reason and judgment. He analyses *li* into three aspects: first, an ordering of society such that each individual knows his rights and duties, so that obedience to the natural order will naturally ensue; second, a code of morality which, being based on human nature, operates not by external control but through individual conscience; third, *li* provides an ideal of social harmony emphasizing the individual's obligation to society.[4] The common element in all these theories seems to be that *li* implies the performance of right actions because, through habituation, they are felt to be right, and without external compulsion.

Mencius went further than Confucius in advocating the adoption of positive measures to stimulate prosperity, regulate agriculture and promote education. But even he favoured only the minimum of interference necessary to enable people to follow their own nature, which he believed to be fundamentally good. He did not believe in forcing them to do what the state required. He said to the king of Liang:

> If your majesty will indeed dispense a benevolent government to the people, being sparing in the use of punishments and fines [*hsing fa*], and making the taxes and levies light, so causing that the fields shall be ploughed deep and the weeding of them carefully attended to, and that the strong-bodied, during their days of leisure, shall cultivate their filial piety, fraternal respectfulness, sincerity and truthfulness, serving thereby, at home, their fathers and elder brothers, and, abroad, their elders and superiors; you will then have a people who can be employed, with sticks which they have pre-

[1] Waley (1938), p. 66. [2] Hu (1948), p. 53.

[3] Needham (1956), p. 519. This volume contains a section on the *Fa chia* or Legalists (in which numerous quotations are translated) and a masterly summary of 'the main features of the history of law in Chinese civilization' (pp. 521 ff.), written with sociological insight.

[4] Hsü (1932), pp. 93–99, 'The Meaning and the Programme of Li'.

pared, to oppose the strong mail and sharp weapons of the troops of Ch'in and Ch'u.[1]

It will be noticed that punishments had a place but were to be used sparingly, merely to supplement moral discipline. The Confucian view was that punishment without education amounted to tyranny. Moreover, in any doubt, the judge should err on the side of leniency.[2]

Hsün-tzu, who was the Confucian philosopher closest to the Realists, did not believe that human nature was naturally good, but held that it could be made good by cultivation and that this was the function of the *li*. According to Hsün-tzu, it was part of human nature to have desires which, if unchecked, would lead to strife and disorder. 'The cure for strife and disorder is to lay down rules concerning the position and status of individuals and classes in society. This would define what everyone is entitled to and the precedence of the different claimants. This is Shyuntzyy's [Hsün-tzu] conception of morality, which is to enable people to reap the benefit of living in society while avoiding the accompanying evils.'[3] It is clear from the Chinese that the 'rules' referred to are those of morality (*li* and *i*), not laws (*fa*).

The Realists, on the other hand, recognized both the evil of men's nature and the changed character of society (since the days of the legendary virtuous rulers to whom the Confucianists were always harking back) as facts to be accepted, and designed a positivist theory of government to deal with them.

In his rule of a state, the sage does not depend on men doing good themselves, but brings it about that they can do no wrong. Within the frontiers of a state there are no more than ten people who will do good of themselves; nevertheless, if one brings it about that the people can do no wrong, the entire state can be kept peaceful. He who rules a country makes use of the majority and neglects the few, and so does not concern himself with virtue but with law.[4]

A ruler, according to the Realists, did not need to bother with setting a virtuous example; his weapons were: *fa*, defined as 'that which is recorded in the registers, set up in the government offices, and promulgated among the people',[5] and *shu*, 'the true arts of kingship',[6] which consisted chiefly in establishing objective criteria for judging men and policies so as to make the rules independent of flattery and corruption, arbitrariness and personal foibles. Rewards and punishments were the two 'handles of the ruler'.

In ruling the world, one must act in accordance with human nature. In human nature there are the feelings of liking and disliking, and hence

[1] Legge (1895), ii, p. 135. [2] See Hsü (1932), ch. viii, 'Law and Justice'.
[3] Lau (1953), p. 556.
[4] Fung (trans. Bodde) (1948), p. 160, quoting Han Fei-tzu.
[5] Fung (1948), p. 160. [6] Waley (1939), pp. 232–7.

rewards and punishments are effective. When rewards and punishments are effective, interdicts and commands can be established, and the way of government is complete.[1]

In spite of its logical and other imperfections, this philosophy served its turn when the Ch'in rulers were building up their power to subdue their neighbours, and they were able, by putting it into practice, to unify China in 221 B.C. Nevertheless their triumph was short-lived, and, when they were superseded by the Han, their methods were discredited,[2] and their philosophy gave way to that of their rivals. However, just as Roman Catholicism underwent changes in Protestant countries under the impact of the Reformation, the Confucianism which now became the accepted orthodoxy was transformed by the Han scholars into an amalgam which, besides being a reinterpretation of the Confucian philosophers, included an admixture of *Fa Chia* Realism. According to Tung Chung-shu,[3] for example, as there are four seasons, there are four ways of government—beneficence, rewards, punishments and executions—and four grades of government official, to be used according to their natural grades of virtue and ability. When Confucianism is mentioned in contexts that refer to the Han and later times, it is this eclectic blend of hitherto conflicting schools that must be understood.

This refurbished Confucianism was the basis on which the Han dynasty laid the foundations of the Imperial system which, though further developed by later dynasties—notably the T'ang (618–906)—remained as the Chinese governmental system until recent times. Imperial China devised a system of governing through a hierarchical bureaucracy schooled in the ethical writings of the philosophers, the notion underlying the whole edifice being that those who observed the *li* should be treated with benevolence and rewarded, while harsh punishments and executions should be applied to those who were too uncouth or too obtuse to do so. The unpopularity of the Realists—after the hardships suffered by the Chinese under the Ch'in dynasty—from that time onward coloured the attitude of the Chinese to law, which was regarded as their legacy. Law, equated with a system of punishments, was in its nature harsh and to be avoided by reasonable men.[4]

[1] Fung (1948), p. 162.

[2] On the harsh punishments and other oppressive policies of Ch'in, see Bodde (1938), pp. 166–75.

[3] Tung Chung-shu's dates are variously given as 179–104 B.C. and 175–105 B.C. On his writings and place among Confucianists, see Fung-Bodde (1953), vol. ii, pp. 16–19, and Wright (1959), pp. 11–16.

[4] This chapter was completed before I read Bünger (1952) which covers much the same ground. At the end of this, the interesting question is raised as to how far Chinese and other oriental views of law must be taken into account by the international organizations of our 'one world' if misunderstandings and conflict are to be avoided. It concludes: 'Oder ist es möglich oder nötig, dass nur eine Rechtsidee, nämlich die abendländische, in internationale Besprechungen zugrunde gelegt wird?'

FUNCTIONS OF GOVERNMENT IN CHINA

The functions of government as understood by the Chinese through successive dynasties may be deduced from the governmental institutions encountered in Chinese history as well as from the writings of their social philosophers. They may be outlined as follows.

The first duty of a ruler was to maintain harmony with the other elements in the universe. Though this had the widest implications, it was symbolized by the carrying out of certain propitiatory rites. At the appropriate season, for example, the Emperor went out to the temples of earth and heaven and sacrificed at them, and then ceremonially ploughed the first furrow—to win heaven's favour for agricultural operations throughout the Empire for the year. Such ceremonials gave further emphasis to the agriculturalists' need for an exactly calculated calendar. The belief that heaven's pleasure or otherwise with the Emperor's performance of his duties could be judged from the occurrence of certain phenomena of nature, such as eclipses and sun-spots, led the Emperor to take an interest in them and appoint officials whose duties[1] included the careful observation of such portents. (Interpreting their meaning gave opportunities for veiled criticism of the ruler: a memorial could be sent to the Emperor drawing attention to the warning from heaven and suggesting a change in policy.)[2]

Next a ruler was expected to encourage virtue, industry and learning among all his subjects both by example and precept. The practice of filial piety demonstrated in the ceremonial of venerating the Imperial ancestors and observance of mourning[3] may be seen as setting his subjects an example in these most important matters.[4] From time to time exhortations to virtue were also published with instructions that they should be publicly read at *yamens* throughout the Empire. In particular, the Sacred Edict of the K'ang-hsi Emperor, amplified by his successor, Yung-cheng (with a paraphrase by Wang Yu-pu, significantly, in colloquial Chinese) set out in sixteen sections a code of behaviour covering most aspects of life.[5] Official encouragement was given to learning, in particular to classical

[1] The acceptance of the Jesuits at the (Ming) Chinese court on account of their superior knowledge of astronomy testifies to the importance attached to this office.

[2] In Bielenstein (1950) it is shown (for the Han dynasty) that this was done selectively: not all portents were the subject of memorials, but only those which occurred when it was felt that there was cause for criticism.

[3] The rules for mourning were set out in elaborate detail in the *Li Chi* (Book of Rites) and *I Li* (Book of Etiquette and Ceremonial). See bibliography under Couvreur and Steele.

[4] cf. 'When the love and reverence (of the Son of Heaven) are thus carried to the utmost in the service of his parents, the lessons of his virtue affect all the people . . .' in the *Hsiao King* (Classic of Filial Piety), see Legge (1899), p. 467.

[5] Trans. by Milne (1817); Baller (1892); summarized in Chang Chung-li (1955), p. 65 n. On the way clan rules reinforced these injunctions, see Liu (1959)[a] pp. 72–74.

studies—and consequently to the ethical tradition—by the establishment in the national and provincial capitals and other cities of schools for the public (though this only provided for a small proportion of China's population), and indirectly by making success in competitive examination the chief criterion for admission to the governing bureaucracy.

The belief in education as an aid to virtue, or at least to peaceable behaviour, is indicated by the reply of the Emperor to a memorial of the Governor of Canton (1831) about bands of vagabonds. The Emperor assented to the proposal that uncultivated land should be given to the dissident elements, but desired also that attention be given to the half-monthly reading of the Sacred Edict and to the formation of free schools.[1]

If precept and example failed to produce among the people behaviour consonant with the required harmonious order, responsibility had to be assigned and offenders punished. Militia were maintained in all parts of the Empire to prevent or suppress rebellion, and local officials were charged with the duties of identifying and punishing wrong-doers of all kinds in accordance with the provisions of a published code of laws. These operations will be dealt with in detail in Chapter 6.

Exhortations to industry—if any were needed in China—abound in the Confucian classics, and practical treatises on methods of rice cultivation, on the rearing of silkworms and on other aspects of agricultural production were issued and re-issued (with government imprimatur) throughout the centuries. From early times in China the government has helped to create prosperity by undertaking the construction and maintenance of canals and irrigation works which have always been the pre-condition of water control and irrigated agriculture.[2]

For the support of the Imperial family, army and officials, and the upkeep of administrative establishments and other public works, revenue had to be raised. The chief sources were (*a*) direct taxation of land or persons, (*b*) tribute of grain or local products, (*c*) government monopolies and licensing systems, such as those on salt, wine, etc., (*d*) customs duties, and (*e*) miscellaneous fees for licences. Of these, (*a*), (*b*) and (*e*) were dealt with by local offices of the general administration; (*c*) and (*d*) had special ad hoc local offices at places where they were needed.[3] Traditionally Chinese authorities also exacted labour services from the mass of the population: the character and incidence of these duties varied at different times and from place to place. Reliance on these sources of revenue and labour involved the periodic enrolment of the population and registration of lands.

[1] *Chinese Repository*, vol. iv (1832), p. 424.

[2] Floods and consequent famine could in this sense be attributed to inefficiency on the part of the administration and thus served as logical justification for the belief that they were signs of the departure of Heaven's mandate.

[3] Details of the taxation system in Ch'ing times are given in Morse (1921) and Ch'en (1914).

The transmission of revenue, whether as money or in kind, principally grain, was a complicated matter which absorbed a considerable amount of the administration's energy. Less bulky, but also a responsibility of the administration, was the transmission throughout the Empire of official correspondence.

The principle on which successive Chinese dynasties conducted relations with peoples outside China was consistent with the relationship between government and the governed within China itself. Those neighbouring peoples who showed themselves capable of civilized relations—demonstrated chiefly by sending envoys with tribute in token of submission to the Chinese Emperor, thus confirming the latter's claim to rule all under heaven—were treated with graciousness, gifts were sent in return, their ruler's title was authenticated, and help was extended to them if they stood in need of it. This tributary system, like the rest of Chinese government, was regulated down to the smallest detail (how often, and how many, envoys should appear at the Chinese court, by what routes they should travel, what form their tribute should take, how they should behave at court, and so on). This was the Confucian world-order in the Far East, 'the way in which barbarous non-Chinese regions were given their place in the all-embracing Chinese political, and therefore ethical, scheme of things'.[1] There was no compulsion on peoples to enter the system, but if they did—and there were material inducements[2] to persuade them to do so—it had to be as China's vassals. Equality had no place in China's international relationships. The long list of countries which became tributaries to China[3] testifies to the advantages they derived: the gain to the Chinese was confirmation of their moral supremacy, and economy in frontier defence. This system, which was the pattern into which relationships with European countries were also expected to fit, lasted into the nineteenth century, when, after the first Anglo-Chinese war, the legend of Chinese supremacy could no longer be sustained.

For the performance of all these functions throughout the extent of the Empire, whoever held heaven's mandate to govern it needed the services of capable men. China early evolved a system of selecting officials by competitive examination, and throughout the imperial epoch this remained yet another of the functions of government in the Chinese system. More will be said of this in Chapter 4.

[1] Fairbank and Teng (1941), p. 139.

[2] Professor Fairbank has shown that a considerable volume of trade went on under cover of these exchanges and that during the Ch'ing period trade undertaken by the Chinese was expanding while tribute decreased. See Fairbank (1953), ch. ii, 'Tribute and the Growth of Trade'. That some trade was countenanced can be seen from the inclusion of regulations about tributary missions in the chapters of the Penal Code that deal with trade. See Lind (1887), pp. 54–55, in which the relevant passages are translated.

[3] Fairbank and Teng (1941), p. 174.

3

The Structure of the Administration

THE machinery of government as re-created by the Han out of what they inherited from earlier periods, to suit the needs of their unified empire, received later additions and refinements, notably in the T'ang period; minor modifications continued to be made by later dynasties, but its essential characteristics remained recognizable throughout the imperial period. The names of offices were changed, the size and number of local government areas was constantly being altered to suit local conditions, but the machine as a whole was never scrapped and replaced. By the Ch'ing period, therefore, though certain innovations were introduced by that dynasty, the institutions of government had the strength and acceptance that come of long establishment. Until the second half of the nineteenth century any opposition which existed was mainly of two kinds: first, anti-dynastic sentiment expressed in secret societies, aimed at expelling the alien Manchus and replacing them by a Chinese dynasty; second, spontaneous local uprisings[1]—peasant or tribal—neither of which aimed at transforming the whole government machine.

I shall try to give a simplified account of the three tiers of the administration—at the capital, in the Provinces and on the spot.[2]

THE CENTRE

At the head of the government hierarchy was the Emperor, surrounded by various court officials and certain bureaux for managing the affairs of the court and the imperial family.[3] The Emperor himself was no mere figurehead but was daily consulted and daily gave decisions on cases sent up from all parts of the Empire.

The centralized control of the system of government for the whole Empire was chiefly in the hands of two councils: the *Nei Ko*, which deliberated and offered proposals on matters to be submitted for the

[1] See Meadows (1856), ch. x, on the '. . . origin of Chinese insurrections and rebellions generally', and Wright (1957), ch. vi, 'The Suppression of Rebellion'. After describing four major rebellions, she says, 'The government had to deal with revolt in virtually every province.'

[2] For a fuller account of the government structure and powers, the reader is referred to works (listed in the bibliography) by Mayers, Ch'en Shao-kwan, Hsieh or Morse.

[3] Mayers–Playfair (1896) lists over one hundred titles of ranks or offices.

Emperor's decision, and the Council of State (*Chün Chi Ch'u*), which conferred with the Emperor, recorded his decisions and made them known throughout the Empire in the Gazette of the Capital (*Ching Pao*). Members of these councils frequently held other substantive office. Below these were what were known as the Six Departments[1] whose names—Department of Civil Office (*Li Pu*), Department of Revenue[2] (*Hu Pu*), Department of Ceremonies (*Li Pu*), Department of War (*Ping Pu*), Department of Punishments (*Hsing Pu*) and Department of Public Works (*Kung Pu*)—indicate the functional division of public business. During this dynasty, each department had two presidents and vice-presidents, one Manchu and one Chinese. Except for certain sections dealing with technical matters peculiar to the particular department, the internal organization of each was exactly similar to that of the others.

A further three bodies were sometimes grouped with the Six Departments, making what were known as the Nine Chief Ministries (*Ta Chiu Ch'ing*). These were the Censorate (*Tu Ch'a Yüan*), which had the duty of examining all actions of central and provincial government, theoretically at least from the Emperor downwards, and of criticizing where necessary in memorials addressed to the Emperor[3]; the Court of Revision (*Ta Li Ssu*), charged with the supervision of the administration of the criminal law[4]; and the Office of Transmission (*T'ung Cheng Ssu*), through which memorials addressed to the Emperor were routed. There were in addition two bodies, with their subsidiaries, which had various scholarly duties, the Imperial Academy (*Kuo Tzu Chien*) and the College of Literature (*Han Lin Yüan*), one office of which engaged in the custody and preparation of historical archives and the compilation of official biographies of eminent public servants. Another body, the *Li Fan Yüan*, was responsible for the control of tributary and subjected peoples outside the eighteen provinces, for example, the outlying provinces of Tibet and Mongolia (as distinct from tributary tribes within China Proper). Such, with the addition of a number of lesser bureaux, was the structure of the administration at its centre.

THE PROVINCES

The territory within the frontiers of the Empire was divided for adminis-

[1] Often referred to as Boards after the model of nineteenth-century England. The Chinese word has the meaning of section or part, so I have preferred 'Department'.

[2] Ch'en (1914) has drawn attention to the key role of this Department in determining the administrative structure in the Provinces (p. 16).

[3] The fact that ex-officio Governors of Provinces had the rank of Associate Vice-President of the Censorate, and Governors-General the rank of Associate President, must have acted as a curb on the censor's freedom to criticize, unless the seriousness of some matter warranted making an issue of it.

[4] The Dept. of Punishments, Censorate and *Ta Li Ssu* together constituted *San Fa Ssu* (literally, Three Legal Offices), which was the supreme Appeal Court. See p. 68.

trative purposes on a roughly homogeneous pattern. The whole was divided into Provinces (*Sheng*), the number of which rose from thirteen in Yüan times to fifteen in Ming, while further regrouping during the Ch'ing dynasty increased the total to eighteen.[1] The hierarchy of government in each provincial capital (*Sheng ch'eng*) was a replica of that to be found in its co-ordinate provincial capitals.

The nominal head of the civil government, in charge also of the military forces in the Province, might be either a Governor-General (*Tsung-tu*, sometimes translated as Viceroy, who could be shared with an adjoining province) or a Governor (*Hsün-fu*); or it might be the two officers side by side.[2] The super-imposition of this layer was a Ch'ing innovation, and historical accident or political expediency was doubtless responsible for the actual constitution at the summit in each province.

The most important offices of the provincial administration, and their holders, were:

Pu cheng shih ssu, Treasurer and Head of the Provincial Civil Service
An ch'a shih ssu, Provincial Judicial Commissioner
Yen yün shih ssu, Salt Comptroller
Liang Tao, Grain Intendant

These were formed into a Provincial Board of Reorganization after the T'ai P'ing rebellion, but even before that, with the Provincial Governor (and/or Governor-General), they had as a body been known as the Provincial Government (*Tu Fu Ssu Tao*). Below them came various grades of assistants, secretaries, archivists, receivers of money, and so on.

The seniority of the Provincial Treasurer and Judicial Commissioner over other officials was indicated in the title by which they were together known: the Two Chief Commissioners (*Fan Nieh Liang Ssu*). They were appointed directly by the Emperor and were responsible respectively to the Department of Revenue and the Department of Punishments at Peking. Each had the right to memorialize the throne directly, and, in the course of a duty visit to Peking at the end of his three-year term, he was granted an audience, at which he could report on the affairs of the province

[1] Chih-li, Kiangsu, Anhui, Kiangsi, Shantung, Shansi, Honan, Shensi, Kansu, Fukien, Chekiang, Hupeh, Hunan, Szechwan, Kuangtung, Kuangsi, Yunnan, Kweichou. This does not include Manchuria, the homeland of the Ch'ing, or Manchu, dynasty, which was known as the Eastern Three Provinces (*Tung San Sheng*) and continued to be separately administered, the most northerly part on a military basis, the southern part on lines approximating to the rest of China. The title given to Mukden, Sheng-ching, indicates its parity of status with Peking, and its Five Departments (omitting one of civil office) were modelled on those of Peking. The description that follows should generally be understood as not applying to Manchuria.

[2] Shantung, Shansi and Honan had no Governor-General. Chih-li and Szechwan were administered by a Governor-General directly with no Governor. Accounts agree in stressing the fact that the relationship between the Governor and Governor-General was that of colleagues rather than of subordinate/superior. In Chih-li and Szechwan, for example, the Governor-General exercised the powers of both.

—and on his erstwhile colleagues. The independence of the Two Chief Commissioners provided a check on the power of the Provincial Governor.

Another high official at the provincial capital, always a scholar of high literary degrees, was the Literary Chancellor (*Hsüeh Cheng*). He was not thought of as forming part of the provincial government but as being seconded from the central government in Peking to preside over the examinations held in *fu* cities (*an lin*) for the *hsiu ts'ai* degree. (This qualified successful candidates for admission to the triennial examination at the provincial capital, but the official who presided over each of these was specially appointed for the occasion from Peking.) The Literary Chancellor also had jurisdiction over titled scholars living in the province: they could be tried by local magistrates but could not be punished unless the Literary Chancellor had first deprived them of their rank.

Outside the provincial capital the administrative structure of the province was a complicated system. Looked at from the bottom upwards, the administrative unit lowest in the governmental hierarchy was the *hsien*,[1] district or county, comprising all the land and people of the villages within its area, and the city which formed its administrative centre. These *hsien* were grouped into *fu* (sometimes called 'prefectures'). For certain purposes another grouping of two or more *fu*, the *tao* (often translated as 'circuit') was interposed between the *fu* and the province, though it was not, for other matters, a stage in the hierarchy. So at the simplest, the province might be divided into *fu*, and each *fu* divided into a number of *hsien*; or, if one includes the *tao*, the sequence in descending order would be:– province, *tao*, *fu*, *hsien*. However, the matter is complicated because some of both the larger *hsien* and smaller *fu* were called *chou* or *t'ing*, and thus, while some *chou* and *t'ing* were independent of *fu*, and the *chou* might have *hsien* dependent on them, other *chou* and *t'ing* were themselves dependent on *fu* and co-ordinate with *hsien*.

The *fu*, *chou* and *hsien* magistrates were the general administrative body of the provincial civil service. Their tasks included the collection of revenue, the maintenance of order and the primary dispensation of justice, as well as the conduct of literary examinations and of the government postal service—in short, all the immediate functions of public administration. 'They are commonly spoken of as *Fu Mu Kuan*, or officials . . . who are the "father and mother" of the people.'[2]

The counter over which 'the government' did business with 'the people' was the magistrate's *yamen*, whether that at the lowest level was called *hsien*, *chou* or *t'ing*.

[1] The word *hsien* is used in three ways: for the district, for the city which was its administrative centre, and sometimes as an abbreviation for the *chih hsien*, the magistrate.

To translate the titles of Chinese administrative areas is difficult and the arbitrary choice of equivalents by western scholars seems to me to lead to confusion. I have thought it best to retain the Chinese term.

[2] Mayers–Playfair (1896), p. 40.

The next superior office—whether *fu* or *chou*—acted as court of appeal for legal cases[1] sent up by the *hsien* magistrate and also dealt with affairs in the administration of which control over a larger area than the *hsien* was required: such as, care of waterways necessary for irrigation and communications, certain police duties, coast and river defence. For other business originating in the *hsien yamen*, the *fu* office acted as a forwarding agent, and thus had some knowledge of what went on in the subordinate offices.

Next in the hierarchy came the *tao*, which had administrative control, particularly in matters relating to the salt monopoly and transport of grain; its chief officer, the *tao t'ai* (as he is usually known: more properly *Fen hsün tao*) exercised control over the military forces, waterways and customs and acted as a link between civil officials and military officers[2] in his area. Then came the provincial government, functionally divided as has already been described, which co-ordinated the administration of the whole province. This pyramid of authority provided a chain of communication from the central government to the lowest administrative unit.

One *hsien* city in each *fu* (called *shou hsien*, head *hsien*) was also the seat of government for the *fu*, and one *fu* city in each province (*shou fu*, head *fu*) was also that of the provincial capital, which then had the offices of various government layers side by side. (Cf. various levels of local and central government to be found at Westminster.) Doolittle describes[3] an impressive concentration at Foochow, which contained the establishments of the Viceroy of two provinces, Fukien and Chekiang; Governor-General of Fukien; Prefect of Fuchou-fu; two District Magistrates; and the Manchu military commander.

A steady flow of returns, reports, memorials and proposed decisions in legal cases came in to the provincial government from the *fu* or independent *chou*, as they did to each of these from subordinate offices. These were dealt with, according to competence in each matter, either locally or by transmission to the appropriate department at the capital, with other documents which they had themselves initiated. A flow of edicts, replies to memorials, new regulations, decisions on legal cases submitted, came back in the reverse direction for communication to the subordinate offices. And, as usual in China, a chain of authority was also a chain of responsibility. Each office was responsible to the one above it for what happened within its area and would hold its subordinate responsible in turn.

Many observers, impressed with the powers of the provincial govern-

[1] See p. 67 for a slight qualification of this.

[2] '. . . he was the man to judge when it was necessary to use arms for the suppression of riots, the execution of laws and the administration of justice. He had the power to direct and supervise the prefects and magistrates and to demand the help of Chinese forces in his circuit.' Ch'en (1914), p. 25.

[3] Doolittle (1865), pp. 18–19.

ments to raise armies, to issue coins and paper money and to contract loans, have concluded that provincial governments were practically autonomous. Of course, governments in charge of areas the size of European kingdoms were powerful bodies. Within limits, however, the government at the capital had effective methods of control at its disposal if it wished to use them. The provincial governments had to carry out orders from the capital, were subject to supervision and criticism, and, most important, their officials were appointed and dismissed from Peking. It was often convenient in dealing with the special problems of widely different regions to make matters the responsibility of the provincial governments in whose area they arose. In particular, the imperial government preferred to keep itself somewhat remote by insisting that relations with Europeans be handled through the province. However, other events of the nineteenth century demonstrated that weakness of the central government did not always mean a gain in strength for the Provincial Governor: he might try to make innovations, but, unless Peking appointed to his staff officials sympathetic to them, such schemes could not get very far. So far as legal cases were concerned, while wide powers were delegated, control was completely centralized and all the most serious cases had to be referred to the capital.[1]

OFFICIAL ADMINISTRATION AT THE LOCAL LEVEL

The *yamen* of the District Magistrate (usually the *hsien* magistrate, but as has already been explained, sometimes called *chou* or *t'ing*) was the point furthest from the centre to which the official hierarchy reached, the point therefore at which people and officialdom were in contact.[2]

In all the eighteen Provinces there were some fourteen hundred *hsien*, which underwent regrouping from time to time, particularly after disturbances. *Hsien* varied widely in area and population, some including only a dozen villages, others hundreds. Of these, some would be only a mile or so away from the *hsien* city, while others were up to twenty or thirty miles away. In Ting Hsien the *hsien* city was fairly centrally situated in relation to its total area (480 sq. miles) but this was by no means always the case. *Hsien* were classified according to various criteria—such as wealth, volume of business, litigiousness of local population—so a magistrate knew in advance something about the post he was going to.[3]

[1] See later, p. 66 f. for procedure. Wright (1957) examines (at pp. 57–59) the tendencies towards regionalism and centralism in nineteenth-century China and reaches conclusions which are in substantial agreement with what has been said above. Hsieh (1925), pp. 294–7, traces shifts in the balance between provinces and centre during the course of the dynasty.

[2] It is often incorrectly stated that the *hsien* magistrate was the lowest official appointed by the central government. In fact, there were several grades of assistant *hsien* magistrate also filled by holders of official rank (eighth and ninth rank, whereas the *hsien* magistrate was upper seventh).

[3] On the way in which magistrates were appointed, see p. 53.

Except for a few special or technical services operated by *yamens* senior to the *hsien* (see above p. 41) so far as all the inhabitants of his area were concerned, town-dwellers and villagers alike, the *hsien* magistrate *was* the government. It was to his *yamen* that taxes and labour services were due, it was his *yamen* that kept registers of population, and that registered changes in land ownership; the same *yamen* was charged with maintaining public order and served as court of first instance for the hearing of lawsuits; official provision locally, if any were made, in such matters as education and flood relief had also to be undertaken by the *hsien* magistrate.[1]

Because of the all-embracing nature of the *hsien* magistrate's duties, it is necessary to know something of the general organization of the *hsien yamen*, in order to understand the legal machinery which functioned through it.

First, as to the financial arrangements: the *hsien* magistrate was responsible for collecting taxes, the chief of which was the land tax, for the whole *hsien* and for remitting an assessed sum to the office senior to him. He was also expected to send, as a matter of routine, appropriate amounts as presents to his superiors. He received a fixed allowance to provide for his own salary and for maintaining the establishment necessary to conduct the business of the *yamen*. No one pretended that this allowance was sufficient for the purpose (in Ch'ing times, at least), and it was understood on all sides that the magistrate would raise the excess by adding various 'accretions' to the tax assessments, part of which at least were recognized as legitimate. The K'ang-hsi Emperor wrote to the Governor of Honan in 1709:

> It is impossible for any magistrate to support his family and to pay for the services rendered by his secretaries and servants without charging a single cash in excess. A magistrate charging ten per cent in excess of the regular taxes may be considered a good official.[2]

On another view,

> The magistrates are mainly bound by old custom, what has been done before is tolerated, but there is always a tendency to seize on every occasion to try to obtain a little more. This, if too much, provokes a riot, the magistrate gets into trouble with the people, and a haggling ensues until either the extra impost is abandoned or a *modus vivendi* is arrived at on some middle ground.[3]

Some light is thrown on the financial aspects of traditional local government by Edgar Snow who, when in China in the nineteen-thirties, came across a *hsien* magistrate—a native of east China holding an appointment in the west—who was imbued with reforming zeal and battling against the weight of centuries. Thirty years after the revolution which brought

[1] cf. Appendix 4, no. 33: 'Although within the *yamen* duties fall into different categories, to those outside, one person, the *hsien* magistrate, is responsible for all.'

[2] Quoted in Ch'en (1914), p. 54.

[3] Morse (1921), p. 99, quoting Jamieson on taxation in Honan in 1905.

the Empire to an end, the *hsien* government remained unchanged, he found. When he arrived, he told Snow, he found tax-collectors, whose families had occupied the position for generations, who had their own secret records of land ownership and collected according to reckonings made out by the gentry. They had to be beaten to pay over taxes to the magistrate. Magistrate Chen sacked these collectors, made a new land-survey, and sent out officials to the villages to advise each owner and tenant what they should pay and invited them to do so on a personal visit to the *yamen*. The innovations were popular with the majority. Chen also raised the salaries of his staff and introduced a book-keeping system by which accounts were balanced daily. (This enabled him to clear himself of charges of embezzlement which a few angry residents made against him to the Provincial Governor.) In spite of economies, he found himself in debt to the treasury at the end of the first year. '. . . Now there are honest officials, but what can they do against a system like this?'[1]

The system was arbitrary in its incidence, and its employment makes accurate estimates of yield almost impossible (there are wide variations in the estimates offered by writers like Jamieson, Parker, etc.),[2] but it was probably a fairly cheap method of collection.

The *yamen* was both official residence of the magistrate and office for the transaction of public business, the inner rooms or courts serving as the former, while those more accessible to the roadway were used as offices. The size of the building and the staff employed naturally depended on the size and importance of the place. The offices in every *yamen*, however, reflected in some way the functional division of public affairs observed in the government departments at the capital. In the larger *yamens* (and in all *fu yamens*) there were actually six offices, each with its staff, to correspond to the Six Departments at Peking. Where the volume of work did not warrant organization on this scale a smaller staff divided the duties between them.[3] Besides the clerks there were various messengers and attendants, runners and gaolers.[4]

Though not themselves well paid, these positions opened up other avenues of profit and, while all affected to despise them, the posts were greatly sought after by the poor. Theoretically the magistrate was free to choose his own staff and to dismiss them, but in practice the breadth of his duties and the fact that he was appointed to a province other than his native one made him very much dependent on his staff and gave them a corresponding measure of independence. A new incumbent would come as a stranger to take up his appointment, ignorant of local custom and precedent, and it would be most natural to re-employ those who had had experience under his predecessors and who wished to serve under him.

[1] Snow (1941, London), pp. 295–8.
[2] See Morse (1921), pp. 100–10.
[3] cf. Appendix 4, no. 33.
[4] Meadows (1847), Note IX 'On the yamun . . .', pp. 101–16, has a vivid description of the scene and the various grades of staff inside a *yamen*.

Owing to the incomprehensibility of many Chinese dialects to natives of other parts, in many places he would also need the help of his staff as interpreters.[1] It was possible for holders of such posts to entrench themselves in the service of the *yamen* and sometimes particular posts became the monopoly of certain local families.

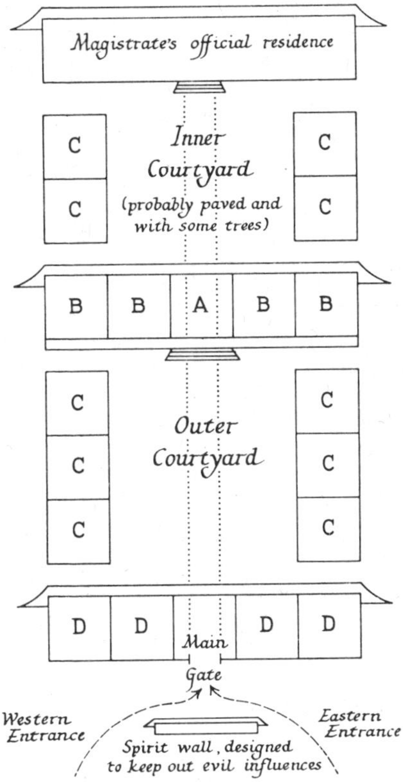

Sketch-plan to show the standard layout of a magistrate's *yamen*

A: Main hall of *yamen*, used as entrance hall and way of access to magistrate's residence—transformed into a court-room on days when legal cases were to be heard. B: Offices (*shu*), including the *yamen* treasury. In larger *yamens* there would be two rows of offices, an outer and an inner, and the magistrate's own office and rooms for entertaining visiting higher officials would be in the inner row. C: Side rooms for attendants and servants, most of whom would also live on the premises. D: Rooms for door-keeper, messengers, etc.; also rooms used to house accused persons awaiting trial.

With acknowledgment to Professor Amakai for inspiration derived from his article in *Toyo Bunka*, 1958. Meadows (1847, pp. 101 ff.) has also given some details of the use of the different buildings that comprised the *yamen*.

[1] See p. 75 for the power exercised by these in legal cases.

Partly to protect himself against this situation, and also because of the impossibility of any one human being mastering all the intricacies of all aspects of government, the magistrate also appointed to his service certain specialist advisors who acted as his personal assistants within the sphere of their competence. Of these the most important were the legal advisor and the financial advisor.

> In every Chih hsien [District Magistrate]'s yamen a complete staff would include the following persons: First, there are the *mu yu* whose Chinese titles indicate that they are individuals in intimate official relationship with the incumbent of the post. The most important of the staff are two, the *Hsing ming shih yeh* or law secretary and the *Chien ku shih yeh*, or revenue secretary. These men are nearly always from the Chekiang province and usually come from Shaoshingfu.[1] A secretary in a yamen has always some pupils or articled clerks with him, and these in course of time are recommended for employment to magistrates or other officials in want of secretaries. In this way the office of secretary in all yamens has almost become a monopoly of the Chekiang province and it is as much in the natural order of things for a yamen secretary to be a Chekiang man as for a banker to be a native of Shanshi. The magistrate is entirely in the hands of his legal and financial advisors in their respective departments. He goes to his first post utterly ignorant of the duties he will have to perform and to an extent which could find no parallel in our own services he is merely a responsible figurehead at the mercy of his trained subordinates.[2]

We shall have occasion to refer again to this legal advisor or law secretary (in Chapter 6): it will be seen that the magistrate was not alone in being entirely in his hands.[3]

In the *hsien* area subject to the magistrate, two separate strands of local government can be distinguished—the one self-government of natural growth, the other imposed by the authorities for their own purposes.[4] Communities managed their own affairs under the leadership of family and lineage heads, village leaders, guild officials or organizers of ad hoc associations (who owed their position to seniority, prestige or competence). So long as certain minimum official requirements were complied with when put forward, the authorities did not interfere. For the purposes of communication between *yamen* and village, and in order to constitute a link where there would otherwise be a gap in the chain of responsibility which reached from family head to Emperor, the magistrate recognized one person in each village as his agent there. This agent, usually known as the *ti pao* or *pao chang*, had the duty of passing on to his fellow-residents

[1] It is interesting that Wang Hui-tsu, whose advice to 'those who assist in governing' (based on his own experience as legal advisor to many magistrates) I have translated in Appendix 4, came from Hsiao-shan, which is in Shao-hsing-fu, Chekiang.

[2] Brenan (1897), p. 45; for a fuller account of the staff and its functions, see Boulais (1924), pp. 47–48.

[3] See later, p. 69; also Appendix 4, p. 138.

[4] Hsiao (1953) stresses the aspect of administrative convenience.

the demands of the *yamen*, and he was also held responsible by it for their compliance—whether the matter were taxation, household registers, transfers of land or producing offenders or witnesses for legal hearings. Nominally the *ti pao* stood at the head of a pyramid: families were supposed to be grouped according to a neat pattern, ten households making a *p'ai*, ten *p'ai* a *chia*, and ten *chia* a *pao* or *li* (in towns, *fang* and *hsiang*). The edict of 1708 reviving this system—which represented a tightening up of the previous rather loose organization—stressed the principle of group responsibility for misdeeds of members, an idea with deep roots in China. Besides his other duties, the *ti pao* was supposed to read out the Sacred Edict[1] to the people on the first and fifteenth of each month, and in 1757 an edict pointed out that the *pao-chia* system had been instituted to suppress sedition and keep peace among the law-abiding, and ordered the people to choose sincere and educated persons as *ti pao*. However, apart from the latter's serving as a channel of communication between village and magistrate, the system seems to have declined and remained largely an official fiction. When, as time went on, disturbances occurred, the authorities had to raise bands of militia to deal with them, thus acknowledging the inadequacy of the *pao-chia* machinery.[2]

According to Boulais's description of the system as it was supposed to operate after the ordinance of 1852, the head of *pao* or *chia* was responsible for reporting brigands, thieves, members of illicit religious sects, known cases of playing at dice, gambling, raping of women, counterfeiting of money, illicit salt trade and any other suspicious circumstances. Rich and poor families were alike under his supervision, also religious communities, and the comings and goings of all their members. Particulars of travellers and itinerant merchants had to be given to the magistrate, and a record of boats arriving and place of origin of their personnel. Boulais comments: 'Tel est le système adopté partout en Chine pour la police: il n'est ni fort compliqué ni fort dispendieux, mais il faut aussi l'avouer, il laisse bien en paix les habiles et les riches criminels.'[3]

The post of *ti pao* did not carry official remuneration, but the *ti pao* found compensation for his work and the risks attendant on his responsibility (in the technical sense) in various ways: by charging fees for 'chopping' title deeds—without which sales of land were not valid—and by what he could make out of his fellows for all the intermediary services he performed on their behalf. His position conferred a degree of power over his neighbours, but he was not usually one of the most influential persons;

[1] See above, p. 34.

[2] See Wen (1935), pp. 216–24, in which Wen divides the history of the *pao-chia* system into three phases and ascribes its decline to population and other changes. Hsiao I-shan describes the interaction between the *pao-chia* and organic local self-government, citing as his authority Liang Jen-kung's *History of Chinese Civilisation* (in Chinese), section on village self-government, which I have not myself seen. See Hsiao (1947), pp. 102–3.

[3] Boulais (1924), pp. 162–4.

for a scholarly person to have encounters of a routine nature with a fellow scholar who held a position of authority might cause embarrassment to both sides, while it was not in keeping with such a person's dignity to have to deal with official underlings. Influential persons in the locality would sooner use the *ti pao* as their mouthpiece, and pay the penalties involved, than occupy the position themselves.

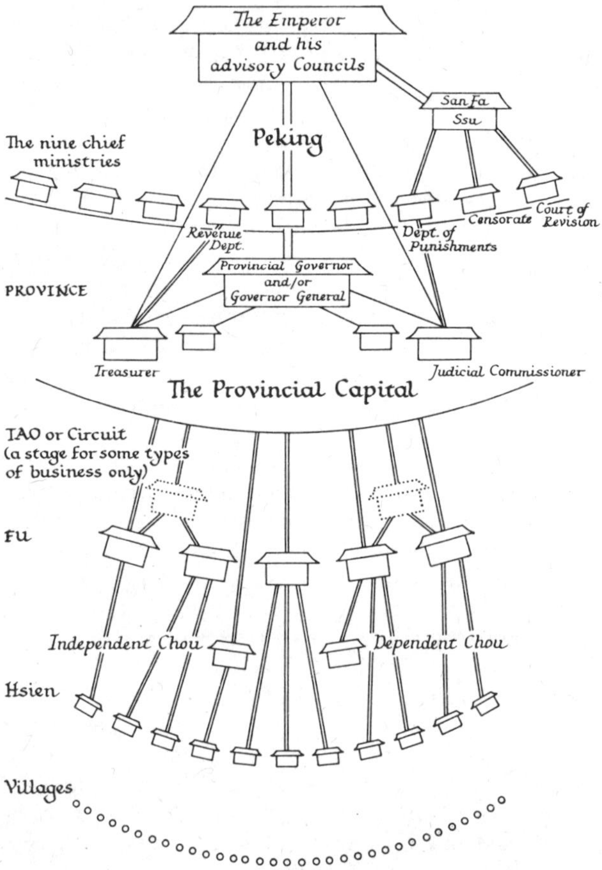

Diagram to show the structure of government
and channels of official communication

The system of rural self-government taken as a whole had the advantages of economy, the magistrate being saved the expense of establishing local sub-offices in every village.

For administrative purposes towns and cities were divided into wards (the inner wards called *fang* and the outer *hsiang*) each with its head—*fang chang* or *ti fang*, etc. In matters which concerned a ward as such, or the collection of tax on agricultural land within its area, the *yamen* dealt with the *ti fang* in the same way as it dealt with the *ti pao* in the village. The powers of the *ti fang* must, however, have been proportionately less, since *yamen* levies on goods, relatively more important in the town, were made by merchants and artisans through their respective guilds. In the *hsien* etc., *fu* and provincial capital cities, the presence of the *yamen* on the spot must in any case have left less to the agency of the *ti fang*, whose duties seem to have been chiefly of the nature of police,[1] as contrasted with the more comprehensive duties of the *ti pao* in the village. Most discussions I have found which purport to be of municipal government are in fact concerned with the local administration of the central government, not local self-government. Urban self-government was for practical purposes concentrated in the hands of guilds. (See Chapter 7.)

Exceptionally, areas in which there were enclaves of non-Han aboriginal peoples (chiefly in the southern and south-western provinces) were dealt with on one of two systems, *T'u kuan* and *T'u ssu*—native or local magistracies and chieftainships, in both of which appointments were hereditary.

In the first of these, *fu*, *chou* and *hsien* magistracies were arranged on the standard pattern, but, subject to satisfactory performance, the magistracies were hereditary, though not necessarily filled from indigenous families.[2] It was laid down in the Administrative Statutes[3] which member of the family should succeed, the Governor of the province being responsible for reporting the names of office-holders to the Department of Civil Office.

Of the *T'u ssu* Mayers wrote:

> The government of the semi-independent tribes in general is left in the hands of their hereditary chieftains, upon whom high-sounding titles of various degrees are bestowed in accordance with a system introduced originally by the Mongol conquerors of China. According to the size and importance of the territory they rule over, these chieftains are invested with different gradations of rank. . . .[4]

It was laid down that the Governor of Kuangsi, for example, was to inspect and report on all the *T'u ssu* in his area once in three years, and a later decree ordered Provincial Governors generally to make such reports at any time without waiting for the three-yearly inspection.

In this way autonomous or semi-autonomous areas were fitted into the over-all administrative pattern.[5]

[1] See Meadows (1847), Note X 'On the Ti Pau . . .'. This observer was impressed most with the functions of the *ti pao* as policeman and informer, but the scene described seems to be urban.

[2] A few posts in Yünnan and Kuangsi were monopolized by families from Chekiang and Shantung. See Mayers (1896), p. 45.

[3] *Ta Ch'ing Hui Tien Shih-li*, ch. 121. On this code generally see later, p. 56 f.

[4] Mayers (1896), p. 4.

[5] A fuller account of the *T'u ssu* system may be found in Wiens (1954), ch. vii.

4

The Personnel of the Administration

THE body of men who filled the country's civil service posts, from the Councils and central ministries down to the *hsien* magistracies, formed a distinct and influential group in Chinese society. Mayers speaks of them as 'the most active and important element in the national life of China'.[1] As entry into the civil service was theoretically open to all,[2] its members cannot be regarded as constituting a closed caste. The community of scholar-officials at any given period formed, nevertheless, a body apart, formally distinguished from 'the people', strongly conscious of its own separate character, and imbued with a marked *esprit de corps*. The system of public examinations, which was the chief agency employed in the selection of officials, set its stamp on those who passed through it; and this, together with shared interests, functions and privileges, gave the bureaucracy a considerable measure of homogeneity and a formidable solidarity. In this chapter I shall be mainly concerned with the strictly official functions of the bureaucracy, leaving for later consideration their role in wider social activities.

The principle of selecting suitable candidates for appointment to the civil service by literary examination goes back to the Former Han dynasty,[3] though it achieved formal institutional expression only under the T'ang, in the early seventh century. From then on the system continued through successive dynasties down to the beginning of the present century. For more than a thousand years these public examinations, with their emphasis on the Four Books and Five Classics and the Histories, have determined the character and goals of Chinese education.[4]

The public examination system comprised a series of graded competitive examinations designed to select for the government service the most talented of the scholars in each province. A man wishing to enter upon an official career had first to attain the title of *hsiu-ts'ai*, literally

[1] Mayers–Playfair (1896), p. 123.

[2] Or nearly all. Those who had undergone legal punishment, or who were in mourning for a parent, were excluded from the examinations. So also were prostitutes, actors, *yamen* servants, mortuary attendants, musicians, post-office grooms, etc., and their children. See Zi (1894), pp. 21 and 24–25.

[3] An imperial edict of 165 B.C. See Dubs (1938), i, p. 259.

[4] See for example Biot (1847); or Ch'en (1937), chs. 13, 16, 19, 21, 23 (in Chinese). On the texts, see above, footnote 1 on p. 9.

'budding talent'. (This was the popular term: the official title was *sheng-yüan.*) To secure this qualification, which may be thought of as corresponding to our B.A., the candidate had to pass three tests: one at his native county seat, and two more at the *fu* city. These were presided over by the *hsien* and *fu* magistrates, and the Provincial Literary Chancellor respectively, the latter visiting the *fu* cities in the province twice in the course of three years for the purpose. Great solemnity and publicity attended everything to do with the examinations: those who succeeded in becoming *hsiu ts'ai* in the *fu* examinations were invited to a banquet by the magistrate in their *hsien* on their return and were henceforward marked out from the ordinary run of men. Their status conferred the right to wear the official style of dress and headwear and, so long as they did nothing to forfeit the immunity, exemption from corporal punishment and corvée services, but it also involved certain obligations. They were registered at the *yamen* and required to observe certain principles of conduct, the essence of which was loyalty to government and respect for learning.[1]

Many scholars were satisfied to have lifted themselves above the common level, but those with ambition for office went on to sit for the examination held triennially at the provincial capital, under the direction of the Provincial Governor but presided over by an Examiner (*Cheng K'ao Kuan*) sent specially from Peking, for the title of *chü jen*—literally 'a man raised up'. The candidates were required to attend at the provincial examination halls throughout the Empire on the ninth, twelfth and fifteenth of the eighth month and submit their knowledge of the classics and ability to compose essays on given themes to stringent tests. A quota was fixed for each province, and those placed within that number at the head of the list were awarded the degree. Competition was severe, thousands of candidates competing for sixty or seventy places,[2] and great excitement prevailed in the capital cities both while the examinations were in progress and when the list of successful candidates was published. Many scholars found the physical and emotional strain too great and had to drop out before the end.

Those successful were allowed to compete in the metropolitan examination held in Peking in the spring of the next year, followed by a Palace examination, on the result of which the degree of *chin shih* was awarded and scholars were selected to serve in the *Han Lin Yüan.*[3]

Finally there was a Court examination at which the Emperor set the papers; this was largely a formality but symbolized the imperial interest in the whole system. To come out among the first three *chin shih* was

[1] A mandarin's wife was also awarded an imperial distinction, *Kao-Feng*, which could only be accorded to any woman once, so more stringent rules governed the betrothal of an official than were observed by other people, and the wife had greater protection against repudiation. (Hoang (1915), pp. 30 and 112.)

[2] See Chang Chung-li (1955), pp. 169–70.

[3] College of Literature at the capital. See above, p. 38; also Mayers–Playfair (1896), pp. 24 and 28.

almost the highest honour that one could achieve, an honour shared by the whole province of the successful candidate; and to be chosen to serve in the *Han Lin* College was also thought to be a great distinction—for the candidate's family and district as well as the candidate himself.[1]

Chin shih not selected for the *Han Lin* College were appointed either to posts in the Departments at Peking or to magistracies in the provinces, the older men being sent to *hsien* magistracies. *Chü jen* could also be specially selected for *hsien* and *chou* posts.[2]

Neither age nor previous failure were barriers to entering the competition, and many scholars spent much of their lives as examination candidates.[3] The examinations were elaborately regulated and the whole activity—allowing for the work of examiners and the scholars they called on to advise them, writers who copied essays (to preserve the anonymity of candidates) and servants who attended on them while in residence—must have been a major Chinese industry. It certainly absorbed the energies of large numbers of people who might otherwise have engaged in opposition to the régime, and secured continuous attention for ethical texts which might otherwise have fallen into oblivion.

The intellectual exercises required of the candidates were modified from time to time, but the form remained broadly the same. They were required to write essays in a highly stylized manner, and a poem, on a number of themes selected either from the canon of the Confucian classics or from the official dynastic histories. The last head might, according to Wells Williams, include 'doubtful matters of government, such problems as might arise in law or finance, customs of the Empire in former times, etc.'[4]

Chang Chung-li throws doubt on the idea that equality of opportunity was achieved through the examinations and shows[5] that certain classes of candidate were more favourably placed to succeed than others; notably, the sons and brothers of high officials, and salt merchants and their heirs. It was also possible to purchase titles which, though they did not automatically admit to office, did qualify their possessors to enter the provincial examinations and so accelerated their progress. *Chü jen* degrees and official positions were also conferred, without examination,

[1] cf. Hutson (1921, p. 112): 'In Ch'ung-ch'ing chou districts . . . yamen runners . . . control the literati. In Kuan-hsien the case is reversed, because that district has produced two or three *Han-lin* scholars, thus raising the status of the literati. Ch'ung-ch'ing has only produced *chin shih*. The result is that the yamen runners' oppression is intolerable in one place while it may be mitigated in another. . . .

[2] See Chang (1955), pp. 25–26. I believe however that the whole question of selection for appointment was considerably more complicated than he suggests.

[3] Chang (1955), Part III: 'The Examination Life of the Gentry'.

[4] Williams (1900) gives some of the themes set in 1828 (vol. i, p. 552), and Wright (1957) quotes some of the questions from the Palace examination of 1868 on the development of Chinese criminal law and methods candidates would recommend to reduce the amount of crime (p. 83).

[5] See Chang (1955), pp. 183–5.

on heirs of high officials or as a reward for loyal service to the dynasty.

Appointment to office did not follow automatically on gaining the required qualifications: sometimes a long interval elapsed between the two, and 'officials in expectancy' played a considerable role in Chinese society. Nor was the order of ranking of successful candidates followed in making appointments. During the course of a visit to Peking (calculated to impress them with the power of the central government, no doubt) the newly qualified candidates cast lots to decide to which province they should be assigned. Arrived at that provincial capital, they again cast lots to decide their ranking on the provincial list, which further distinguished between those who had qualified by examination, purchase, transfer or promotion. The 'expectants' then waited for offices to fall vacant and theoretically could expect appointment in turn, but this did not always work out and we hear of some remaining expectants for the rest of their lives. Hsieh remarks, 'The whole business consisted of a gambling chance for the expectant as well as for the people, and the appointment seems to have been made for the benefit of the official, not for the good of the people.'[1] This should doubtless be amended to read: '. . . the benefit of officials with influence.' Personal recommendation and well-directed presents eased the path of the aspiring official, and in practice flexibility —at variance with the intention implicit in the initial lot-casting procedure —opened the way to various abuses.

The hierarchy of Imperial officials was divided into nine ranks, all further divided into an upper and a lower grade, each distinguishable in the details of its official dress. A given rank attached to each office, and only holders of that rank, or those who could be promoted to it, could hold that particular post.

All officials were reported on at regular intervals to the Department of Civil Office, by and through their superior officers, and, as time went on, were promoted to higher rank or demoted on their record.[2] An official who had himself committed a crime could not be charged in the ordinary court without the prior permission of the Emperor, and then, if found guilty, was exempt from the physical punishments laid down in the Code. (These were convertible, in the case of officials, in terms of loss of salary or degradation according to a fixed tariff.[3]) A distinction was made between offences committed in a private and official capacity, the latter being more lightly sanctioned. For serious offences magistrates could of course be deprived of office, and, when thus reduced to the status of a commoner (*wei min*), they would be liable to the ordinary punishments.[4]

[1] Hsieh (1925), p. 308.

[2] See 'Disciplining the bureaucracy' in Wright (1957), pp. 87–88.

[3] Sections 7 and 8 of the Penal Code. The custom of exchanging office against punishment—*kuan tang*—goes back at least to the Sui dynasty; see Balazs (1954), note 237, p. 167.

[4] Section 14 of Code. For an example of such a punishment, see that inflicted

There were certain recognized conditions attaching to official employment, apparently designed to promote the disinterested discharge of duties, though on occasion they may have been honoured in the breach. An official was not eligible to hold office in his native province, and was subject to periodical transfer; he was not allowed to marry a woman of the district to which he was assigned, nor to own property there. One other custom which passing centuries did nothing to undermine was that of retiring for a prescribed period of mourning on the occasion of the death of either of the official's parents. They also occasionally withdrew to care for sick parents, but the degree of their solicitude was probably not unconnected with the exigencies of official life.[1]

After dealing with the recruitment of officials and the conditions attaching to their employment, it may be well at this point to consider their attitude to their official career once they had entered on it.

Young men were attracted to an official career as being the way to prestige and fame, and by hopes of security or even wealth—in brief, personal ambition and loyalty to kin. Service to the wider public did not usually enter into their thoughts. By the time they reached their first official appointment, the majority had spent many years—and some of them decades—in concentrating on a prescribed course of studies and style of writing. Their training had fostered habits of industry and perseverance, but it had not given them a wide general knowledge or originality of mind. Many of them had accumulated debts, at least debts of honour, to those who had supported them through the years of their studies and now expected some return for their sacrifice.

Official life was not without its hazards, and these had to be surmounted if the goal of security was to be reached. Negatively, it was important to avoid criticism or adverse report. More positively, all officials would try to satisfy their superiors by fulfilling tax and grain quotas expected of them in any given district and to give an impression of order and well-being in the area under their charge to superiors or itinerant inspectors. These were the criteria on which depended, first, security of tenure and then advancement.

In addition, the official would have the personal objective, which it would probably have been agreed on all sides that he owed to his family

on a magistrate guilty of fornication with a woman of the people; Hoang (1915), p. 217.

[1] cf. Teng Ssu-yu, in Hummel (1943): 'In 1852 (Tseng Kuo-fan) was sent to conduct the provincial examination of Kiangsi, but learning on his way south of the death of his mother, he was granted leave to return home to observe the customary mourning . . .' (p. 751).

'Tseng Kuo-fan's father died on 27th Feb., 1857, making it necessary for him to return temporarily for mourning. . . . He was recalled before the period of mourning had elapsed . . . to suppress the Taiping revolt' (p. 753). 'In 1862 Pao Ch'ao . . . was so occupied that he had no chance to take leave even when his mother died. . . . In 1864 . . . he was given two months' leave to inter his mother's remains . . .' (p. 609).

and patrons—in order to return benefits received—of amassing as much wealth as possible. Success in official life consisted in holding the balance between these conflicting aims.

It was natural for officials to be guided in their public conduct by considering every action in the light of its relation to these goals: doing what could be justified in terms of rules and instructions, or evading them to the extent they could 'get away with it'; maintaining or restoring an appearance of order; reporting to superiors what the latter would like to hear; while never missing any opportunity to add to the funds in their official treasury, which, after necessary official expenses and expectations from above had been met, represented the rewards of their services.

It has seemed useful to examine the character and attitudes of officials as a group, since the majority, in the discharge of their largely undifferentiated duties, were concerned with the investigation and adjudication of legal cases, or with their revision.

5

Codified Law

BESIDES the uniformity of outlook which prevailed among the administrators as a result of their training, selection and goals, standardized administrative procedure was laid down by successive dynasties in two compilations which together comprised the body of laws to which the bureaucracy throughout the Empire was required to give effect. The first of these, the collected Administrative Statutes of the dynasty (for the Manchu dynasty, *Ta Ch'ing Hui Tien*), laid down in detail the establishment and functions of all departments and offices throughout the Empire, and prescribed the sphere and extent of the activities they should undertake *vis-à-vis* the general public on one hand and official bodies on the other. The second compilation was what is usually known as the Penal Code of the dynasty (for the Manchu dynasty, *Ta Ch'ing Lü Li*) and prescribed the official action to be taken whenever the conduct of either officials or people failed to conform to what was required of them—by the official system. The lay-out of both compilations therefore reflected that of the government organization.

The codes of the Ch'ing dynasty were closely modelled on those of their immediate predecessors, the Ming, which themselves reproduced features of earlier dynasties—especially the Sung—for which the T'ang codes were the basic models.

In addition to the laws contained in these two codes, edicts were being issued continuously by the Emperor, and published for the information of magistrates in the *Ching Pao* (gazette of the capital), and there would at most times have been a number of these, not yet incorporated in a revision of the code, of which a magistrate would have to take notice.[1]

The *Ta Ch'ing Hui Tien* (a work varying in size from 80 to 250 chapters, according to the edition) listed, straightforwardly and comprehensively, the various bodies of which the government was composed, from the Imperial Court, Councils and the Six Departments down to the minor courts. It set out in each case the establishment, the subdivisions and the

[1] When E. Alabaster purchased the retiring Hupei Judicial Commissioner's compendium of the Penal Code (printed 1872) in 1912, it was interleaved with neatly written slips giving the wording of (then) new Edicts, memorials, etc. and, more rarely, additional explanatory matter by the Judicial Commissioner. (See Alabaster, 1936, p. 426.)

staff employed, with their various functions and duties. The government structure was looked at centrally, but the provinces were dealt with also under the appropriate central departments. For example, the Department of Civil Office section included civil service posts in all provinces—first, offices with general responsibility down to 1,293[1] *hsien* magistrates (every *hsien* being named), then those with special responsibility for education, waterways, prisons and the courier service; while the Department of Revenue (*Hu Pu*) dealt with the registration of population (including the census figures for each area), revenue collection, granaries and coinage throughout the Empire.

The descriptions follow a standard pattern, as, for example:

The Department of Civil Office, with one Manchu and one Chinese President and senior and junior Vice-presidents, is responsible [*chang*] for the appointment of civil officials throughout the Empire, thus assisting the Emperor in governing the mass of the people. . . .

or, in the case of the *Nei Ko*:

. . . in dealing with general affairs.

The Department of Punishments section, after listing the posts at the head, continued as follows:

. . . is in charge of the administration of punishments throughout the Empire thus assisting the Emperor in governing the mass of the people.

All questions concerning the severity appropriate to the different *lü* and *li*[2], the conduct of hearings and judgments, the immediate execution or remission of sentence, pursuit of stolen goods and amount of fines, should be notified to the Department so that important matters can be decided by the Presidents etc. and their staff, while lesser matters can be recorded for the whole country. In all capital cases the *San Fa Ssu*[3] meet to decide the sentence. . . .

Then follow in smaller characters the list of crimes this is intended to include, and similarly after the next main item, the holding of the Autumn Assizes,[4] details of the time and place and who should attend. And so on through every office of every Department, council, academy and court.

Each of the Six Departments also had its own compilation of departmental regulations dealing with technical matters, internal organization and cases to be taken as precedents, known as the Department's *Tse Li*.

The *Ta Ch'ing Hui Tien* was published five times during the dynasty —in 1690, 1732, 1764, 1818 and 1899.[5] The edition of 1764 was accompanied by the publication of the *tse li* (see above), and the editions of

[1] In the edition of 1818.
[2] See later, pp. 59 f.
[3] Supreme Court, see above, p. 38, later, p. 68.
[4] See later, p. 68.
[5] See Fairbank (1952), pp. 59–60.
An account of the contents of the *Ta Ch'ing Hui Tien* (the edition of 1764, I think) by Preston, C. F., appeared in the *China Review*, vol. vi, 1877–8, under the title, 'The Constitutional Law of China'.

1818 and 1899 by *Shih Li*, which describe changes that have taken place in establishments and procedure. If one wants to know therefore, for example, about the administration of non-Han peoples, one finds in any edition of the *Ta Ch'ing Hui Tien* an account of the system in force at the date of its compilation; for the changes the system underwent, and the dates and circumstances, one must look at the *Ta Ch'ing Hui Tien Shih Li*. There can have been few better documented administrative systems.

The *Ta Ch'ing Lü Li*[1]—or Penal Code—was divided in the main into seven sections.[2] The first contained general considerations and sets out the standard punishments and how they should be applied or mitigated in particular circumstances and to certain categories of persons. Then followed six sections, one for each of the Six Departments of the central government, in each of which were collected the laws on matters which were the preserve of that Department. Thus the *Li Pu* (Department of Civil Office) section, a short one, dealt with irregularities in official conduct and had no bearing on the lives of ordinary people. The next covered all matters which were the ultimate concern of the *Hu Pu* (Department of Revenue)—viz., irregularities by magistrate or people in the registration of population and lands, payment of land and other taxes, custody of public property, performance of marriage ceremonies and, more sketchily, offences against the public interest in the manufacture and exchange of goods.[3] Then followed the *Li Pu* (Department of Ceremonies) section, including improprieties in official worship, court ceremonial, mourning etiquette and offences against sumptuary laws. The *Ping Pu* (Department of War) section dealt with the security of the palace, imperial roads (the concern here being, significantly, for the Emperor's person, not the safety of the citizen), city walls, use of the military, misuse of supplies or military horses, conduct of soldiers, protection of the frontiers and the government postal service. Next came what Sir George Staunton translated as 'Criminal Laws', that is, the *Hsing Pu* (Department of Punishments) section, included in which are crimes such as robbery and theft, treason, homicide, violence, arson, abusive language; bribery, corruption, offences arising out of prosecution, trial and custody of prisoners, execution of judgment; forgery, falsification and fraud in official matters; incest and adultery. The final section is that of the *Kung Pu* (Department of Public Works) and covered such matters as neglect of public buildings, river embankments, bridges and highways; failure of magistrates to occupy their official residences or to report plans before

[1] There are two readily accessible translations of this code, though neither is complete. Staunton (1810), as the title of his work (*Ta Tsing Leu Lee; being the Fundamental Laws and a selection from the Supplementary Statutes*) suggests, translated all the *lü* but few of the *li*. Boulais (1924) gives more of the *li*.

[2] There were actually two further sections dealing with the Emperor's Manchu subjects, an innovation of the Ch'ing Dynasty which hardly affected the rest of the Empire.

[3] See footnote 2, p. 60.

undertaking public works; offences by officials and others to do with the manufacture of silk or other products in official factories.

The whole is preceded by prefatory edicts to the original (1647) and later (1679 and 1725) editions setting out the aims of the code: 'to secure the peace and tranquillity of an honest and unoffending community by helping magistrates to decide the proper punishment of wrong-doers' so that 'magistrates and people look up with awe and submission to the justice of these institutions', '. . . the transgressor will not fail to suffer a strict expiation for his offences and will be the instrument of deterring others from similar misconduct'.[1] After these edicts were included tables of relationships, a scale of degrees of punishment (for use when increase or decrease of punishment was prescribed), another which showed the rate at which physical punishments could be commuted to money payments, according to rank, and a list of instruments of punishment and confinement.

Throughout all sections the arrangement is consistent: a *lü* or general law is stated and then followed by *li*, specific conditions for its application or for exemption from its provisions, and then by commentary to explain both.[2] Sir George Staunton wrote in the introduction to his translation:

> The *Leu* or Fundamental Laws, are those of which the Penal Code upon its formation soon after the accession of the present dynasty appears originally to have consisted, and which, being, at least nominally, permanent, are reprinted in each successive edition, without either alteration or amendment.
>
> The *Lee*, or Supplementary Laws, are the modifications, extensions and restrictions of the Fundamental Laws, which after undergoing a deliberate examination in the Supreme Councils, and receiving the sanction of the Sovereign, are inserted in the form of clauses at the end of each article or section of the Code, in order that they might, together with the Fundamental Laws, be equally known and observed. They are generally revised every fifth year,[3] and subjected to such alterations as the wisdom of the government determines to be expedient.

Actually the *lü* were of considerably more ancient origin. As Dr Meijer wrote:[4]

> The *lü* (436 in number) were the laws considered to be valid for all time. Some of them are said to originate in the first code of *Li K'uei*, made for the Marquis *Wen* (424–387 B.C.) of the State *Wei*. Most of them occurred already in the T'ang code (653–4), but in exceptional cases a new *lü* was added, as e.g. in the beginning of the Manchu dynasty, when the Manchus

[1] Staunton (1810), p. lxvii.

[2] See Appendix 1 for example of lay-out.

[3] In the earlier part of the dynasty the Code was re-edited at intervals of 10 years while a lesser revision was made half-way through that period. In 1830 however it was decided that the edition of that year should be altered as little as possible by decisions of the supreme courts, departments, etc., but that such decisions as they were obliged to make should be submitted immediately for imperial approval and promulgation throughout the Empire without delay.

[4] Meijer (1949), p. 4.

were exempted from transportation. The *li* (numbering about 1800) were rules of a more heterogeneous character. They contained many rules for special occasions when it seemed necessary to aggravate or alleviate the *lü*, when new rules were needed for new situations, or when new leading cases were established. . . . The *li*, called 'clauses' by Staunton, 'articles supplémentaires' by Boulais, changed or hollowed out the *lü* freely. The word means precedent, example, rule. . . . They were appended to the *lü* which were considered of a cognate character.

Sometimes what Meijer has called 'hollowing out freely' amounted to contradiction. For example, as Jamieson pointed out, cross-cousin marriage was forbidden by the *lü* but permitted by the *li*. Thus the *lü* has:

> A man cannot marry the children of his aunt on his father's side or of his uncle or aunt on his mother's side, because being of the same generation they are within the fifth degree of mourning. . . .

while one of the *li* reads:

> In the interests of the people it is permitted to marry with the children of a paternal aunt or a maternal uncle or aunt.[1]

New *li* were also classified rather surprisingly under articles with which they seem to have little connection; e.g. a *li* prohibiting the working of coal-mines in the Western Hills near Peking appended to *lü* no. 93 which prohibits fraudulent sale of lands and houses.

One cannot know what the law on any point was, therefore, without studying the *li* as well as the *lü*[2] (and this makes Staunton's translation an inadequate guide to the law then in force on any particular point). However, the *li* rarely made as much difference to the original intention as the one quoted above on cross-cousin marriage; they represented partial adaptation to particular circumstances, in order to make the law fit all eventualities, rather than fundamental developments in legal thinking.

The *lü* are stated in (broadly) one of three ways:

(i) Whoever commits *x* shall be given the punishment *y* (i.e., punishment for an act of commission).

[1] This particular point is dealt with in *China Review*, vol. x (1882–3), at p. 83. There seems to have been some vacillation on this matter. The first edition of the Ming dynasty Code forbade cross-cousin marriage, but a *li* of 1385 allowed it (because, the commentary explains, the prohibition had given rise to so many accusations and lawsuits). The first edition of the Ch'ing code reverted to the prohibition without the contradicting *li*, until in 1729 the *li* was re-enacted. See van der Valk (1956), p. 27. On the advantages of cross-cousin marriage and the preferred type (in the Lower Yangtze area he studied), see Fei (1939), pp. 50–51. The evidence of cross-cousin marriage in different parts of China is surveyed in Freedman (1958), p. 96–99.

[2] Five *lü*, with their *li* and commentary (relating to trade and commerce), are translated in full in Lind (1887), which also gives the Chinese text of these sections.

(ii) Whoever performs *a*, *b*, or *c* actions in an *x* (improper) manner shall be given punishment *y*. (Here the manner of carrying out the action is the occasion for punishment.)

(iii) *a*, *b*, or *c* should be done. Whoever fails to do them, or fails to do them in a fitting manner, shall be given punishment *y* (i.e., punishment for an act of omission or for the manner of commission).

The wording of the *lü* usually begins (in type (iii) above, of course after a preliminary): 'All persons who . . .', (*fan* = all, generally), 'Any person who . . .', 'In all cases in which a man does (not) . . .', 'Any official who connives . . .', 'Any magistrate or any other person who . . .', and ends '. . . shall receive punishment *y*.' In spite of this form of words, however, equality of all persons before the law was not a principle of the Chinese system. Before arriving at a calculation for *y* (the proper punishment in a given case), various details such as a person's age, sex, rank, position in family, relationship to plaintiff or victim—as elaborated in Section I of the Code—had to be taken into consideration. Much can be deduced about the Chinese system of values from the relative weight allowed to these considerations.

The list of recognized punishments is also given in Section 1 of the Code. They were of five kinds,[1] but prescribed according to a graduated scale of intensity:

(1) Correction with the lesser bamboo (*ch'ih*) in five degrees of intensity, only a proportion of which was to be inflicted:

1st	degree nominally	10	blows of which	4	were to be inflicted.
2nd		20		5	
3rd		30		10	
4th		40		15	
5th		50		20	

(2) Punishment with the larger bamboo (*chang*) in five degrees:

1st	degree nominally	60	blows of which	20	were to be inflicted.
2nd		70		25	
3rd		80		30	
4th		90		35	
5th		100		40	

[1] The term *wu hsing*, the five punishments, is the standard expression used for the system of punishments in force in China at any time. In Han times they were: branding, cutting off the nose, castration, chopping off the feet, and the death penalty. In succeeding periods the number five was symbolically retained, however much the content changed and however they might be subdivided and supplemented to fit in the actual punishments. It will be observed that in the Ch'ing code neither the punishment of the 'lingering death' nor that of branding was included in the five punishments, though they were prescribed by certain articles of the Code (see p. 62).

(3) Temporary banishment (*hsi* or *t'u*) to a distance not exceeding 500 *li*[1]:

Banishment	–1 –1½ –2 –2½ –3	years and	60 70 80 90 100	blows reduced as above.

(4) Perpetual Banishment (*liu*), after 100 blows, to a distance of

2,000 *li* 2,500 *li* 3,000 *li*	with forced labour.

(5) Death, by strangulation or decapitation.

Imprisonment was not in itself a punishment in China but a means of detaining the accused for trial or pending settlement of his case. Chinese prisons, however, were often unwholesome places and many prisoners died in gaol.

In addition to the punishment prescribed for stealing (which was graded in proportion to the value of goods stolen) it was provided that those convicted of this crime should be branded on the arm with the characters for 'thief' (*ch'iang tuo*).[2] Branding was also to be inflicted for embezzlement of public property or theft of official seals or edicts.[3]

The forms of the death sentence themselves represented an ascending scale of intensity. Strangulation was considered preferable to beheading as it did not involve mutilation of the body, while the most ignominious was the dreaded *ling ch'ih*—slow and painful execution, inflicted on those convicted of parricide or high treason.[4] This involved the offender's being tied to a cross while, by a series of painful but not themselves mortal cuts, his body was sliced beyond recognition, after which the head was exposed for a period.[5] As the intention was to prevent the continued existence of the criminal's spirit in recognizable form, the slicing would still be carried out even if he had committed suicide.

What the *lü* prescribe, as amplified by the *li*, is the kind and degree of punishment to be inflicted for any offence of omission or commission and the circumstances in which it should be mitigated or intensified. Where it

[1] Say, 150–70 miles. The *li* varied in length in different parts of China.

[2] Staunton (1810), pp. 283–4; Boulais (1924), p. 494.

[3] Staunton (1810), pp. 274, 275, 278, 279.

[4] Staunton (1810), p. 269, 305–6. Boulais (1924), p. 464.

[5] See Alabaster (1899), pp. 57–58. One tradition dates the introduction of this punishment to the reign of the Sung Emperor Shen-tsung (1068–85). See Ratchnevsky (1937), pp. 8–9. Nearly two centuries later Ma Tuan-lin referred to it (*Wen hsien t'ung k'ao*, ch. 166) as an extra-legal punishment, basing himself on a reply from Emperor Chen-tsung, c. 1015. It was first officially included as a punishment in the code of the Yüan dynasty (second half of the thirteenth century).

appeared that two *lü* might both be applicable, it was provided that the more serious offence should have precedence. Offences were not classified into broad categories, but each variety of any crime was separately provided for, and its evaluation depended on particular circumstances. Meijer lists 15 types of homicide, distinguished according to relationship of killer and victim, motive and method.

The possibility that the compilers themselves should have been guilty of any omissions was provided for at least twice in the body of the Code. It was laid down[1] that where no statute was precisely applicable, cases should be determined by analogical application, 'by an accurate comparison with others which are already provided for, and which approach most nearly to those under investigation . . .', while Section 386 (in Staunton's translation) reads:

> Whoever is guilty of improper conduct and such as is contrary to the spirit of the laws, though not a breach of any specific article, shall be punished at the least with 40 blows and when the impropriety is of a serious nature with 80 blows.[2]

This article contained no *li*—no exceptions or amplifications.

Meijer[3] has pointed to the link between the need to redress the criminal fact in order to restore the natural order on the one hand, and the symbolic character of the punishments, and their gradation, on the other. As against this, Hulsewé has suggested[4] that the idea that punishment is an act to redress the harmony of nature which has been disturbed by the crime was itself already archaic in Han times, except when crimes were qualified as impious or nefarious (*pu tao*, *pu ching* or *ta ni*), but that this fundamental idea lived on in the terminology and particularly the notion that the punishment should fit the crime.

The Administrative Statutes and the Penal Code together provided the bureaucracy with comprehensive statements of what the central authorities required both of them and of the people resident in the areas of their jurisdiction, the measures to be taken to promote the desired results and the legal steps necessary to deal with lapses from the officially required

[1] In the first (general) section of the Code, see Staunton (1810), p. 43.

[2] The title of this section, *pu ying wei*, may be translated as 'things one ought not to do' or 'things one ought not to have done'.

Hoang (1915) gives the following examples of what was classified as *pu ying wei*:

- Selling one's wife, but with the justification of pressure of poverty (p. 127).
- Not to report the adultery of a daughter-in-law (in which one has not connived and has no pecuniary interest) (p. 138).
- To kill one's wife's lover in the act of escaping from the house after committing adultery (p. 140).
- A wife who sells herself to provide money to bury her deceased husband (p. 161).
- Not to arrange a marriage for a slave-girl who has reached the age of 23 (p. 226).

[3] Meijer (1949), p. 3.

[4] Hulsewé (1955), p. 81.

standard if other methods had failed. The form of these codes has been described here in detail so that comment on them may be intelligible.

A government structure covering so extensive an area as the Chinese Empire, employing so many officials in such diverse work clearly needed written regulations for its own functioning. The *Ta Ch'ing Hui Tien* and its subsidiary compilations correspond roughly to the Departmental Regulations—Army Regulations, Post Office Rules etc.—well known in our own government departments, i.e., codified instructions for the guidance of servants in those departments, but in China these included sections on court etiquette, religious observances, etc. Such regulations are not normally subject to actions in the courts of the land and in this China was no exception.

It will be seen that as far as the *Ta Ch'ing Lü Li* is concerned, every law is formulated at least in part in the manner of a penal law: 'Anyone who does *x* is to receive punishment *y*.' In many cases, however, the same *lü* that prescribes punishment for a lapse first sets out in some detail the procedure which ought to be followed—either by the citizen or official or both. For example, Section 55 of the Penal Code[1] sets out the manner in which officials should proceed to a new post and how the transfer of the *yamen* accounts from old to new incumbents should be dealt with; Sections 119 and 120 describe the procedure to be followed in collecting revenue in kind; Section 397 states the time within which sentence should be executed after judgment has been reached and approved; Section 405 gives the procedure to be followed in a case in which accomplices are brought to trial under a jurisdiction other than that which is trying the original suspect. If the *lü* is not of this form, an implicit statement of what the positive law is can often be deduced from the statement of what constitutes an infringement of it—e.g. Section 149: '. . . If a creditor whose debtor has failed to fulfil his agreement, *instead of applying for redress at the tribunal of the magistrate of the district*, relies on his own power and authority, and attempts to reimburse himself by seizing violently the cattle, furniture or other property of such debtor, he shall be punished with 80 blows. . . .' (The prohibitions in such cases probably give a fairly clear indication of what usually went on.) Or Section 62: 'Wherever an Imperial Edict is issued on any subject, whoever wilfully omits the execution of anything that is commanded therein shall be punished . . .' i.e., Edicts should be obeyed. Thus the so-called Penal Code contains much that would be classified as administrative or procedural law in other systems.

When first brought to the notice of western readers, the Code was praised, though not without other criticisms, for its directness and lucidity.[2] In fact, the anxiety of the compilers to cover every possible contingency made at times for vagueness which must have caused a

[1] Section numbers refer to Staunton's translation.

[2] *Edinburgh Review*, August 1810.

magistrate trying to interpret its articles great difficulty. Very often what appears at first sight as a clear rule is very much weakened by what follows. For example, Section 387 states clearly that those officers charged with pursuit and arrest of offenders should discharge this duty within thirty days of the order's being issued by the magistrate—or suffer punishment. 'Nevertheless,' it goes on, '. . . if more than half the offenders . . . be overtaken, or even any less proportion, provided that such proportion includes the most guilty, the original neglect and misconduct of the responsible police officer shall be pardoned. . . .' Evasion of this article should not have taxed the ingenuity of those responsible for the pursuit. Many articles required the magistrate to judge of motives and conduct without even indicating by what objective criteria these should be judged. Section 289, for example, reads: 'All persons rearing venomous animals, or preparing drugs of a poisonous nature *for the purpose of applying them to the destruction of man*, or instructing others so to do, shall be beheaded although no person is actually killed by means of such drugs or animals . . . The head inhabitant of the village or the district when privy to and failing to give information of this crime shall suffer a punishment of 100 blows *but if really ignorant thereof* shall be excused. . . .'[1] Judgments in such cases could not be other than arbitrary and such articles lent themselves to abuse.

There was some incongruity in prescribing in detail both the standard of behaviour required and the methods to be adopted to achieve it—the assumption being that A must mechanically produce B—and then, after allowing the magistrate no discretion, holding him responsible for what he had failed to prevent.

[1] My italics. S. v.d. S.

6

Judicial Procedure*

ANYONE had the right to petition the magistrate of the area in which he lived to investigate a case and punish offenders against the laws, and all had the duty to report crimes within the area of their responsibility. Only if a magistrate refused to enter a case for investigation could the petitioner present a plea direct to a higher authority, though there was provision for a case to be transferred to another court if either accused or accuser were related to the magistrate.

Certain days in the month were named for the receipt of such petitions, but, provided that the matter was serious and that the petitioner was not guilty of making a false or malicious accusation, the petition could be presented to the magistrate at any time, in the course of the latter's public progress or by beating the drum placed at the entrance to the *yamen* for the purpose. The petition had to be in writing (thus creating work for scribes, *tai shu*,[1] versed in the drawing up of plaints, though they had no training in law) and the petitioner's identity had to be authenticated by *ti pao* (or *fang chang* etc.) of his locality. After the petition had passed through various hands in the *yamen*, the defendant would be required to submit a written defence[2] and would subsequently be summoned by the *yamen* police to appear for trial. Local headmen were required to produce culprits, under threat of punishment if they failed to do so, and local gentry frequently handed over criminals who were caught with proofs of guilt or reasons for suspicion about them. Customary forms of surety operated, under threat of penalty for guaranteeing a real offender. Thus, remarked an anonymous nineteenth-century observer, 'the guilt or innocence of the parties is left to be decided very much by their natural protectors, their own relatives and friends. If they refuse to give security for them, the chances are that the case is a very bad one'.[3]

The magistrate, assisted by his subordinates, was then required to conduct an enquiry both by private investigation and court hearing to ascertain (*a*) whether the defendant was in fact guilty of the action of which he stood accused (and, if so, a confession of guilt had to be extracted

* For a postscript (1977) to this chapter see p. 164 below.

[1] See Meadows (1847), 'On the . . . *tai shu*', pp. 121–3.

[2] The evidence of Arab travellers suggests that the system of written accusation and defence dates back at least to the ninth century. (See *Chinese Repository*, 1832, p. 13.)

[3] 'Lex' (1873), p. 238.

from him); (*b*) which section of the *Ta Ch'ing Lü Li* covered this misdeed; and (*c*) circumstances which were relevant to determining his degree of criminality. He then had to decide according to (*b*) and (*c*) what punishment was appropriate. If, in the light of his investigation, he decided that the accused was innocent, he had instead to prosecute the accuser—for bringing a false and/or malicious accusation.[1] In cases for which the punishment was the bamboo, he was empowered, after allowing appeal—if desired—up to the level of the Provincial Governor, to have the sentence executed himself, and required to do so without delay. For more serious crimes he had to forward the papers to his next superior magistracy with his recommendations as to the appropriate section of the code and the sentence warranted, or, if he were in doubt, he could ask guidance as to the proper course. This would be decided at higher levels, the judicial hierarchy being almost the same as the administrative but for slight specialization at the summit, while the competence of the different tribunals varied according to the gravity of the case (measured by the punishment provided for it).

Most writers on Chinese government speak of legal cases being referred for revision to the next superior office in the bureaucratic hierarchy. According to Meijer,[2] however, the six stages that this would involve in the provincial hierarchy—*hsien*, *chou*, *fu*, *tao*, Provincial Judicial Commissioner (*An Ch'a shih*), Provincial Governor—were usually reduced in practice to four. Thus if we regard the *hsien* or *fu* magistrate's *yamen* as the court of first instance for the least important cases, the court of second instance or first revision was the office of the *Tao-t'ai*. Next came the court of the Provincial Judicial Commissioner and, fourth, the court of the Governor-General or Governor of the Province.[3] Cases not involving loss of life and not leading to a punishment more severe than temporary banishment would be finally dealt with by the provincial government, and an annual report of such cases was sent to the Board of Punishments at Peking for information. Cases involving loss of life would be passed by the lower courts to the Governor of the Province, whose suggestion would be submitted to the Board of Punishments for approval. The latter had original jurisdiction over cases punishable by perpetual banishment, military deportation or transportation outside China Proper.

The Emperor himself sentenced capital cases, but only after revision

[1] An interesting principle of Chinese law was that anyone who made an accusation deemed to be false was required to suffer the punishment which the crime he denounced would have merited (*fan tso*). See Staunton (1810), p. 364; Balazs (1954), p. 170, note 257. This provision which prima facie appears to be in the interests of justice probably in fact worked against it, i.e. as a deterrent to denouncing the influential but no protection to those who needed it.

[2] Meijer (1949), p. 6.

[3] The statement in the Legal Monograph of the Ch'ing History of the maximum delay permitted in forwarding cases up the hierarchy also gives four stages, thus: *hsien/chou; chou/fu; ssu* (Judicial Commissioner); Governor. See *Ch'ing Shih Kao, Hsing Fa Chih*, ch. 3, p. 6.

by the Supreme Court, *San Fa Ssu*.[1] Wherever in the code the death sentence was prescribed, it was always specified whether it should be carried out immediately (for crimes like treason and rebellion) or delayed (for various types of homicide). The *San Fa Ssu* could be convened at any time to deal with cases in the former category; for the rest, there was an elaborate revision procedure. Cases of prisoners under sentence of death had to be reported to Peking by all Provincial Governors for review at the Autumn Assizes (*Ch'iu Shen*), a court made up of the heads of the Nine Chief Ministries together with officers of the Censorate for the Departments and Provinces. The result of their deliberations was communicated to the Emperor, who ceremonially endorsed it with vermilion brush. Prisoners whose names he had marked were then executed; a lucky few were pardoned; the rest waited for the same procedure the next year.[2] Any who survived this submission procedure in three successive years would have their sentence commuted.

On such occasions as the Emperor's marriage, his jubilee or other memorable events, a general amnesty was proclaimed. This could be of two kinds: a special amnesty, *ta she*, which cancelled the record of the crime as well as remitting punishment; and an ordinary amnesty, *ch'ang she*, which only remitted punishment. Not all crimes could be pardoned, and, for those that could, sometimes bambooing or branding was administered as a substitute for the prescribed punishment.[3] One advantage of the lengthy revision procedure was the chance it gave the prisoner of surviving until the next amnesty.

Several points about the manner of conducting trials in China must be mentioned. First, that though it was hedged about with restrictions under threat of punishment, the employment of torture as a means of obtaining a confession was officially permitted[4]—but only during the court trial.

Secondly, the magistrate himself conducted the examination of the defendant, questioning and cross-questioning to get at the true facts, and, as Professor Gluckman has pointed out in reference to Lozi trial procedure,[5] this form of trial makes it *appear* that the defendant is assumed guilty unless he can prove his innocence, instead of the contrary.

Thirdly, apart from certain specified categories of persons (those over 80 or under 10 years of age, who could not be convicted of perjury), all persons, including the prisoner, might give evidence.[6] Cases were decided however not according to the weight of the evidence but rather according to the conviction of the judge.[7] There are cases on record in which the evidence was set aside.

[1] See above, p. 38, note 4.
[2] See also Appendix 4, no. 18.
[3] See Alabaster (1899), pp. 115–31.
[4] See Staunton (1810), pp. 441–2, 488–90; Boulais (1924), p. 716. This was no new thing in China. A sixth-century debate on the conditions in which torture could be used effectively is translated in Balazs (1954) as appendix 3, pp. 195–206.
[5] Gluckman, (1955) p. 96.
[6] See Alabaster (1899), pp. 15–16.
[7] I consider the question of evidence further on p. 75.

Fourthly, the court proceedings were designed to uphold the majesty of the law, the magistrate being the Emperor's representative in his district, and to emphasize the unworthiness of all other persons. Contemporary prints usually show the parties and witnesses in a kneeling posture, often with *yamen* staff looking on menacingly, bamboo in hand. (Frontispiece.)

Fifthly, the form of the proceedings *in all cases* is accusatory. A accused B of some action forbidden by the code and, if proved guilty, B would be punished as directed in the code. He might also be ordered to make restitution to A. Revision before a higher court only followed where severe punishments were appropriate (or if the defendant felt it worth while to appeal against the sentence, but if this were bambooing, the chances are that he would not do so, having already suffered a number of strokes during the course of trial). Many cases that would fall into the category of civil suits in English law would not carry a penalty entitling them to benefit of revision and thus, as Sir John Barrow remarked in 1804, such cases were not submitted to the scrutiny of a revising judge more impartial to the issue than was the local magistrate.

Lastly, the unavoidable consequence of a legal case once started was punishment for at least one person. It could end in punishment for the accused, if judged guilty; if he were not, punishment would be assigned to the unjustified accuser; it was also likely that witnesses would, during the course of the proceedings, incur punishment, while the magistrate was exposed throughout the case to the risk of reprimand or degradation for making a mistake in procedure or in application of the code.[1]

The *hsien* magistrate who had to undertake these onerous legal proceedings, fraught as they were with risks to himself—and it will be remembered that these were only part of his total official duties—was naturally very much dependent on his staff, and magistrates customarily employed two expert advisors, one of whom specialized in legal matters. This man, whose knowledge of the code and experience of precedents was at the disposal of the magistrate, was the only person openly concerned in the action whose job it was to know the law. The emergence of a legal profession to serve the interest of litigants, either for pleading or offering opinions on points of law, was officially discouraged by articles in the *Ta Ch'ing Lü Li* which penalized those who incited others to undertake litigation or made a profit out of managing a lawsuit. This restriction of professional activity to official advisors or clandestine lawyers was clearly a barrier to the technical development of law in China.

Though the Chinese code was criticized on the grounds of attempting to regulate everything with 'excessive and unprofitable accuracy'[2] and of aiming at repressing disorder rather than promoting individual freedom, certain aspects have recommended themselves to foreign students—

[1] And the magistrates of superior *yamens* who acquiesced in his decision. See, for example, a case quoted in Hsieh (1925), pp. 231–2.

[2] *Edinburgh Review*, August 1810.

notably the attempt to make the punishment fit the criminal. The application of a uniform code for all to know throughout an Empire the size of China was a feat in itself, in strong contrast with the usual ideas of oriental despotism, and the Chinese are recorded as having been justly proud of their laws.[1] Only reform in nineteenth-century England and elsewhere made even the substance of Chinese laws appear, by contrast, less humane.[2]

The real weakness of the Chinese system sprang from the fact that the application of the law was entrusted to the administrative officers of the Empire. The court of law was, like the militia, part of the machinery for maintaining order and good behaviour throughout the district. It provided no check on the executive power, and this the system as a whole provided only very indirectly through the power possessed by administrative officials to punish other administrative officials. When government was efficient, legal machinery functioned efficiently; when it was not, legal machinery offered no correction and was itself corrupt. In a trial of what would be a civil suit in English law, the magistrate would have little interest in doing justice as between the parties, except in so far as it was more likely that a just decision would lead to peace and harmony in the neighbourhood. The legal system subserved administrative ends.

Being enmeshed in the administrative machinery involved other disadvantages for the law. Enough has been said of the financial arrangements of the administration to show that local magistrates and, more especially, their staff, were constantly on the watch for opportunities to earn fees or otherwise add to their resources. To embark on a legal case involved the certainty of fees to various officials through whose hands it passed, the probable necessity of hospitality to those sent by the magistrate[3] to enquire into the circumstances, the possibility of expense on journeys and meals away from home while the case was being heard, and, if the case were protracted,[4] the risk of 'opportunity costs' through loss of earnings. Once started, it was difficult to get a case withdrawn, even though it led to financial ruin for both parties.

Delay was inherent in a system which allowed so much opportunity for revision, but seems also to have occurred through arrears piling up.[5] We are told of Tseng Kuo-fan, for example, that as Governor-General of Chih-li he '. . . cleared up a large number of long-pending legal cases'.[6]

[1] Alabaster, an authority to be respected, offers a defence of the Chinese system on many points for which it has been adversely criticized, but even he admits some weaknesses. See Alabaster (1899), Introduction, pp. lxii, lxiii, lxviii.

[2] Anyone who is shocked at the inadequacies of Chinese trial procedure is recommended to read Holdsworth (1928), in which this authority questions whether the English procedure described by Dickens lasted quite as long as Dickens claimed. He does admit its truth however for a slightly earlier period, which would make it contemporary with China in the middle of the Manchu dynasty. Reminders of its harshness are not lacking in Australia.

[3] See proverbs, Appendix 3.

[4] Appendix 4, no. 13.

[5] Appendix 4, no. 28.

[6] See Hummel (1944).

Presumably lesser men procrastinated in the hope that, if they waited long enough, they would be transferred and they could bequeath difficult cases to their successors.

Expense and delay are characteristics of most legal systems. A further defect of the Chinese system was that a litigant had little confidence of obtaining justice in return for his money and suspense. The goals of the system, resting on the basic Chinese idea of natural harmony in the universe and the absence of ideas of natural rights, were to fix responsibility for disturbance (even if it were an accident), to assign punishment to redress the situation, to deter others from committing the same mistake and to restore order. The only justice it could be said to aim at was the awarding of just deserts, and just deserts might include punishment for a person who would according to English law be judged innocent. The very fact that a legal case had arisen was seen as an indication of disturbance, and some action had to be taken to restore the situation. As Escarra put it, '. . . l'ordre est déjà troublé du fait qu'il y a un procès'.[1]

It seems to have been assumed that in the investigation to fix responsibility for what had occurred truth was bound to emerge. (If it did not, responsibility for falsehood or deceit would have to be assigned and punished . . . and so on in an endless regression.) In practice, other factors in the total social situation made this difficult and provided motives for the opposite to result. A number of persons had an interest in the truth *not* emerging.

Wrong-doers conscious of their guilt had obvious reasons for misrepresenting facts, and in addition were usually willing to pay witnesses who would testify to their innocence[2] (possibly also to some other person's guilt), and, in a population among whom many lived at the margin of subsistence, there were some willing to serve in this way. There were even some who made a living by confessing guilt and submitting on behalf of real offenders to corporal punishment,[3] and we hear of 'a band of devoted men' in the neighbourhood of Canton prepared to risk transportation and even death for the sake of the payment to their families. If '. . . investigation becomes inevitable, the case is by no means so hopeless for the guilty as might be expected where the laws against murder are so strict as in China'.[4] R. M. Martin also testified to this practice.[5] He reported a case in 1829 of multiple murder at sea and concludes, 'Seventeen men suffered for the murder. . . . The subsequent confession of the pardoned culprit discloses an extraordinary fact, that six of those

[1] Escarra (1936), p. 255.

[2] Alabaster quotes the case of a scholar who was found out and punished for acting as intermediary in getting a case of assault entered as suicide (receiving payment from the assaulter's family—and no doubt passing some of it to that of the victim, though that is not stated). He lost his privileges as a scholar and was sentenced to be beaten with the bamboo. See Alabaster (1936), pp. 435–6.

[3] 'Lex' (1873), p. 240.

[4] *Chinese Repository*, vol. iv (1836), p. 412.

[5] Martin (1847), vol. i, p. 165.

that suffered death were bought substitutes.' In the Instructions to Coroners, translated by Giles from the *Hsi Yüan Lu*,[1] the following passage occurs:

> In all cases where prosecutor and accused are men of the slightest influence or position, choose experienced and trusty assistants, taking them along with you and never letting them out of your sight even to eat or drink, unless watched by someone, but adjourn the case for a while until they may have finished. Unless you do this, these men will be tampered with, and there will be an end to all justice or redress. This cannot be too cautiously guarded against. . . .

Various articles in the code charged the *ti pao* of a locality with the obligation to report crimes—those involving the death of the victim or magical practices, for example—to the *hsien* magistrate. To do so would involve the *ti pao* in trouble and expense, so frequently cases were hushed up for this reason. In the case of certain crimes, apparently those judged to be a threat to the existence of the government, a reward was payable to anyone who filed information about them, e.g., the (justified) accuser received the confiscated goods of a person convicted of treason, and a fixed sum was payable for indicting anyone who had counterfeited coin. These inducements were presumably offered as compensation for the risk such informants incurred if their information was proved groundless and to encourage people to overcome their reluctance to have anything to do with court proceedings, but even so they may not always have secured their objective. Alabaster commented on the capacity of the Chinese to turn a blind eye when crimes were being committed against their neighbours:

> A subject of horror to foreigners is the apathy with which Chinese generally will stand by and see offences committed. It may be true to explain this away in the usual manner by attributing this to languor; but it would be more correct to say that it is due to fear of the Law. It is laid down that persons must not interfere unless they have a *right* to do so by reason of relationship or otherwise.[2]

It is clear from the context that Alabaster had in mind personal aid rendered to the victim of a crime—he quotes the case of a man who gave such assistance and received a sentence for his action—but presumably this fear of getting involved in the unpleasant consequences of a legal action acted also as a deterrent to reporting crime, if one could avoid obvious knowledge of it. Nor was the magistrate himself a disinterested party in this respect, even supposing him to be above bribery by guilty parties. The report of a legal case, especially a serious one, drew attention

[1] *Ḥsi Yüan Lu:* 'Instructions to Coroners' (compiled by Commissioner of Justice Sung Tz'u in reign of Shun Yu (1241–53) and steadily improved on by the Board of Punishments), translated in Giles (1874).

[2] Alabaster (1899), Introduction, p. lvii. These ideas are developed further in notes in the author's own copy (now in Cambridge University Library) intended no doubt for publication in a revised edition.

to his area as being one where all was not well; if harmony was disturbed, this implied that he was incompetent and blemished his record, and a mistake in dealing with the case might bring unwelcome consequences for himself. It was therefore in his interest to suppress cases altogether, or in his submission to alter details of fact to make them appear less serious than the true facts would have been, or even to make the case under consideration appear similar to one previously dealt with without hazard. The ultimate was reached in a case quoted by Staunton in which, he says, the basis of proceedings was a fabricated story which Chinese merchants invented, which the Europeans were reported to concur in (though they did not), which the witnesses adopted, which the magistrate accepted and finally the Emperor appears to have acquiesced in—all without examination.[1]

Another reason for reluctance within the *yamen* to pursuing crimes impartially was fear of personal reprisals by influential local families, some of whose members, if they held official office, would almost certainly out-rank the local magistrate. In the early Ch'ing novel, *The Dream of the Red Chamber*, a magistrate newly arrived at his post (and particularly conscientious since he has just been reinstated after losing a previous appointment on account of his unsatisfactory conduct) is full of zeal to arrest a murderer, until he discovers that the suspect is related to one of the families which, his staff inform him, should on no account be implicated. Every *yamen*, it is explained, has its '*hu kuan fu*'[2], magistrate's protective charm, that is, a list of families who have important connections with government circles (or at least have relatives who hold important posts elsewhere) against whom the magistrate would proceed at his peril. In this instance the magistrate reluctantly heeds the warning and allows the criminal to escape; he saves face by claiming that the murderer has already been atoned for by the victim's avenging spirit having inflicted a malignant disease on the murderer. That this incident should figure in a popular novel suggests that it must have had credibility for the reader or listener.[3]

As may be supposed, some magistrates rose above the difficulties and temptations that surrounded them. A small number of officials actually acquired a reputation for their handling of legal cases. It is reported that one 'during his magistracy showed such ability in handling lawsuits that a number of important cases were assigned to him . . .'; of another that he 'showed special skill in handling judicial cases'; while a third 'was known for his legal skill and reform of criminal law and procedure'.[4]

[1] Staunton (1810), p. 516.

[2] A *hu fu* was a protective charm to ward off demons, so *hu kuan fu* equals 'protect-magistrate charm'.

[3] McHugh (trans.) (1958), pp. 34 ff. In the Chinese, Mao Tun (ed. 1935), vol. i, pp. 21 ff.

[4] See Hummel (ed. 1943) under Wang Yün-chi [1642–1715], Chang Ch'i [1765–1833] and Tai Tun-yüan [1768–1834].

These seem, however, to have been the exceptions that prove the rule. In popular fiction the clever and just magistrate was a hero, probably just because he was so rarely encountered in real life. In the short story, 'The Judgment of Magistrate Teng', for example, a dying official, fearing that his elder son will cheat his young half-brother out of his inheritance, says: 'Wait until an upright and intelligent official is appointed. Then take this [magical] scroll to him and tell him all about your case. . . .' By good luck, many years later the son chanced on a neighbouring village holding a sacrifice, which they had vowed to do if ever a magistrate were appointed from whom they could obtain justice. The story ends with the magistrate doing justice between the brothers, but at the cost of a large slice of the inheritance which he himself kept as a reward for adjudicating the matter.[1]

Detective work and trial, being both performed by the magistrate, tended to merge. In Chinese detective stories, in which of course the hero is the magistrate, the magistrate who can get to the bottom of a case is depicted as a *very* clever chap—there were so many people who had to be outwitted. The man who could won fame and popularity.[2]

Legal systems in which the major role in trial procedure is played by the judge have not had the spur to developing clear rules of evidence which jury trial provided in England, viz., the need to guide lay jurors. Only in 'civil' disputes arising out of antecedent transactions did customary forms of concluding the transaction (i.e., by means of documents: deeds of sale signed by witnesses, title deeds to land bearing the official seal) provide a reasonably reliable measure of the true facts. In the case of real crimes there was none. Nor were Chinese medical and scientific knowledge advanced enough to be of assistance in assessing evidence (or, if the level of knowledge reached was enough, it was not harnessed to this use.) The colour of the corpse for example was taken as evidence of the manner of death.[3] It was for the Chinese judge to elicit all the information available to help him to reach his decision and to avoid being misled by interested parties. And, never having arrived at a conception of what constituted proof 'beyond reasonable doubt', the Chinese relied on extorting a confession of guilt from the accused, by torture if necessary. The best Chinese judges were aware of the pitfalls of accepting a confession of guilt. The collections of model cases include some in which the judge continued his investigation because he was not satisfied with the confession he had obtained—and usually his doubts proved to have been justified[4]; but such conscientiousness was probably exceptional.

[1] See bibliography, under Howell. [2] See, for example, van Gulik (1949).

[3] 'Instructions to Coroners', trans. Giles. See bibliography, Giles (1874).

[4] There are fifteen cases of unjustified confession in the 144 cases quoted in the *T'ang-Yin-Pi-Shih*. See bibliography, van Gulik (1956).

Before passing sentence at the Autumn Assizes, the judges had to be convinced that confession had not been made merely because of torture. See Alabaster (1936), p. 431.

Dr A. L. Epstein has considered the problem of what constitutes valid evidence in relation to the urban native courts in Northern Rhodesia.[1] After pointing out that the technical rules of our law of evidence can only be explained in terms of the jury system, he has suggested that in African courts the fact-finding process is nevertheless guided by rules and that the courts have some conception of relevance. In Chinese courts judgment was, I believe, more arbitrary, the proportion of the true facts that emerged depending to a great extent on the capacity of the particular magistrate and his advisor.

A further difficulty in regard to the hearing of evidence arose out of the nature of the Chinese language. As the dialects of spoken Chinese are not usually mutually intelligible, the fact that the magistrate himself did not always know the dialect of the people in his jurisdiction made him dependent on his *yamen* staff for the version of the evidence he received, and thus gave the staff considerable opportunities for distortion in the process of verbal interpretation. It does not seem likely that his legal advisor could have included protection against this danger among the services he performed for his master, since these posts tended to be the preserve of men from one particular area, and we do not hear of a study of dialects being part of their equipment.

The malpractices of *yamen* staff were notorious. It appears that constables who succeeded in arresting suspects who were subsequently convicted received an official reward and that this led to the practice of constables 'loosely arresting the wrong person whether for revenge or hope of reward . . .' and themselves using illegal instruments of torture to extract a confession in advance of trial. This was forbidden by an edict of 1814.[2] There were complaints by censors that constables sent to arrest thieves were themselves indulging in theft. In 1832 the Governor of Chihli proposed to raise a loan for the purpose of paying *yamen* staff better so that constables would side with the government instead of siding with the thieves. A corpse, we are told, was regarded as a prize by the underlings who would use it as a means to extort money from neighbours and relatives of the deceased. In 1827, 23,921 'retainers' of courts 'dreaded by the people as much as wolves and tigers' were dismissed in the province of Chihli alone.[3]

[1] Epstein (1954), p. 7. [2] See Alabaster (1936), p. 433.

[3] See 'Notices of Modern China' by 'R. I.' in *Chinese Repository*, vol. iv, pp. 214–29. Wittfogel writes: 'In all sizable agro-bureaucratic despotisms the underlings are numerous. During the last period of imperial China about 40,000 ranking (civil) officials had at their disposal over 1,200,000 clerks and over 500,000 runners —that is, a total of more than 1,700,000 underlings, or something more than forty underlings to one ranking official.' These estimates have been made, he says, as part of the Ch'ing work on the Chinese History Project, by Lien-che Tu Fang. As I have not been able to find any readily accessible authority against which to compare the figure quoted, I do not feel competent to challenge Mrs Fang's reliability (particularly as I admire other of her work) but 40,000 as the total of civil officials sounds high to me. The *Hsü Wen Hsien T'ung K'ao*, ch. 51, gives

In all the circumstances it seems hardly to be wondered at if the truth did not always emerge.

Even supposing that a plaintiff were successful in obtaining a just verdict, Chinese law was deficient in remedies and machinery for enforcement of judgment. Alabaster quotes[1] the Ch'ien-lung Emperor as having said:

> The object of law is to avoid the necessity for private vengeance, and the law once satisfied, it would never do to allow the individual to take further action.

Chinese law lacked the strength that should attend such resolution, if it was to be effective. It did provide for payment to relatives in case of accidental homicide, and restitution of goods or money illegally extorted (Section 349), but in general the provisions of the Code stopped at assessing punishment meet for the wrong-doer without concern for damage suffered by the person wronged; e.g. after providing fairly precise criteria for what constitutes rape (Section 366) there follows this sentence: 'The woman on whom rape is committed shall not be liable to any punishment', and (Section 266) 'violation of females on the occasion of a theft' merely increases the punishment to that for robbery.

Though it was not lawful to take the law into one's own hands, the law would take into consideration that one had wrongs to avenge[2]—which appears to amount almost to an implicit inducement. The lack of confidence in legal remedies which left it to plaintiffs to help themselves is indicated in Section 299 of the Code, which in Staunton's translation reads as follows:

> Any person who with a view to accomplish some object such as a marriage contract, the transfer of property, payment of debts and the like, alarms another to such a degree by violent threats that he kills himself in despair, shall whenever reasonable grounds can be shown to have existed for such extreme apprehension on the part of the deceased . . . be punished. . . .

Nor would a successful plaintiff have had much confidence in getting execution of judgment, if the law had provided remedies, since the only staff available to ensure their enforcement would have been the magistrate's rapacious underlings.

Other circumstances attaching to the mode of trial—the humble attitude to be taken up in the presence of a magistrate, the insolence and exactions of *yamen* staff, the use of torture to secure a confession, the exhibition of condemned prisoners to the gaze of the multitude—all made it distasteful to self-respecting people. The K'ang-hsi Emperor (reigned 1662–1723) in replying to a memorial once gave it as his opinion[3]

24,683 civil officials for the previous dynasty. Nor can the other figures be easily tested.

See Wittfogel (1957), p. 307 and note p. 479.

[1] Alabaster (1899), p. 6.
[2] Alabaster (1899), p. 5.
[3] Quoted in Jernigan (1905), at p. 191.

'that law-suits would tend to increase to a frightful amount, if people were not afraid of the tribunals, and if they felt confident of always finding in them ready and perfect justice. As man is apt to delude himself concerning his own interests, contests would then be interminable, and the half of the Empire would not suffice to settle the lawsuits of the other half. I desire therefore that those who have recourse to the tribunals should be treated without any pity, and in such a manner that they shall be disgusted with law, and tremble to appear before a magistrate. . . .' So the unsatisfactory character (from a western point of view) of Chinese courts was to some extent deliberate. There is reason to believe that they also went beyond what was intended. Doolittle, for example, describes methods of torture, other than those mentioned in the Code, which were sometimes employed.[1] 'One who has had a wide experience of land transactions in Shanghai' noted that '. . . immunity . . . from seizures at litigations in the Chinese courts was one of the advantages that persuaded shrewd Chinese to register their land at foreign consulates'.[2] Hu Hsien-ch'in quotes a case of an inter-clan fight resulting from a quarrel about water supply. The contestants agreed not to take the case to the magistrate 'as he might do us much greater harm. We prefer to decide the quarrel ourselves.'[3]

Wang T'ao, a Chinese who visited Europe at the time of the Franco-Prussian war, wrote articles on his return advocating the adoption of western practices. From the things he chose for favourable comment, even after making allowance for exaggeration, one can infer criticism of the corresponding Chinese institutions:

> The real strength of England however lies in the fact that there is a sympathetic understanding between the governing and the governed, a close relationship between the ruler and people. . . . In their treatment of the people the officials never dare use severe punishments, heavy fines, or tyrannical and excessive taxation. Nor dare they accept any bribery . . . or squeeze the blood and flesh of myriads of people in order to fill up their own pockets. The English people are likewise public-spirited and law-abiding; the laws and regulations are hung up high (for everyone to see), and no-one dares violate them. He who violates the law goes to court only to have his confession taken; when the real truth has been obtained, then a verdict is made and he is imprisoned. There has never been such cruelty as torturing and beating him by bamboos and clubs so that his blood and flesh spread all over. In prison the convict is supplied with food and clothing, so that he may not be hungry or cold. He is taught to work and not allowed to become idle. He is visited every seven days by preachers to make him repent and live a new life. He is never maltreated by those in charge of the prison. The excellence of the prison system is what China has never had since the Golden Age. . . .[4]

One wonders if Wang T'ao had ever read the French eighteenth-century philosophers' praise of China!

[1] Doolittle (1868), pp. 341 ff.
[2] Feetham Report, p. 322.
[3] Hu (1948), p. 93.
[4] Quoted in Teng and Fairbank (1954), p. 140.

The provision for commuting physical and other punishments to money payments must have worked very unevenly as between those at different economic levels. Presumably the poorest members of the population would always have had difficulty in availing themselves of the privilege of commutation (and equally in offering sufficient inducements to magistrates to hush up or minimize their offences). It seems probable that in periods of economic distress—times when disorder was likely to be on the increase—this would have applied to the majority, so that in hard times harshness of physical punishments became an extra scourge inflicted by officialdom. This would seem to be one possible explanation of the statement by 'Lex':

> There is an elaborate system by which in certain cases fines may be substituted for other punishments, but it is very seldom that fines are paid in commutation at present.[1]

In the case reported by Staunton already discussed,[2] acceptance of the fiction of accidental homicide permitted the imposition of a fine instead of the sentence of death by strangulation which 'homicide by blows' would have incurred. Could this perhaps explain why it was presented as it was?

To sum up, there was a general predisposition on grounds of expense, uncertainty, risk and harshness not to set the official legal machinery in motion, nor to get involved as witnesses, if it could be avoided, but rather to leave other units of social organization to deal with all matters they were capable of handling, and only to bring the official system into action when they had failed or when some blatantly violent occurrence could not be officially ignored.

This reluctance to go to law itself acted as a barrier to the development of a more serviceable system. Though Chinese merchants were not slow to appreciate the protection of western law when they were brought into contact with it, no influential element in Chinese society had a clear interest in the creation or emergence of an efficient system (as for example the Crown in England had an interest in attracting cases to the King's Courts and offered jury trial as an incentive). Independence could only exist between the meshes of the official system. Innovation by adapting or developing official law-courts to handle new types of case was ruled out as much by the lack of confidence all classes of society felt for the magistrate's *yamen* as by official disinclination to multiply the number of court cases. The idea of a test case, undertaken in a public-spirited way and in awareness of the possible outcome, in order to get a decision which might show the need for fresh legislation, was totally foreign to Chinese ways. Needlessly to expose oneself to the degradation involved in an action would mark out anyone who did so as stupid and cause him to lose face. Nor, for obvious reasons, could the law-court be used to test the legitimacy

[1] 'Lex' (1873), p. 240. [2] See above, p. 73.

of official exactions or to establish the rights of private citizens *vis-à-vis* the administration.

The law remained synonymous with a morally desirable standard: the Chinese never developed it as the concept of an enforceable minimum. As 100 per cent performance was not to be expected, evasion was natural. In fact, the legal system provided very little extra sanction over and above the moral code which infused it. Escarra wrote (in 1935):

> Le droit en Chine, d'après les notions traditionelles, ne se différencie pas de la morale. Il n'est que la mise en œuvre de cette morale. Celle-ci suffit en tant que critérium de répression, le châtiment n'étant qu'un succédané du rite, *li*, qui, normalement, doit avoir la prééminence. Si, ailleurs, les règles morales n'interviennent que pour compléter la force des préceptes juridiques, en Chine, les préceptes juridiques n'interviennent que pour compléter la force des règles morales. Dans l'obligation civile, la règle morale est tout. Les théories anciennes demeurent donc valables aujourd'hui comme hier. Le dynamisme juridique est à peu près inconnu à la mentalité chinoise traditionelle.[1]

The Chinese conception of *fa*[2] stopped at the complementary notions of (i) model, ideal, and (ii) punishment for departure from this. As the laws which contained the laws of procedure had no more binding force than any other laws, they were as freely departed from as the rest and supplied no corrective to the general ineffectiveness of law. All this seems to confirm what Maine and Maitland have said about the development of procedural and substantive law going hand in hand.[3]

Perhaps the surprising thing is that there were *any* actions—other than murder trials. The reasons which induced people, in spite of all, to go to law will be discussed in Chapter 9.

Many collections of cases of doubt and difficulty, privately compiled, had existed for centuries for the guidance of magistrates[4], and several official compilations of cases—of enormous bulk—were made during the Ch'ing period for purposes of reference. The latter provide a body of information as to the substance of the law on the many matters for which decisions are recorded[5], and the former tell us much about magistrates' methods. It remains true nevertheless that to adopt the course of going to law was exceptional in China.

[1] Escarra (1936), p. 70.

[2] That is, in its official sense. It has the meaning in colloquial style of 'way' or 'method', and occurs in common phrases which are the equivalent of 'I'll manage' and 'There's nothing to be done about it'.

[3] See Maitland (1936), p. 1.

[4] Bibliographical details of three such compilations—the *I-yü-chi*, *Che-yü-kuei-chien* and *T'ang-yin-pi-shih*—ranging from the tenth to the thirteenth centuries are given in van Gulik (1956), Introduction, p. 4. Several others are included in the Chinese legal bibliography (see Bibliography at end of this volume under Official Compilations and Reports, 1957), section 6.

[5] See Alabaster (1899), pp. 620–1; and Chinese legal bibliography (1957), section 7.

7

Jurisdictional Aspects of the *Tsu* and the Guild

THE *tsu*

THE imperial government was not alone in exercising jurisdiction over individuals. I come now to two other agencies of control.

The *tsu*[1] is defined as an exogamous patrilineal group of males descended from a founding ancestor, plus their wives and unmarried daughters.[2] It consisted of a number of lines of descent called *fang* (which might be further segmented into *chih*, *p'ai*—meaning branch, sect and so on), each with its constituent *chia* (families); it could include any number of people scattered over several villages, unless the individual *fang*, *p'ai* or *chia* broke away and established new *tsu*. Members of a *tsu* shared the same surname, though it was exceptional for this to be exclusive to them; what was distinctive in a particular *tsu*—and a guide to seniority—was the giving of the same character, often in the order of the words in a poem, to members of the same generation as part of the personal name, *ming*.[3] Genealogies were kept, showing how descent was traced and how members were related both to one another and, by marriage, to other *tsu*. In prosperous *tsu* these were printed.

Out of shared obligations to common ancestors grew a solidarity which spread easily to other aspects of life. A *tsu* usually owned some land, the income from which was used for the upkeep of the ancestral hall, graves and the performance of rites, and, for the purposes of management and organization, formal leaders were appointed on the basis of seniority and/or capacity. In addition, many *tsu* collectively owned larger areas of land, to the tenancy of which *tsu* members had first claim—itself a privilege in a land-hungry economy.

The income from such lands was used for a variety of purposes, cor-

[1] See above, p. 17.

[2] As Professor van der Valk puts it (1956, p. 60), on marriage, a woman's ties with her *tsu* of origin became 'if not altogether disrupted, at least of much less importance'.

[3] The generation character is called *p'ai ming* and the set of characters *tzu p'ai*. (*P'ai* seems to mean sometimes 'generation' and sometimes 'branch', which seems confusing but is understandable in terms of lines of descent which can be traced back to the same branching-off point.)

porately determined, such as relief of poorer members, education of boys and assistance to the more promising with the expense of entering for official examinations, or simply for distribution among *tsu* members. This corporate concern for the well-being of their members extended to assistance if one member were involved in an official lawsuit, probably including payment for useful testimony or confessions, as well as informal representations by fellow-members likely to have influence with the authorities. As well as these tangible benefits, to have behind one the strength of a reputable *tsu* was useful in many different ways, from choice of marriage partners to commercial transactions. The *tsu* therefore had a corporate interest—in addition to the more general one arising from the Chinese idea that the leaders of a group can be held responsible for the misdeeds of its members—that strength should not be dissipated in quarrels between *tsu* members and that they should neither besmirch its good name nor fritter away their own substance. Instruction of the young in traditional morality was therefore one of the functions of the *tsu*.

The inculcation of personal virtues—such as filial piety, deferring to one's seniors, supporting parents in old age, the merits of *jang*—that is, yielding to others for the sake of avoiding dissension—began in childhood in the constituent *chia*, lapses being punished by the *chia chang*, by a sort of delegated political authority. Greater weight and solemnity was given to this teaching by pronouncements at a full meeting of the *tsu* before the ancestral tablets; and it was also reinforced, sometimes by commemorating the lives of worthy *tsu* members by inscriptions on wooden plaques hung in the ancestral hall, sometimes by suggesting moral qualifications for position of leadership in the *tsu*.[1]

Most *tsu* also adopted formal rules which can be classified under three main heads: rules for the organization of the *tsu*—a *tsu* constitution, as it were—secondly, rules for the management of *tsu* business, and thirdly, rules for the personal conduct of members.[2] The first of these, which were frequently incorporated in the genealogy, included instructions on such matters as how the genealogy should be kept, the manner of choosing the *tsu*-head, criteria for admission to the *tsu* and for deciding who should take part in ritual. Occasionally it included a reference to other *tsu* considered so closely related that the rule of exogamy operated against intermarriage. A separate set of rules was often adopted when *tsu* estates were founded, frequently laid down by the founder and then modified from time to time by the *tsu* leadership.[3] These dealt with questions like:

[1] Hu (1948), p. 29. For a brief account of *tsu* organization, see Möllendorff (1893), pp. 170–1.

[2] Liu (1959)[1] and Liu (1959)[2] contain a fuller analysis of the content and function of *tsu* rules.

[3] For a good example of such rules, see Hu (1948), pp. 150–1, Appendix 39, where the regulations concerning the ritual land of the *Chou tsu* in Ch'angshu (Kiangsu) are quoted. Twitchett (1959) describes the gradual accretion of rules governing one very famous clan estate founded in Sung times.

who should be permitted to rent *tsu* land; whether the management should rotate among heads of the *fang* composing the *tsu* or be in the hands of a permanent manager, and, if the latter, how he should be appointed; registration of members of the *tsu*, and how income from *tsu* land should be allocated; what loans might be made and whether benefits should be extended to others than *tsu* members. This set of rules often stated the penalties for infraction and sometimes suggested remedies to be adopted (in case of embezzlement, for example), and some *tsu* registered these rules with the local *hsien* magistrate. The *tsu* code of conduct might be interspersed among the other provisions of the genealogy and *tsu* estate regulations, or might be separately written or hung in the ancestral hall as a reminder to all members. The Chinese themselves did not keep the three categories I have suggested distinct: regulations dealing mainly with *tsu* land frequently included instructions to avoid crime and other moral injunctions.

Perhaps the list of punishable offences for the I *tsu* in Hopei (North China) may be taken to illustrate the third class[1]:

(1) Anyone who commits one of the ten big offences[2] according to the criminal code, is to be 'expelled'.
(2) The head of a family who cannot maintain order in his *chia* so that his sons commit theft or frequent prostitutes . . . is to be 'expelled'.
(3) A person who leaves the coffin of his parents unburied and the graves of his ancestors to decay, while erecting building for conspicuous display . . . is to be 'expelled'.
(4) A man who marries a widow in the *tsu*, or marries a servant, and thus confuses the lines of descent and dishonors the ancestors . . . is to be 'expelled'.
(5) A person who will not carry on his vocation, but gives way to violence and indulges his evil desires, thus ruining his *chia*, wasting his property, and finally ending as a vagabond, dishonors the *tsu* and should be 'expelled'.
(6) A person who, because of selfish motives discards the valuable institutions of his forebears, disregards the rules of conduct (they instituted) and in consequence causes a calamity, is very unfilial indeed, and should be 'expelled'.

[1] Quoted in Hu (1948), pp. 134–5.

[2] 'Offences of a treasonable nature' (Staunton); 'abominations' (Boulais). They were: rebellion, disloyalty to the imperial house, desertion of duty, parricide, massacre, sacrilege, lack of filial piety, discord within the family, insubordination to officials and incest. See Staunton (1810), pp. 3–5; Boulais (1924), pp. 28–31. For the history of this classification, see Ratchnevsky (1937), pp. 13–16, and Balazs (1954), n. 184, pp. 142–5. The latter points out that, as the list of crimes can be traced back to the Han, it is incorrect to regard it as the legacy of one of the barbarian dynasties. He observed that the essence of all ten crimes was disobedience to constituted authority (just as the key virtue *hsiao*, usually translated —misleadingly—as 'filial piety', really amounted to complete submissiveness to one's seniors and superiors).

(7) A son who does not provide a descendant for his father is regarded as terminating the generation; should a grandson (presumably the only son of an only son) lack offspring, the family will be said to be terminated for generations. Although it is said this is the worst filial impiety the individual is not responsible himself and his name should be listed in the genealogy. Those who become monks and nuns are not to be mentioned.

(8) Those who forget their origin while living with their relatives-in-law [1] and do not make up their mind to return to their *tsu* are to be omitted from the genealogy.

(9) Those who are wealthy, yet do not assist their poor relatives within the mourning degrees of five months to one year,[2] so that these cannot celebrate funerals and weddings properly, are to be omitted, even though their conduct otherwise may be proper.

(10) A woman who has a son and yet remarries fails in her duty. Still, her name may be listed, so that her son may know by whom he was born. Should she have no son, she is to be 'expelled'.

(11) A woman who, aside from the seven offences that lead to divorce,[3] disregards the *li-fa* (rules of *li*), that is, if she troubles and annoys the elders, maltreats the young, sows discord between 'bone-and-flesh' (family members), and starts quarrels with the neighbors, should be divorced. But if she does not misbehave too flagrantly, it is alright to leave her name. If she has no son, she should be 'expelled'.

(12) One who has committed offences punishable by 'expulsion' is ousted and not included in the *tsu*. His name is not included in the genealogy. If among his sons and grandsons there are some wise and virtuous ones, after investigation of their lines of descent, the *tsu* is allowed to show mercy and take them back into the genealogy. . . . Should the father, grandfather or other ascendants of the offender at any time have brought benefits to the ancestors (that is, the *tsu*), then these merits and virtues should be discussed. The persons editing the genealogy should consult with the elders and the head of the *tsu*, weigh the extent of the crimes and deliberate the question whether the guilty party is to be expunged from the genealogy or not. This has to be decided by taking into account all circumstances. No hard and fast rules can be laid down beforehand.

As Hu Hsien-chin points out, the first clause serves to reinforce the Penal Law of the Empire; the rest deals with 'offences that disturb family solidarity or cause its decay'. There is evidence in some of the *tsu* codes of attempts to deal with social evils prevalent in the locality. According to Hu, the code of the Tseng *tsu* and two others in the neighbourhood in

[1] See above, p. 17, note 4.

[2] The length of the obligatory mourning period indicated the degree of relationship and this was a common way of referring to classes of relatives. For the relatives included in these degrees, see Ratchnevsky (1937), p. 11. I think that third and fourth degrees must be intended.

[3] See Lang (1946), pp. 40–41; Staunton (1810), p. 120.

Hunan show concern with female infanticide, and the first adopted the practical measure of affording relief to poor families on the birth of a daughter.

A special form of benefit enjoyed in virtue of membership in certain *tsu* was use of a good library, a privilege highly valued in China. We are told that the great editor and bibliophile, Sun Hsing-yen (1753–1818) of Yang-hu, Kiangsu, 'unlike other book collectors, lodged his library in his ancestral temple in order to make it accessible to members of his own clan'.[1] In cases like this, the *tsu* also had library rules, and Taam[2] quotes the rules of one *tsu* (from the Ming period) as follows:

1. Keys of this library are distributed to the male members of the family.
2. Removal of any book from the building is prohibited.
3. Unless all the representative male members are present, no single person is allowed to open the library.
4. If one member is found to have entered it secretly, he will be punished by losing his participation in the ancestral worship.
5. If one is found to have brought friends and relatives to the library secretly and to have opened the book-cases, the same punishment will be given to him for a period of one year.
6. If one is found to have lent books out, the same punishment will be given for a period of three years.
7. If one be found to have sold some books he will be banished from the family and never be allowed to participate in the ancestral worship.

Most of the *tsu* codes forbade members to engage in litigation in the official courts before submitting their case to the *tsu* leaders, and laid on *tsu* members the duty of avoiding quarrels within and conflicts without, and taking early steps to settle such differences; e.g.[3]:

When quarrels arise in the *tsu* out of small resentment and disputes about landed property and money debts, the parties are to go to the ancestral hall and hand in a petition. (Then) the matter is to be brought to clarity and resolved in peace. Only when the decision is difficult is it permitted to bring a complaint before the authorities, so that they may examine and decide the case. Should anyone bring action against another person by bypassing the head of the *tsu*, without petitioning him first, this person is to be fined five ounces of silver to be added to the public funds of the ancestral hall.

Throughout the *tsu* it is forbidden to stir up litigations. When people are angry with each other for a time, it rests with the mediators to arbitrate and bring about a conciliation. There is a kind of person fond of mischief, who takes every chance to instigate lawsuits either to reap benefits for himself or to take personal vengeance, who enjoys calamities and misfortune that strike others, and likes to see both parties fail and sustain damage. The harm he does is not small. Such a person, after his guilt has been ascertained, is to be given thirty strokes.

[1] Taam (1935), p. 51. [2] Taam (1935), p. 10. [3] Hu (1948), p. 132.

Quarrels broke out sometimes, nevertheless, which were not capable of settlement by casual mediation by other *tsu* members, frequent causes being disputes over division of property, right of access to graveyard land, dissatisfaction of near relatives over adoption of heirs. In spite of exhortation and regulation, some *tsu* members broke the rules. When this happened, the formal *tsu* leaders would meet with the educated or otherwise influential members 'to open the ancestral hall', i.e., constitute themselves a court to sit in judgment. Hu quotes the rules of one *tsu* as follows:

> Should there be some in the *tsu* who commit such unlawful and unjust acts as being disobedient and unfilial, deceiving their elders or oppressing the young, quarrelling for wealth or litigating in court, getting drunk or gambling, the *tsu* is to be convened in the ancestral hall and deliberate publicly the right and wrong (of such conduct).[1]

The offences most frequently dealt with were apparently 'unfilial conduct, lawless behaviour as theft and robbery, and disputes regarding property.'

Within the *tsu*, Lin Yueh-hwa[2] traces the process of adjudication up from the *chia chang* through successively more inclusive segments of the lineage until the *tsu* head is reached. It probably depended on the character of the different leaders whether this sequence was observed or not, but there was clearly an advantage in dealing with a dispute in the smallest inclusive group to which the disputants belonged.

To be summoned to appear before the whole *tsu* or its leaders was a humiliation in itself, even if the offender were let off with a caution. The action taken by them would vary according to the particular rules of the *tsu* and the seriousness of the offence. Physical punishments were administered with bamboo or wooden boards; fines could be exacted; his name might be marked in the genealogy to record his offence; he might be deprived for a time of his share in the *tsu* income, and in some cases near relatives had also to be punished. To be omitted from the genealogy altogether was a serious matter,[3] but according to Hu the most severe and effective punishment of all was that of expulsion from the *tsu*, involving loss of all the privileges attaching to membership.[4] Anyone who had been expelled could not take part in rituals, or enjoy material benefits during his lifetime, and after death his name would not be included in the *tsu* genealogy nor his tablet in the ancestral hall, and no one would perform rites for him. This was to be 'shut out from the community of the living and of the dead members of the *tsu*'.

For a Chinese this would represent failure in the most important things in life, and without the support of his own relatives, it would be difficult

[1] Hu (1948), p. 59.
[2] Lin (1936), an article to which my attention was drawn by Dr Freedman.
[3] Hu (1948), App. 33. [4] Hu (1948), p. 61.

to make a success of anything else. If a man so expelled later mended his ways, most *tsu*, we are told, would re-admit him.

The rules of some *tsu* laid down that, if the *tsu* found one of its members guilty of some serious and indictable offence, in addition to the punishment awarded by the *tsu*, a charge against this member should also be laid before the *hsien* magistrate. In cases such as this where, instead of rallying to the support of their fellow-member, the *tsu* was the accuser, it can be imagined that the accused would be certain to be treated with all the harshness of which official law was capable. The sanctions of the two systems combined constituted a threat to be taken seriously.

The verdict of the two courts would not always coincide. If the *tsu* decided that the *hsien* magistrate had wrongly convicted one of their members, even though the offence was serious, his name would not be expunged from the genealogy.

The principles on which the *tsu* would decide these matters would no doubt have been standards of conduct to be reasonably expected of one in a given role and particular circumstances. They were in a better position than the *hsien* magistrate to know both their man and the facts, and familiarity must have imposed practical limits on perfectionist standards.

There is evidence that these powers were exercised with the approval of the administrative authorities and of the members themselves, with the exception no doubt of the recalcitrant. Proverbial sayings testify to general agreement that family quarrels were best dealt with privately, while magistrates clearly had an interest in avoiding the work and the difficulties such cases would have involved. Hu[1] instances a *tsu* member who continued to feel let down because the *tsu* leadership failed to settle a bitter inheritance struggle, which consequently involved great expense to the disputing parties and thus weakened the whole *tsu*.

It may be doubted whether the rules made by *tsu* were any more effective than official law and whether techniques of evasion were not applied to them also. Some of the moral injunctions were doubtless reminders of the path of virtue—that *tsu* members should not gamble or get intoxicated, for example—and while they may have exercised some slight restraint, it may be assumed from common knowledge of Chinese society that they were frequently honoured in the breach. It will be remembered that the *tsu* was, *inter alia*, a religious group and these prescriptions may perhaps be compared with the high morality of other religions. Others were pointers to discretion—advice to *tsu* members to pay taxes by the due date, not to pledge their land as security for debt—and underlined the interest of the whole *tsu* in their members avoiding trouble. Some were so vague as to make action on them almost impossible; they merely assert rights of jurisdiction of the *tsu* leadership over members. E.g.:

A descendant who misbehaves and is degenerate, thus dishonoring the

[1] Hu (1948), p. 57.

ancestors, and who conducts himself in every way contrary to ethical precepts, is to be punished by the whole *tsu* in a spirit of righteousness.[1]

Many of the rules however do contain criteria for their interpretation, as, for example, in the I *tsu* rules already quoted,

> The head of a family who cannot maintain order in his *chia, so that his sons commit theft or frequent prostitutes* . . . is to be 'expelled'.[2]

And particularly as regards property regulations, the remedies suggested are practicable. Moreover the *tsu* had at its disposal sanctions which the *yamen* did not wield—withdrawal of positive benefits, disavowal by those who were one's natural supporters in time of difficulty, and the threat of denial of rites after death.

A case of ritual sanctions being employed to enforce *tsu* land regulations is described by Chen Han-seng:

> A remarkable case of the seriousness with which the ancients have tried to impress it [i.e. that clan land should remain intact] is to be found in one of the villages in the delta region of the Yang-tze. Here the deeds of the clan land are kept not in paper form, but were from the beginning carved on stone tablets. These tablets were then set into the walls of the clan temple, so that members can hardly divide the land among themselves without a grievous offence against their religion, nor can they easily effect the sale of that land. . . .[3]

Hsü mentions several types of sanction which were adopted in cases of incest: supernatural,[4] ritual, beating by a senior relative, social disapproval, loss of benefits of reputation and friendship, and ridicule. All these were applied, while the government law (which, of course, contained prohibitions against incest) might not have existed.[5]

Relatives would have possessed close knowledge of the details of fellow-members' personal lives which would, for example, have made sudden and inexplicable increases in wealth cause for suspicion; and people who shared continually in so many activities must have been averse from losing the good opinion of their fellows. For all these reasons, it seems fair to assume that the *tsu* was a more effective agency of control than the *yamen*, while, as suggested above, the greatest degree of control was exercised by the combined threat of sanctions by both.

The degree of control over members exercised by the *tsu* varied considerably between different *tsu*. Generally it seems to have been effective. 'Quarrels and fights were rare', writes Hu, but naturally they attracted more comment than peaceful settlements. Occasionally the advice of leaders was ignored by unruly members and *tsu* loyalties were sometimes

[1] Quoted in Hu (1948), p. 136.
[2] Hu (1948), p. 134 (my italics).
[3] Chen (1936), p. 28.
[4] For the police functions of the kitchen god, see also Fei (1939), pp. 101–2.
[5] Hsü (1940), pp. 126, 127, 134. He describes the situation in Republican times, but this is a matter in which usage was probably long-established.

enlisted in keeping alive inter-*tsu* feuds. Martin Yang[1] has suggested a correlation between strength of authority and general prosperity of the group; there would, he thinks, be greater interest among members in the reputation of the *tsu* ('clan' in his terminology), when its fortunes were improving and correspondingly less when they were on the wane. Other writers have suggested local variations.

It is well known that the *tsu* as an institution varied in strength and significance in different parts of China; in particular, that *tsu* solidarity was a more important factor in society in South China than in the north. There, larger aggregates continued in membership in preference to breaking away to found independent *tsu* and cases are known where fictive links were introduced into genealogies for the sake of increasing the numerical strength of the *tsu* membership. This should not, I think, be taken to mean that internal *tsu* jurisdiction was necessarily weaker in the north.

It happened in the south far more than in the north that the boundaries of villages and *tsu* coincided. This no doubt obscured the division of functions between *tsu* leaders and village leaders, though these were not necessarily identical, and prevented conscious transference of disputes, for example, from one to the other. In the north it was more usual for a village to be composed of two, three or four *tsu*, and because of the preference for choosing marriage partners outside the village, there were few cross-links of kinship between them. Adjustment of disputes between persons in different *tsu* would have been the function of the local leaders, and this may have created a habit of approaching the latter at all times in preference to *tsu* leaders, especially if someone outside the *tsu* had acquired a name for being able to settle disputes. This may have been a factor in weakening the *tsu*, but I have found no firm evidence of this. Hu Hsien-chin gives examples of *tsu* regulations which, though the south-east and Yang-tze provinces provide the majority, are drawn from nine (out of eighteen) provinces, including Hopei in the north and Szechwan in the west, while Martin Yang illustrates practice in Shantung, also in the north. As the list includes most of the areas of dense population, it seems reasonable to assert that *tsu* jurisdiction was no local phenomenon but applied to the majority of Chinese people. Chinese in all areas depended on relatives for support in all matters of importance or difficulty, and it may well be that the restriction of explicit relationship to a smaller number of kinsmen may have concentrated loyalty and strengthened dependence on those—and therefore obedience. In the larger groups these would be more diffuse, and it is likely that backing by factions within the *tsu* enabled members to ignore the restraining counsel of the *tsu* leaders. It is a fact that strength of numbers could be used for aggressive purposes and was at times feared by the authorities. In recent times several new factors have contributed to undermine *tsu* organization among many of the Chinese: notably, first, economic development on the coast which has provided

[1] Yang (1948), pp. 141–2.

opportunities for employment away from home, relatively independent of *tsu* support, and wealth disproportionate to other *tsu* values; secondly, the growth of new forms of social organization, like university communities, which provide alternatives to the *tsu* in matters both of welfare and loyalty. It is in terms of such developments as these rather than traditional weakness in a given area that I should explain M. Fried's observation (in 1948) of weak development and ineffectiveness of the clan in central (coastal) China.

It is noteworthy that the *tsu* regulations do not seem confident of asserting the same measure of control over non-members. It is frequently suggested in regulations about the property that the manager appointed should be a man of substance and therefore, the implication is, not tempted to be dishonest. Sometimes it is stated that in case of embezzlement, '*he should be forced to restore*' what he had wrongfully taken, without specifying how this force should be applied other than by recourse to the *yamen* court.

The question of adjudication in cases of inter-*tsu* friction will be taken up later.[1]

CRAFT AND MERCHANT GUILDS

Western observers have frequently expressed surprise that the Chinese, who have such a reputation as traders, should have been so reticent on the subjects of commerce and industry in their legal codes. In the Ch'ing code only a few articles deal with these matters (and these come at the end of the *Hu Pu* section, rather as if our commercial law were an appendix to the Inland Revenue Department regulations). Section 149 fixed the maximum rate of interest at 3 per cent per month (!) and punished creditors who took private action against defaulting debtors. Section 150 prescribed punishments for those who embezzled property entrusted to them, and section 151 provided that lost property should be handed over to the authorities. Sections 152 and 153 required merchants in various branches of trade to register officially and to value their merchandise for tax purposes, while the *li* added some somewhat unsystematic prohibitions against sales of rice at variance with government pricing policy. Section 154 forbade individuals to monopolize a commodity or otherwise trade unfairly. The list ends with two rather pious-sounding sections, one providing for the official inspection of weights and measures—which remained notoriously ineffective[2]—and the last prescribing a rather nominal punishment of fifty blows for private traders whose manufactures (textiles are apparently intended) failed to come up to the established or customary standard.[3]

[1] See p. 120.

[2] Demonstrated by the fact that individual guilds kept their own. See p. 93.

[3] The Chinese text and commentary, with an English translation, of Sections 152 to 156 are given in Lind (1887).

The reason for this relative reticence in the codes is that detailed regulation was left to the associations of craftsmen and merchants concerned. These are usually known as *hongs* or guilds.

Several strands in Chinese history had coalesced by the Ch'ing period to produce these associations: their development is an interesting and complicated story.[1] The practice of artisans who shared the same craft and dealers in the same commodity combining in associations goes back to the T'ang period or earlier. In ancient times shops in the same trade were concentrated in one street, and after this ceased to be the rule (though until quite recently it remained true of some places and trades), merchants engaged in the same trade formed themselves into associations for which they retained the name *hang* (or *hong*), line. This appears to have been a natural outgrowth of what began as shared activity in religious festivals and continued as co-operation in business matters for their mutual benefit; they adopted a tighter form of organization in Sung times when the trade needed to act as a body to resist government demands and to maintain their monopoly.[2] The outcome of this conflict seems to have been an uneasy truce, the government allowing the merchants the privilege of monopolizing (and controlling) their trade in return for recognition of their collective responsibility for paying the *hang-i*, i.e. regular dues in lieu of goods and services, plus other sums according to what the traffic could be made to bear. Though *hang* merchants did not always work in perfect accord,[3] they could act together—no doubt with veiled coercion by stronger members—to further common interests.[4]

It was also a long-established usage for those who came from the same part of China and found themselves together in a place where they were unfamiliar with people, custom and perhaps even dialect, to band together for mutual support and companionship. Candidates who went up to the capital for the official examinations lodged together with their fellow-provincials, and others who travelled on business or settled in parts where they were strangers sought the help and backing which bonds of locality entitled them to expect. Local 'clannishness' of the host community was met by 'clannishness' of the settlers. (In both, *tsu* loyalties played a part, though members of rival *tsu* at home probably sank their differences and discovered an overriding local solidarity in face of the solidarity of *tsu* in the neighbourhood where they were now trading.)

By Ch'ing times two main types of association[5] existed in most large

[1] For which see Kato (1936). [2] Kato (1936), pp. 62–64.

[3] Kato gives instances of powerful tea merchants and comb dealers in K'aifeng exploiting their co-traders, pp. 68–69.

[4] The *hong* best known to foreigners in Ch'ing times was the *cohong* (*kung hang*) of export-import merchants at Canton through whom they were compelled to trade. A good description will be found in Hunter (1882) and (1885).

[5] Unless otherwise stated, most of the information about these is drawn from MacGowan (1886). Morse's book, *The Gilds of China*, is based very largely on this article.

towns, viz., first, local tradesmen organized according to their special skill or product, and second, associations of merchants who came from the same place (and who very often were traders on a larger scale). Thus in Ningpo, for example, one would find local associations of carpenters, barbers and other craftsmen as well as associations of merchants from Canton, Fuchou and elsewhere.[1] In practice the distinction between these two types is somewhat blurred. Certain fairly menial occupations were the preserve of people from a particular part of the country: for example, water carriers in Peking all came from Shantung. And sometimes a 'merchant guild', in addition to the bond of being fellow natives of a particular place, had a specialized function as, for example, the Shansi guilds of bankers to be found in most important towns. Somewhere between these came the Fukien guild in Ningpo which had three sections, two of which concentrated on trade in sugar and timber respectively while the third was miscellaneous. In general one can say that, though the basis of association might be a blend of the two types, in each guild one principle —shared trade on one hand or common local origin on the other—was more important. One gets the impression also of a difference of temper between the memberships of the two types. If we forget for a moment the luxury crafts of Peking, we may say that members of craft guilds were in general poorer than those of the merchant guilds; their skills were in some cases fairly easily acquired and little capital was needed to enter the occupation. Consequently they needed to organise jealously and were easily aroused, either against one another or to resist the authorities. The settler merchants were likely to be people of substance, offered hospitality to visiting scholars and officials, and could afford the luxury of better discipline and more subtle methods of influencing authority.

The chief functions of the craft guilds were mutual protection (by controlling the conditions of trade, nominally in the interests of all) and resistance to official demands in excess of what custom allowed—whether for corvée services or higher taxes on sales. In order to control the craft or trade, they had to control their own members, and in order to maintain solidarity in their ranks in the face of officialdom, they had an interest in minimizing friction between their members. The guild therefore acted as an agency for enforcing control and a tribunal for settling disputes. Guilds sometimes also undertook relief among their needy members and other charitable projects. There must have been considerable variation in aims and organization between the different guilds, which covered the whole

[1] These two types are frequently referred to as *hui kuan* and *kung suo* after their assembly buildings, and these are frequently translated as 'guild' (often qualified by 'compatriot') and 'trade union'. Kato has suggested that the associations should more properly be called *hang* (literally, 'line'). I shall use 'craft guild' for the association of craftsmen and traders in the same commodity and 'merchant guild' for the association of settlers (including others besides merchants) from a common place of origin.

range of occupations from unskilled—e.g. water-carriers—to highly skilled—jade workers, for example.

Membership was not obligatory in every occupation but was wide enough for the guild to exercise effective control over all engaged in it in a given town. Authority was exercised by a group of headmen, for which posts all members were eligible, but seniority and ability to represent their fellows effectively were no doubt factors in their selection or self-appointment. As happened in the *tsu*, their authority was enhanced by leadership in ritual associated with the group cult—in this case veneration of the founding craftsman, *tsu shih* (literally, ancestor craftsman) of the guild.[1] Both masters and men belonged to the same guild; if employees had a common grievance against their employers they might hold a separate meeting about the issue, decide to strike and then, when this had had its effect, unity was restored.

Every guild had its regulations printed on red paper and hung in stores and workshops. These covered such matters as hours of work—e.g., weavers were not permitted to work after 9 p.m.; conditions of apprenticeship—the number permitted, premium, period, their working conditions and hours; quality of product (e.g. pewterers and umbrella-makers) in order to keep up prices; seasonal adjustment of prices (dyers); fair weight (fishmongers); and measures to maintain members' existing shares in the trade[2]—customers who transferred to a new barber, for example, were supposed to be charged a higher price than they had paid their original man. Guild regulations also required members to submit their disputes to the guild before going to the official courts.

Gamble[3] reports a case, which, though he attended it in 1918 or 1919, is probably typical of the traditional operation of guild courts, which according to him are better thought of as informal boards of arbitration than as formal courts.

> The committee, the interested parties and their witnesses met in a temple. There the goods concerning which the case had arisen were set in front of the committee, and each side briefly gave its testimony. The witnesses were heard, and after a short conference the committee gave its decision. This was accepted as final, both parties arose, bowed to the committee and to each other and the matter was closed. A half-hour sufficed to settle satisfactorily a case which, if taken before the official, would have meant at least a day's travel for all of the parties concerned, besides possible delays and inconveniences.

The penalties inflicted on members who broke guild regulations varied according to the craft and the offence. The sanction might take the form of direct action by the offender's fellows; e.g. (the barbers' guild at Peking): 'Anyone found breaking these rules is liable to have his tools and

[1] See Wou (1931), ch. ii (L'âme de la corporation).
[2] This seems also to be the intention of part of Article 154 in the Penal Code.
[3] Gamble (1921), pp. 194–5.

furniture thrown on the street.' Or it could be a fine, sometimes payable as so many bundles of incense to be burnt on the altar of the god of the guild, or, for more serious offences, being fined the cost of a feast or theatrical performance for his fellow members. In the last resort, an intransigent offender could be expelled and, after expulsion, boycotted. If he was a master, he would then find that suppliers and customers alike would avoid his shop: an employee would be unable to find work. Anyone unwise enough to defy the boycott would be included in it. Control was, in fact, effective. In return, if any member of a guild were involved in a trading dispute with someone outside his guild, the guild leaders would undertake negotiations for him. Or if he found himself summoned to the *yamen* court, he could expect the support of his guild.

The administration of the merchants' guilds was usually in the hands of a general manager and committee—who were elected annually but were eligible for re-election—and a permanent secretary who held a key position. The man appointed to this post was almost always a titled scholar and therefore able to deal with the mandarinate on fairly equal terms.

The guild levied contributions from members, usually as a percentage on their business, according to the value of commodities sold or the number of junks unloaded. For this purpose the books of every establishment were examined monthly, the examination being made by clerks of various firms in rotation. One of the uses to which this money was put was the assistance of members who were involved in legal cases.

The merchant guild, being a body distinguishable from local residents, was regarded as responsible for its members' behaviour. Guilds therefore exhorted their members not to get into trouble with the authorities by tax evasion or fraud; if they did, the guild would not support the guilty person. They undertook to assist in the recovery of stolen property, and urged members not to retain it or to conceal robbery, under threat of fine or expulsion.

The merchant guilds also had formal rules. Some of these dealt with their own constitution and management; for example, how committee and secretary should be appointed, or how guild funds should be invested. Others, when put together, constituted codes of trading practice. They fixed such things as the time to be allowed for payment after delivery, the time the buyer might leave goods to be warehoused by the seller, the weight to be deducted for packaging, and responsibility for loss of goods through fire after sale. Each guild usually kept its own set of weights and measures to which its members were required to conform—again under threat of a fine. Fines, to be paid into the guild treasury, were in fact the most used penalty. They were frequently fixed at so many times the value of the offending transaction or consignment, thus emphasizing their relevance to the 'crime'. If guild members disobeyed regulations, or when disputes arose between them, the guild constituted itself a court to judge the case. Members were expressly forbidden to appeal to the magistrate without first giving the guild court the chance to adjudicate. The reason for this may have been the desire of the stronger members to keep control in their own hands without unwelcome publicity or the unpredictable interference of the *yamen*; or it may have been the need to maintain internal cohesion and prevent, if possible, the bitterness that would arise if members were ranged opposite one another in a court action; or fear of endangering the good name and future influence of the whole guild by an irresponsible action against an outsider; or it may have been a combination of these motives.

> It is agreed that members having disputes about money matters with each other shall submit their cases to arbitration at a meeting of the guild where the utmost will be done to arrive at a satisfactory settlement of the dispute. If it be impossible to arrive at an understanding, appeal may be made to the authorities; but if the complainant have recourse to the official direct, without first referring to the guild, he shall be subjected to a public reprimand and any future case he may present for the opinion of the guild will be dismissed without a hearing.[1]

So reads the rule of one guild. Another was the following:

> It is impossible to say that disputes may not arise. . . . If anything of the sort occurs, the guild shall settle the difficulty in the manner most advantageous to all. Justice shall be observed and the facts of the case brought to light, and the matter be decided according to what is right. No concealment must be employed that justice may be manifested.[2]

The guilds had other sanctions at their disposal to enforce obedience on their members. One which they frequently used was to fine an offender the cost of a feast or a theatrical performance for the entertainment of the membership. This penalized the guilty party but allowed him to regain dignity by playing the part of host and so re-establish himself in the affections of his fellows. If on the other hand the guild were set at defiance by a recalcitrant member, they could expel him, which would mean that he would lose the benefits of membership and would have instead to face the hostility of the guild—that is, of his organized competitors. This would probably make it impossible for him to continue in business in that place.

If members who were amenable to guild discipline got into trouble outside the guild, the guild would come to their assistance. The statutes of the Canton merchant guild at Pakhoi began with a preamble describing the lawlessness of the local people and the need to maintain a common front against them as mutual protection (which imperial law apparently could not be expected to afford to unorganized individuals). They then continued that the guild undertook:

> to prosecute in behalf of their members when satisfactory proof is afforded of the equity of their claims. Members having occasion to go to law to obtain

[1] MacGowan (1886), pp. 140–1. [2] ibid.

redress for a real grievance, and finding their resources inadequate to carry on the suit, the Guild will address a joint petition to the Court praying for an adjustment of the case. Half the expense of legal proceedings will be defrayed from the funds of the association; but if it is discovered that the plaintiff has an unworthy case and no resources, or that his trouble originates from gambling or dissolute life, all claims to assistance will be dismissed. Members going to law to effect a settlement of claims will have three-tenths of the cost defrayed by the Guild, the balance being defrayed by the litigants. But before legal proceedings are commenced, the unanimous consent of a meeting of members for approval of action shall be obtained. . . . When the claim sued is sufficient to liquidate costs, no grant will be made—not with a view to the saving of expenditure, but with the object of preventing advantage being taken of this rule for the sake of gain and to repress the spirit of persistency in litigation among members.[1]

It was for the work of advocacy that the guild chose its secretary so carefully. By employing a scholar whose social standing was such that he could interview mandarins personally, they forged a link between themselves and the magistrate without going through the lower ranks of officialdom. The secretary was 'a medium of all correspondence, and at the *Yamens* appears as the Guild's legal representative, pleading for its interests, demanding redress for its injured members, defending and protecting his constituents as occasion requires. He is useful to local authorities in soliciting from his Guild subscriptions for public works, charities and extraordinary exigencies,'[2] and no doubt developed considerable finesse in turning such services to good account.

What has been said of the attitudes of both members and authorities to jurisdiction by the *tsu* applies also to that by guilds. Their tribunals operated with the knowledge and approval of magistrates and saved them a great deal of trouble. Guild regulations were quoted and regarded as authoritative in official courts, and magistrates would refer questions to guilds for their opinion or even send cases which had bypassed the guild to them for decision.[3]

From the point of view of their members, guild jurisdiction had disadvantages, especially for the weaker, who could be dominated by their fellows. But in general, *the official courts being what they were*, guild members were probably satisfied to be judged by their peers, though this does not mean that they would have preferred it to judgment in a civil court, if impartial and efficient courts had been available. (The enormous growth of Chinese business in the foreign concessions in the nineteenth century testifies to the fact that Chinese business men appreciated a more efficient system of law when they saw it.)

Vis-à-vis the rest of society, activity by guilds on behalf of their members who were engaged in court cases may at times have constituted an

[1] MacGowan (1886), pp. 136–7. [2] MacGowan, op. cit., p. 138.
[3] See Kotenev (1925), p. 255 on bankruptcy cases; also Jamieson (1888), p. 147.

exercise of arbitrary power, but on balance it probably increased the chances of justice being done. For the sake of preserving its influence, a guild would have been careful not to back unjust claims, and, among the sources which the magistrate could draw on for information about a case, the guild secretary—on account of his training and care for his reputation—was probably one of the most reliable. If, on the other hand, the guild informed against a member or failed to intervene in his defence, this would no doubt have been taken as a fairly clear indication of his guilt. The following comment by Alabaster[1] on the subject of the delegated authority of the clan (*tsu*) applies equally, I think, to both *tsu* and guild:

> The authority of a parent or grandparent is, touching family matters, paramount within the family: and as the family increased in numbers and became a clan, the authority passed to the most capable member—usually a *literatus*. So we find throughout China groups of persons subjected to a very real authority. But the effect of this liberal admixture of local government has been misconceived: it is commonly supposed to have all the force of an *imperium in imperio*. The family or clan is, however, much in the position of an English corporation: with powers, *within certain limits*, to frame by-laws: subject to have its local regulations construed by the ordinary tribunals: and liable to the ordinary law for exceeding its powers. As the innermost of two concentric circles is of necessity bounded on all sides by the outer, so is the family or clan circle encircled by the law.

The *tsu* and guild tribunals may perhaps be thought of as subsidiaries of the official courts, exercising delegated powers, the one as a community, the other as an association, in connection with matters which came within their range of operation. On this view, they were part of the hierarchy of courts, from which the magistrate's court constituted the first court of appeal. The defects of the system lay in the inefficiency and corruption of the official court rather than in the exercise of delegated authority.

[1] Alabaster (1899), p. lvi.

8

Local and Customary Jurisdiction

THOUGH both *tsu* and guild were important for the control they exercised over their members, large and important areas of life fell outside their scope. Whereas ancestral ceremonies had to be performed only at intervals, and regulating the condition of work or sale in given trades directly affected only people working in them, the mass of the population was concerned all the year round with the processes of agriculture and the routine transactions of rural life. They were engaged in a continuous struggle to add to their holdings of land if they could, either by purchase or lease, since this was the surest way of increasing income; disposing of it or borrowing against this land as security, if driven by pressing need for money; all the time defending their enjoyment of possession or use and guarding their plots against intrusion. Those who belonged to *tsu* which owned large areas of land would no doubt have engaged in all these activities without entering into relations with anyone outside their own *tsu*, but most families had at times to have dealings with outsiders. On account of *tsu* exogamy, all had to, when marriage was contemplated. These transactions were carried on according to custom, and adjudication of disputes arising out of them was the province of leaders in the locality where they arose—usually the village leaders,[1] though within a large village there might also be leaders for the different subdivisions of the village. To these leaders also fell the solution of other inter-personal or inter-*tsu* conflicts in their area: for example, cases of marriage and divorce, which because of *tsu* exogamy necessarily involved two *tsu*; questions of inheritance, if *tsu* solidarity and authority was not strong enough to prevent quarrels; and, sometimes, friction between members of different *tsu* or neighbourhoods who had entered into customary relationships with one another for specific purposes (e.g., co-operative loan societies and burial clubs) in the course of which grievances against one another had developed.

The significance of the village in Chinese social organization has been

[1] For the sake of simplicity, throughout this chapter I have written 'village' and 'village leaders' to mean organization based on locality. I have suggested earlier that I think that this was more important in agricultural areas than commercial centres, but the distinctions were not clear-cut. It was not impossible for a dispute about plot boundaries to arise in a city, so I must ask the reader to add 'or town ward' when appropriate.

stressed and its internal structure discussed briefly in Chapter 1, while the links between the village and the administrative hierarchy were described in Chapter 3. It was mentioned in Chapter 1 that an important part of the duties of village leaders arose out of their powers of jurisdiction over their fellow-residents (while informal leaders owed part of their prestige to their reputation for settling disputes equitably). In contrast to the powers of the *tsu* and the guild, which, though not limited by statute, were limited in practice to groups with defined membership and fairly specific, if wide-ranging, activities, jurisdiction exercised by the village was general and comprehensive. It covered all the people who lived there, or passed through it, and all activities that went on, except for the limited jurisdiction exercised within household, *tsu* or guild by their respective leaders.

The village possessed no rules of incorporation or written by-laws, but a certain amount of organization was necessary for enterprises undertaken by the village as such, involving ad hoc decisions which the leaders enforced. They allotted duties between families in regard to the upkeep of the village temple and performance of ceremonies connected with it; they allocated responsibility for the defence of the village against bandits and robbers, for the safeguarding of crops against thieves, for maintaining irrigation works, or for building a wall round the village, requiring each family to supply either labour services for these purposes or money in lieu; and they decided what share each should pay towards the expense of theatrical performances arranged by the village. Such decisions could usually be enforced by enlisting public opinion in their support; there was in most villages an open space (where the market and theatricals took place, very often in front of the village temple) where villagers assembled to discuss these things, and if informal pressure had failed to persuade a family to undertake its allotted duty, reminder in public and some show of disapproval by fellow-villagers was probably more effective. 'Disapproval . . . is a powerful check. . . . Social isolation is a terrible punishment. Only three or four families whose social position is so low that they are in a sense immune from public opinion are indifferent to disapproval and fear only physical punishment.'[1]

The officially recognized leaders in the villages were held responsible by the administration for the good behaviour of their residents and were required to report crimes of violence, arson, kidnapping and the like, to the *hsien* government. Lesser crimes might be dealt with by them or by 'gentry', according to the relative influence of the different elements locally, penalties being inflicted according to the scale determined by local custom. Petty theft might meet with mere scolding or being held up to public derision; more serious offences might involve extra contributions to the expense of village activities, avoidance by neighbours or even ostracism, which in the context of village life was almost unbearable;

[1] Yang (1945), p. 150.

while there remained the ultimate sanction, denunciation to the *hsien* authorities with all that that implied.

The force of social approval or disapproval as a means of securing conformity to social norms, which is strong in any small community, was greatly strengthened in China by the universal preoccupation with considerations of 'face'. This may be thought of as a constant concern to stand well in the opinions of others and in one's own opinion of oneself by giving in all one's social roles the best performance[1] of which one was capable (best, that is, according to social norms and values). It was as if the individual were acting on a stage and being awarded marks for his performance which would depend both on the performance itself and its reception by the spectators, always with reference to what the role allowed and demanded and to the player's resources. It was conceived of as being always in flux; one's performance was being judged continuously and one could never relax. The business of life was easier for those who kept the respect of their neighbours and their own self-respect, and this desire to think of oneself, and to be thought of by others, as behaving well was a powerful factor in enforcing social norms.

Hu Hsien-chin has suggested[2] that the idea of 'face' is really made up of two related conceptions conveyed by two different words, which both have the meaning of (physical) face but differ in their metaphorical use. *Mien-tzu* is 'face' in the sense of prestige or reputation which can be accumulated (or decreased) and deliberately fostered; *lien* on the other hand is good character, personal integrity, the confidence that others have and that one has oneself in one's conscientious filling of social roles at whatever cost to oneself, and it implies higher demands on those with higher social status. *Mien-tzu* is a stock to be added to or decreased by degrees; *lien* is something to be kept intact or forfeited.

Both *mien-tzu* and *lien* were useful as means to other ends, the one as an avenue to power and wealth, the other to the comfort and convenience that come of solid respectability. Both, but more particularly *lien*, played a part in controlling conduct: 'consciousness that an amorphous public is, so to say, supervising the conduct of ego, relentlessly condemning every breach of morals and punishing with ridicule, has bred extreme sensitivity in some people . . .'[3]; '. . . all infringements of the moral code,

[1] I feel that this habit of passing judgment on another's performance is connected with the attitude of Chinese to theatricals, which were popular alike in village and city. Companies of professional actors toured the villages and young people formed amateur companies in the slack farming season. The enjoyment of the Chinese audience consists, I think, not in identifying themselves with the characters portrayed and sharing their emotions, but in judging the actors' performance *qua* actors.

Officials too must always have been conscious that their performance of their duties was being officially observed and recorded, and so long as scholars were examination candidates their conduct was subject to official supervision (see above, Chapter 4).

[2] Hu (1944), pp. 45 ff.

[3] Hu (1944), p. 46.

all acts contrary to behaviour of a person of ego's status cause a depreciation of character. The loss of esteem is felt acutely and is symbolically expressed as 'loss of *lien*'. The fear of 'losing *lien*' keeps up consciousness of moral boundaries, maintains moral values, and expresses the force of social sanctions.'[1]

The strength of 'face' as a sanction was recognized in such sayings as 'Since he doesn't care for face, what can you do about him?'[2] As Hu puts it:

> *Pu-yao lien*—not to want *lien* is a serious accusation meaning that ego does not care what society thinks of his character, that he is ready to obtain benefits for himself in defiance of moral standards. On such a person social sanctions lose their effect as he does not recognize the rules of the game. Moreover, should he be in the habit of 'not wanting *lien*' his fellows would find it impossible to predict his behaviour. Such an individual few people will care to deal with. . . . Very often the conduct of these people cannot be punished by law, and public censure may not be open, but should a time come when they find themselves in a disadvantageous position, society will withdraw its moral and material support. They can not longer count on the network of social relationships to help them out, for they have isolated themselves by flouting moral standards. Indeed society will point to their failure or misfortune as deserved punishment for defying its injunctions.[3]

So the control mechanism worked in the long run.

The concept of face may be contrasted with the idea of *kan-ch'ing*[4] which was a bond of regard and affection existing between two persons who were not on precisely the same social plane. In its name favours could be asked and pressure exerted. It was consequently useful to have such a good understanding with as many people as possible since this would extend one's influence. To be on good terms with a number of people was also a way of gaining face (*mien-tzu*), especially if they were well thought of, but whereas *kan-ch'ing* was a private and personal relationship, face was a public and fairly objective index. (Compare our expression that 'X's stock stands high', implying a market valuation.) *Kan-ch'ing* would have been invoked in private mediation, but once a dispute or misdemeanour was public, concern for face would be the argument that weighed.

The settlement of disputes in the village formed a large part of the functions of village leaders, more especially of the local 'gentry'. Sometimes these arose suddenly out of a particular action, or failure to act, on the part of one person or family, which another regarded as a wrong against itself; shifting the boundaries between plots, or diverting water before it reached a neighbour's plot, for example. Sometimes the occasion was not a particular action, but marked the stage where patience was exhausted and some repressed annoyance was made an open grievance.

[1] Hu (1944), p. 50. [2] Yang (1945), p. 170. [3] Hu (1944), p. 56.
[4] This relationship is analysed in Fried (1953), pp. 102–9.

Very often it was due to a long-standing feud between two groups which, after simmering below the surface, was suddenly re-opened by some chance incident which then assumed serious proportions on account of previous resentments. Private mediation was often effective in settling such arguments, particularly the sudden quarrel or the cases where breaking-point was reached, but when they were not easily settled or when the contestants required public satisfaction, the village leaders were called in to arbitrate. It was part of the latters' function to know whether the quarrel was a minor squabble, best ignored, or more serious and not likely to heal itself. It was more likely to be serious, in which case the village would be torn by factional loyalties, if the contestants were prominent members of the village, each of whom would feel that his personal dignity or the reputation of his family was at stake. For the sake of harmony in the village the conflict had to be brought to an end, and for the sake of upholding village values, as well as the interests of future peace, it was necessary to find a solution which allowed both parties to save face and which both would therefore accept. Sometimes it was more effective to invite leaders from a neighbouring village to arbitrate. In this case relationship to matrilateral kin might determine the choice of arbitrators.

M. Yang[1] describes what would happen in the village of Tai-tou, Shantung. First, he says, the invited or self-appointed village leaders enquire into the background of the dispute and establish what is really at issue. Then they propose a solution based on past experience of such quarrels. Next comes the task of getting the parties to agree to a compromise, discovering how much each will concede and where agreement can be struck. Then follows a party or a feast to mark the conclusion of the conflict, the expenses being borne by one party, if he admits to having alone been at fault, or shared, if both admit some responsibility. Thus the settlement is reached and publicized. Except among the poorest people, it would be undignified for the wronged party to accept compensation: his victory lies in the general opinion that he has right on his side. In theory the feast is given to repay the mediators, but in fact it is an admission of defeat and an apology.

A party who did not receive satisfaction could appeal to the *hsien* magistrate but, according to Yang, 'very few—perhaps none—of the disputes in this village have been solved by a law-suit'.

Writing about Anhwei (east central China) Fried[2] suggests that there were three ways of dealing with a 'civil' suit. First, appeal could be made to affection and the parties exhorted to settle their differences amicably on the basis of the *kan-ch'ing* existing between them—and most questions about rentals, debts or responsibility for small accidents would be, he claims, settled in this way. Or, if this was not successful, mediators might appeal to reason, hearing all the facts and giving a considered judgment of what they think would be the right solution. Or it could be taken to a

[1] Yang (1945), p. 165. [2] Fried (1953), pp. 209–10.

civil court—but this (in 1948), involving lawyers and scrutiny by unknown persons, was anathema to the average person.

In the nature of things, the details of the procedure varied from village to village, and, within the same village, according to the character of the contestants. The essentials seem always to have been the same: when the efforts of informal mediators had proved ineffective at bringing two parties to agreement, the village leaders would hear the case from the two points of view, find out what would satisy the one and where the other could be persuaded to yield, until, after a lot of patient talking, they brought the two parties to the point where they could agree, and this would be given publicity.

The process can be further analyzed, and its efficacy can, I think, be shown to depend very much on the general acceptance of local custom, in enforcing which the leaders could claim the sanction of public opinion. Their arbitration can be divided as follows. First, they would enquire into the grounds of complaint on one or both sides and hear the replies of the other party. From this it would emerge whether the complainant was trying to assert a customary right (such as respect for ancestral graveland or the right to use water from a canal), or if his complaint arose from a specific agreement, like sale or mortgage, entered into with the second party, which the latter had failed to honour. Behind these discussions, familiar to arbitrators and contestants alike, would be the knowledge of the different customary forms of relationship (landlord and tenant, buyer and seller, for example); the rights and duties of parties so related, as allowed or expected customarily; and the customary forms of entering validly into such relationships. By bringing this knowledge to bear on the evidence of the particular case, they would decide which of the forms of relationship applied to the contestants and what could reasonably be expected of parties so related. Then, whether what was being asserted was a general customary right or a right arising out of the specific relationship between the two parties (as modified of course by special conditions entered into by the particular contestants), the arbitrators would determine which of the parties had right on his side according to custom or where the line of compromise could be drawn between them.

In the vast area of China, it is obvious that there would be wide variations in custom. It seems clear however that there was, in any locality, a range of accepted forms which transactions—like sale, lease or marriage—and the relationships resting on them, had to take if they were to be accepted as valid and the obligations arising out of them enforced. These matters were legislated for, though inadequately, in the official codes, but (to quote Kulp) 'Laws exist but rarely impinge on village life',[1] and (Fei) '. . . law does not apply to those places where custom is paramount'.[2] It appears from Wang Hui-tsu's advice[3] that *yamen* secretaries should not

[1] Kulp (1925), p. 316 [2] Fei (London, 1939, ed.), p. 184.
[3] Appendix 4, no. 35.

act on any law or instruction (*lü or ling*) without seeing that it did not conflict with local custom, that this adherence to custom rather than statute was official policy and not due merely to negligence on the part of the *yamen*.[1] It is clear that the rights and obligations attaching to these customary forms were well understood and accepted. They were frequently summed up in a neat phrase like 'a two : eight field' (to indicate land on which the landlord, in return for supplying seeds and implements, was entitled to four-fifths of the crop); or 'mortgage three, sale four' to indicate the time allowed in each case (in months) for possession to be taken. Their brevity seems to indicate that they needed no explanation to local people.

In view of the degree of acceptance these customs had among the people of a given area and the fact that they were enforced by local leaders with the approval of the local public, I think we are justified in describing them as customary law. This, then, is what the village leaders were administering.

The important place formerly occupied by custom in matters of what we should call civil law was underlined when the modernization of the legal system was attempted in the early years of this century. One of the reformers' objectives appeared to be attained when the power of the judiciary was separated from that of the executive. The newly independent courts found, however, that in civil matters there was little formal law for them to apply. The Supreme Court ruled that cases should be decided according to the express provisions of law, if any existed; in the absence of express provisions, then according to custom; and in the absence of custom, then according to juristic principles.[2]

A compilation of legal custom prevailing in different parts of China was made in the early years of the Republic (1925) for the purposes of drawing up a civil code.[3] It includes provisions for a very wide range of matters among which the section for Shantung,[4] for example, covers: proportions of crop or other produce due to landlord and tenant; conditions on which leased land could be sublet; prohibitions on well-digging or building within a given distance of another's graveland; terms of mortgage and redemption; liability for repairs; repayment of loans in instalments; forward sales of ground-nuts and mulberry leaves; regulations for loan and burial co-operatives; differential rates of interest accord-

[1] Van der Valk, for example, instances places where the legal prohibition against marriage with a deceased wife's sister or deceased brother's wife were customarily ineffective, especially among the poor. (Van der Valk, 1956, p. 29.) I must admit to being puzzled by Père Hoang's comment, in his section on betrothal: 'Il faut observer qu'en Chine aucun usage n'a force en justice contre la loi' (Hoang, 1915, p. 22), which is at variance with the observation of all other authors. The only explanation I can offer would be that marriage more than anything else was regulated by law (see later, p. 112), but even in this area it can be seen from the evidence just quoted that law did not always prevail against custom.

[2] Decision 64, 1913. See Bibliography, Official Compilations (1923), p. 1.

[3] See Bibliography, Official Compilations (1930) to which unfortunately I have not had access.

[4] See Kroker (1955).

ing to amount borrowed; and regulations relating to marriage, separation and inheritance. While a wide diversity of custom is revealed within a single province, it is perhaps worth noting that whereas conditions of land tenure and transfer seem to be different in each *fu*, similar conditions were reported from different parts of the province in regard to such matters as loan co-operatives.[1]

Most of the claims that gave rise to disputes which village leaders were called on to settle rested on an antecedent transaction or settlement which would be called in question as the arbitration proceeded. It may therefore be well to describe the customary form of concluding some of the most important transactions in which village people engaged.

The most notable features of such transactions were, firstly, that they were conducted through the agency of an intermediary, who, when a conclusion satisfactory to both parties had been reached, would arrange the terms of agreement between them; secondly, the terms of the agreement were frequently, though not always, committed to writing; and thirdly, the conclusion of the agreement was marked by considerable publicity.

This was the usual manner of arranging marriages, for example. A third party would be employed as go-between by the heads of families who wished to find wives for their sons or homes for their daughters and he (or she) would shuttle backwards and forwards between the heads of the two families to persuade them of the suitability of a particular match. To one side he would give assurances as to the looks and character of the prospective daughter-in-law; to the other he would stress the comfort the girl would enjoy as a member of the first family—while urging on each the advantages of being allied to the other. These practical considerations were overlaid with concern for the compatibility of the supernatural influences affecting the young people, in terms of which the discussions were overtly conducted and which provided grounds on which negotiations could be broken off by either side without giving offence. If the match was arranged, cards were exchanged, bearing personal details of the prospective marriage partner and the match-maker's name; symbolic presents were also made by each family and distributed among relatives, thus serving as a '*faire part*' of the betrothal. After a lapse of several years, when one of the families felt that a propitious time had come for the marriage to take place, the go-between would be summoned again and asked to fix the day for the ceremony. Two points are note-worthy: first, that though the two families might consult different fortune-tellers on the question of the auspiciousness of the match, both employed the same go-between as negotiator; second, that even families who were well acquainted would use an intermediary if they wished to arrange a betrothal between them. Doolittle comments:

[1] Kroker has also analysed the material in this compilation on customs relating to contractual labour relations in different provinces of China. See Kroker (1957).

Very few instances occur when, both parties having arrived at marriageable age, one refuses to carry out the contract.[1]

Other types of transaction show similar features. When a family was thinking of hiring labour or having a contractor carry out work for them—like the building of a house or the felling of trees—the employer and prospective employee or contractor would probably go through the formality of being introduced to one another and then enter into an agreement. Some of the obligations involved in their relationship would be customary and understood, but details of the particular agreement, like the amount and manner of payment and date for completion of the work, would be subject to negotiation and were usually worked out through an intermediary, who could if necessary witness to the terms agreed on.[2]

Another important transaction would be the division of the family and of the family property at each generation. According to Lin Yüeh-hwa, in Fukien at least, the person on whom it was customary to call to act as arbiter was a maternal uncle.[3] He, it may be supposed, would have had affection for all his sister's children, and so could be relied on to judge impartially between their claims; also that he would have had a certain authority over them all in cases of later disagreement. A written agreement was drawn up, and an offering before the ancestral shrine followed by a feast, at which arbiter and guarantors were guests of honour, gave solemnity to the occasion. Hu Hsien-ch'in speaks of assistance with this division as one of the functions of the elders in the mourning circle.[4]

Although property was freely alienable by Sung and Yüan times, the intention of the owner to transfer title gave certain people the right of pre-emption. As there were essentially three classes of option holders, viz., immediate agnatic relatives,[5] neighbours and 'mortgage' holders[6]—to make a sale valid, it had to be clear that the first two had no objection and that the third was not involved. Sales of land were negotiated through the agency of a middleman who, together with relatives, neighbours and other witnesses, was invited to observe the measuring of the plot changing hands. A deed of sale[7] was drawn up giving details of the land, what was included with it and the agreed price. To avoid later trouble and distinguish this from transactions more akin to mortgage, the sale had to be described

[1] Doolittle (1868), p. 68.

[2] On the form and content of contracts for work and services, see Kroker (1957). Some decisions of the Supreme Court throw light on the background of custom behind the formal contracts. See Bibliography, Official Compilations (1923), pp. 121–3.

[3] Lin (1948), pp. 123–6.

[4] Hu (1948), p. 17.

[5] Section 88 of the Penal Code prescribed punishments for junior relatives who might dispose of family property without permission.

[6] Schurmann (1956), p. 514.

[7] See Appendix 2; also Hoang (1897), of which the second part is devoted to a selection of documents relating to transfer of property in various ways.

as 'absolute sale without power of redemption' (since an edict of 1753) and it was customary for it to be stated that the sale was made with the agreement of the vendor's relatives. The deed was signed by the vendor, the agent and the writer of the contract, and the handing over of this document signified the transfer of ownership, after which neither party could withdraw. Its conclusion was usually marked by a feast, given either by the buyer or by buyer and vendor jointly, to which middleman, writer and witnesses were all invited. The middleman and the writer were further rewarded for their services by receiving a percentage commission on the value of the transaction; the saying 'middleman three, writer two' (*chung san* : *tai erh*) indicates their shares.[1]

The deed was supposed to be registered at the District Magistrate's *yamen* to validate the conveyance (and transfer the tax liability) for which a further fee was payable, but the distinction made by peasants between 'red deeds' (stamped with the *yamen* seal) and 'white deeds' (those without it) indicates that this was not always carried out. One method of partially evading this obligation was to execute two deeds of sale which together made up the purchase price and to register only one of them, thus evading tax on a proportion of the sale.[2] It appears that in rural China people thought that the witnessing of the transfer by relatives and neighbours gave more effective title than any official title deeds.[3]

Besides absolute sale of land, two types of mortgage were customary. The first of these, *tien mai* (mortgage sale), or as H. F. Schurmann would prefer 'sale with limited ownership',[4] was a semi-permanent transfer of land in consideration of a sum of money, the original owner being entitled to recover his land after a given period on repayment of the money. The use of the land was exchanged for the use of the money, no interest or rent being payable, for an indefinite or a specified period. If the land had not been redeemed within thirty years, the sale was regarded as absolute. Contrary to the usual terms of mortgage, it was the land and not the money that could be redeemed. The other form, *tien tang* (or mortgage-pledge), was a temporary loan for which land was pledged as security without changing hands. If the debtor was unable to redeem his land, the permission of the authorities had to be obtained before the creditor could sell or otherwise realize on the land—which made such loans a bad risk. Both of these forms of mortgage were negotiated through an intermediary and were the subject of written agreements, the first type having to be registered with the authorities, while the second required that title deeds were lodged with the agreement, but not official registration.

[1] Niida (1952), p. 308. [2] Jamieson (1921), p. 98. [3] Niida, op. cit., p. 311.

[4] Schurmann (1956), p. 514. Compare 'sale with provision for repurchase' of Indonesian *adat* law. See B. ter Haar (1948), p. 109.

Similar institutions existed also in Japan under names which could be used for them in China as well: *teito*; *shichi ire*; *ten*. See Wigmore (1892), Part II, ch. vi, p. 91.

Niida, summarizing the work of J. L. Buck, Ch'en Han-seng and several Japanese scholars, describes three customary forms of tenancy[1]:

(i) Perpetual tenancy (*yung tien*) which could not be disturbed so long as rent was paid, was not affected by changes of legal ownership and could pass to descendants of the tenant. It did not give right of ownership and the tenant was forbidden to do lasting damage to the soil. Guarantee money was payable at the commencement of the tenancy and was returnable when it ended.
(ii) Tenancy for an indefinite period—which the landlord could terminate at will. This was formerly the most usual type of tenancy.
(iii) Tenancy for a fixed term; in recent years, often for one year; in a considerable number of cases, for periods of three or five years; and even in some for as long as ten or twenty years. These were renewable on expiry at the option of the landlord, the tenant enjoying no security of tenure in case of sale. Sub-letting was forbidden under threat of the land being reclaimed by the landlord.

Both (ii) and (iii) were usually the result of negotiation by a middleman, not directly negotiated, and the agreement was marked by sharing—what was for peasants—a quite elaborate meal. Recent investigations have disclosed that a majority of tenancies rested on unwritten agreements, though evidence of written agreement is available for Ming and T'ang dynasties as well as some for more recent times. In these it is stated how the rent was to be paid—whether as a fixed amount of money or grain, a proportion of the crop or in unremunerated labour for the landlord at the season when it was most needed on the land. The T'ang documents included an indemnity clause for breaking the contract, but this was not usual in those for later periods.

In Ch'u-hsien (in 1948), according to Morton Fried, prospective tenants and landlords might meet in one of three approved ways: the landlord might seek out a suitable tenant, or a prospective tenant might approach a landlord, or—the most popular method—a third party brought the two together. The go-between would most commonly be a friend or relative, and he would negotiate a tenancy agreement for a trial period. Then, if the landlord was satisfied that his tenant was a good farmer, a long-term agreement might be negotiated, after which the tenant would have reasonable security of tenure. While all these arrangements were, by 1948, covered by the legal code, according to Fried, custom and *kan-ch'ing* were more important than formal legal standards. (Fried goes on to assert[2] that in this locality *kan-ch'ing* was more important than custom since there was no agreement among landlords on tenants' rights to security of tenure, but I should guess that this might be connected with twentieth-century dislocations and inflation in land values.)

The employment of an intermediary or agent was standard practice among the Chinese in all parts of China for almost all transactions of any

[1] Niida (1952), pp. 297–301. [2] Fried (1953), p. 108.

consequence. A number of terms were used for this role, some of the commonest being *chung-jen* (middleman), *chieh-mei* (go-between) and *chieh-shao* (introducer). Any competent person might undertake the service—it was not reserved to a separate profession. Some people, of course, acquired a reputation for having suitable contacts or for handling negotiations skilfully; some also for special competence in a particular type of transaction. These people were naturally more sought after than their neighbours when anyone had business to arrange, and some were adept at inspiring transactions in which they could be of service. But in general, the man who arranged one agreement might well be one of the parties to the next. The middleman received a reward for his services, and the fact of being asked to conduct negotiations in itself conferred a certain amount of 'face', as it showed confidence in his ability and trustworthiness. Consequently his concern for his good name and future employment prospects gave him an interest both in his clients' satisfaction with their bargains and in their conscientiousness in honouring their commitments.[1] He also had a legal responsibility, since he was liable, if the transaction was illegal, to suffer punishment only one degree less than that decreed for the contracting parties.[2] His responsibility was indicated by his name appearing on the written agreement: if either party later had grounds for dissatisfaction, there was a ready channel for expressing them, by means of which the matter might be straightened out. The middleman who had arranged the deal ought to know what had been agreed, and he could bring pressure to bear on the defaulting or offending party—to repay his loan, perhaps, or to see that a daughter-in-law was better treated—by arguing that failure to honour the agreement would cause *him* to lose face. He was in a better position than the aggrieved party to enquire dispassionately and discreetly into a defaulter's circumstances, to find out what part of his commitment it was possible for him to fulfil. He could also elicit the minimum the other could be persuaded to accept in lieu of payment in full, and so, with considerable delicacy, arrive at a compromise that would save face all round. Presumably this was accepted as the best settlement obtainable, and it is certain that many arguments were settled in this way without growing to the proportion of serious disputes.

A special case of the employment of an intermediary was the system of guarantee or security, which Niida considers (seen particularly in the context of its influence on surrounding countries) one of the most significant parts of traditional Chinese law. This system was one by which one person's debt to another was guaranteed by a third person. Niida suggests that in its earliest form this was comparable with bail as known in the West, that is, an undertaking that the person guaranteed would not abscond. (It was also used in the case of persons required to be present

[1] In considering marriage contracts, feminine pronouns should be understood. Marriage go-betweens were commonly women.

[2] See, for example, Hoang (1915), p. 125.

for official legal investigations.) In time it was gradually transformed into a guarantee of payment in place of the original debtor if the latter absconded or died without paying, viz.: C undertook to indemnify B if A failed to pay his debt. The two forms of guarantee existed side by side—no doubt varying also with locality—and care had to be exercised (as European merchants found when they came up against the system in the nineteenth century) to know which was intended. Sometimes the responsibility of the guarantor was limited to bringing pressure on the debtor to pay up, as is indicated in a saying current in Hupei, 'A go-between cannot undertake to produce children, a guarantor cannot undertake to repay money.' The roles of middleman and guarantor seem in some cases to have merged, and it was not always clear from the title given to this person in written agreements in just what capacity he was acting. The interchangeable use of characters in the names applied to such people reflects this confusion: a guarantor was usually called *pao jen* (guarantor) but occasionally *chung-pao-jen* (middleman-guarantor) is used. Niida comments:

> The lack of clear definition of rights which characterized these agreements left a vague borderline area in which the assertion of rights depended upon mediation and arbitration, that is, a delicate balance of considerations of saving and losing face by three people, the two parties and the guarantor poised between them.[1]

The principle of underwriting by a third party was extended to mutual guarantees for joint debts. Several people jointly borrowed—very often, though not always, government funds of grain—the proportionate share of each in the total loan being stated. It was the primary responsibility of each to repay only this proportion, but if one defaulted his share would be divided between the others, equally, unless otherwise provided in advance.[2]

Contractual leases were also negotiated when other things were lent and borrowed for productive use on the understanding that a return would be made for their loan.[3] Items included in such agreements were labour, querns for grinding corn, camels, farm animals, boats and carts; various words are used signifying loan, lease, hire and others for rental, wage or fee. The general principle underlying these exchanges was that they rested on negotiated bargains which specified the conditions of loan and the return to be made. Transactions could no doubt be ranked in an ascending scale according to their degree of formality: not all were so formally negotiated as those just described. The contrast between, on the one hand, the customary or contractual relationships formally entered into and, on the other, the privately negotiated bargain or compact points, I think, to an important difference. Morton Fried describes the way peasants negotiated with one another to exchange labour at the busiest

[1] Niida (1952), p. 350. [2] Niida (1952), p. 350. [3] Niida (1952), p. 329.

season, and the informal manner of securing fulfilment. These exchanges were an informal co-operative with fairly stable membership but negotiated afresh each year. One farmer who knew that he would need help at harvest time might approach another suggesting that they should co-operate. If a mutually advantageous exchange could be made, an unwritten agreement would be reached, 'informal but as binding as a contract', specifying the number of persons, dates for the work, and so on. The two originators might then try to draw others into their scheme. Fried suggested to the farmers that someone might unscrupulously try to manipulate the exchange. They denied that it would be in anyone's interest to do this, since he would lose *kan-ch'ing* and become known as one 'who did not want face' . . . and consequently in future he would be unable to get help, which in a real crisis would amount to disaster.[1]

Here the arrangement is a private, though specific, compact, arrived at by the parties themselves, and the sanctions which would support it are persuasion and self-interest. What distinguishes the previously described transactions from this is, first, that the former represent agreements to enter into a relationship the rights and obligations of which are either customary or specified in customary form; and, secondly, their public character, both on the score of being negotiated through the agency of a third party, very often by means of a document accessible for public verification, and by being given deliberate publicity. (I would suggest that the negotiator represented the community interest in a transaction as well as those of his clients, and that an argument in terms of 'loss of face', besides containing ideas of personal humiliation, represents an attempt to enforce standards of conduct that the community would consider reasonable.)

The village leaders had, on account of their duties in connection with registration and taxation of land, to be informed of transfers of land or division of inheritance, while their duties in relation to population registration involved them in knowing of marriages. These were thus theoretically made known to the community as a whole. This was another reason why the local leaders should be called on to adjudicate when, for example, land transactions led to disputes, and so ensured that the latter were dealt with by the local community as formally constituted. These features seem to confer on the conclusion of formal agreements the character of legal acts which were enforced by the authorities of the local community (with the approval of the authorities of the wider public). Their adjudication of local disputes in fact served to distribute rights and obligations, which is one of the functions of law. If in some hypothetical case the mutual assistance compact had broken down and the sanctions of persuasion or economic self-interest had not been enough to enforce it, there would no doubt have been an open quarrel; if informal intervention had failed to settle this, the village leaders would have been called on to

[1] Fried (1953), pp. 117–9.

arbitrate and would have done so in order to restore peace, which they were held responsible for maintaining. In the case of disputes arising out of customary and contractual agreements, there was added to this an additional motive, viz., that custom—which I have suggested is here to be equated with local law—must be upheld and customary contracts must be honoured, if the life of the community was to go on; i.e., the public had an interest in seeing the content of the agreement fulfilled as well as in preventing friction between the parties.

9

The Complex of Legal Institutions Considered as a Whole

THE jurisdictional aspects of the *tsu*, the guild and the village have been examined in some detail, and it has been shown that, taken all together, they offered a substantial extension of the official legal machinery. It can be seen that in China offences were punished and disputes were formally adjudicated by the authority of the group most nearly concerned, and that this was done with the approval of the administration. The *tsu*, the guild and the village may be thought of as operating as subordinate tribunals of the official courts, and the norms they enforced as an extension or amplification of official codes which the official courts, if appealed to, would endorse. On this analysis, specialization took place—though with some blurring at the edges—at the lowest level: the *tsu* dealt with questions of inheritance, adoption and the ancestral cult, the guilds with the regulation of trades, and villages with land law and contracts of sale or tenancy.[1]

Most of life for the majority of people in China fell within the scope of the *tsu*, village or guild organization. Before analysing further the working of this machinery, I shall give a few illustrations to show how the principle of delegated powers of jurisdiction was extended to communities which one might have thought would constitute exceptions: a Buddhist monastery and two examples of non-Han peoples, remote from one another, unassimilated by the Han-Chinese.

The legal status of Buddhist and Taoist religious was set out in the introductory section of the *Ta Ch'ing Lü Li*: the relationship between superiors and subordinates was regarded as equivalent to that between agnatic uncles and nephews.[2] Of one monastery, Jamieson wrote:

[1] Marriage, it will be seen, was in a rather special category. Because of *tsu* exogamy, a marriage was bound to involve more than one *tsu* and usually did involve people from two villages, so it did not fall conveniently within the scope of intra-*tsu* or intra-village jurisdiction. This fact, taken together with the ritual importance attached by the Chinese to the consequent relationships, may explain the more explicit regulation of marriages in the official code—than, say, of trading practices—and the number of cases arising out of them that came into court. (See Hoang (1915), passim.)

[2] See Staunton (1810), sect. 42; Boulais (1924), 189 Loi, p. 96. Other laws relating to religious communities are included in the Revenue Department section of the Code, see Staunton, p. 83, or, for fuller detail, Boulais, pp. 172 ff.

. . . the *Ssu Kang Seng* [head of the Buddhist monastery] who although a *kuan* or government official, scarcely ranks with the magistrate of the district in which he resides. He has exclusive jurisdiction as regards petty offences, but his duties would seem mainly to consist in bringing the misdemeanours of his subordinate priests to the knowledge of the local authorities. By these officials he is selected from the higher grade of priests and recommended to the Board of Ceremonies, from which he holds his appointment, and in case he fails to discover and report on any grave crimes, or even such offences as the illegal taking of probationers or novices by the priests under his control, he is liable to degradation and punishment.[1]

As examples of enclaves of non-Han peoples I shall take the Yao people of Kuangsi and Kuangtung and the Ch'uan Miao in Szechwan. (Both are taken from twentieth-century accounts but on these matters they are probably reliable as guides to the past.) The Yao differ from the Chinese around them in social organization[2]; so much so that the Chinese consider their free ways licentious. They live in nuclear families in villages, and it is with the latter that they identify themselves—neither clan nor tribe has significance for them. The anthropologist who studied them reported that in their villages they managed their own affairs under the leadership of an elected *ngung-chu* (for which the Chinese use the name *chia-chang*, taken from the *pao-chia*[3] terminology), in consultation—on important matters—with a village assembly. The *ngung-chu* represented the village to villages beyond and ultimately to the Chinese authorities, and had to be someone able to speak Cantonese, as that was a lingua franca between speakers of the different Yao dialects, as well as being used for communication with the Chinese. In case of a quarrel between two individuals, or villages, the *ngung-chu* of the village (or the two villages) would try to reconcile the parties, or a council of the leaders of all the Yao villages might be called; and to their decision there could be no resistance. However, the *ngung-chu* would not use his power in an arbitrary fashion—he tried to make his decisions accord with public opinion on the matter in question.

Of the Ch'uan Miao we are told that they have no written laws: crimes are infractions of the customs or mores of the group. Minor disputes when they arise may be settled by the two persons concerned; or their families may try to solve them. If they are more serious, the local headman or a number of older people in the district are called in. They have their own scale of fines for offences and recompenses for grievances—mostly in terms of animals—and also physical punishments. 'It is said that only one or two per cent of the worst cases are ever taken to the Chinese courts. . . . Litigation in a Chinese court is expensive and a Miao . . . is likely to be discriminated against. In addition he is at a disadvantage because he cannot read Chinese characters.'[4] (This was a disadvantage he shared with the majority of Chinese!)

[1] Jamieson (1888), p. 168.
[2] See Wist (1938), pp. 103–7.
[3] See above, pp. 47 ff.
[4] Graham (1937), pp. 28 ff.

Below the formal or near-formal tribunals constituted by all the groups described, a great deal of informal mediation of disputes went on. This might be performed by the middleman responsible for negotiations out of which conflict had arisen, or by respected persons whose help was sought or, if neither of these succeeded in disposing of the quarrel, there were always people ready to gather to hear an argument and offer solutions. Such informal discussions sifted out the less difficult cases before they led to serious rupture, and reduced the need to appeal to official courts. That this was in accordance with official policy is confirmed by the K'ang-hsi Emperor's reply to criticism of the courts:

> . . . the good citizens, who may have difficulties among themselves, will settle them like brothers, *by referring them to the arbitration of some old man or the mayor of the commune*. As for those who are troublesome, obstinate and quarrelsome, let them be ruined in the law-courts—that is the justice that is due to them.[1]

The village 'anti-litigation societies' set up by regulation as part of the community development planned in the nineteen-twenties seem to have been designed to give formal and permanent expression to something that had existed informally and contingently for centuries.[2]

Chinese philosophical predispositions, moreover, favoured the resolving of disputes by mediation and compromise. Positively, the idea of harmony or agreement (*ho*) ranked high in the scale of values; negatively, conflict was feared because it was fraught with risks for all and undermined group strength. In philosophical and religious thought Chinese as individuals were eclectic and tolerant; rather than admit the exclusive claims of any one system of ideas, they preferred a blend of what was valuable in each. Parallel with this, conduct likely to minimize friction or reconcile conflicting interests received general approbation.[3]

It was thought better to yield ground (*jang*) and meet an opponent half-way than to stand on principle: then if both parties behaved in this way compromise would be possible without either of them losing face and thus group cohesion would be maintained. If, of two parties to a dispute, one were willing to give way, while the other insisted rigidly on what was due to him, public opinion would always side with the more accommodating party. The idea found general favour that if losses had to be borne, they should not all fall on one party. In describing the difficulties of securing execution of judgment, Escarra wrote:[4]

[1] Quoted in Jernigan (1905), p. 191 (my italics).

[2] See Gamble (1954), pp. 140, 165.

[3] An observer of nineteenth-century Japan reported a similar predisposition there towards mediation and arbitration and avoidance of official courts, except in larger towns and cities 'where family unity was somewhat weakened'. In villages 'few private disagreements went beyond the family or the *kumi* [local group]'. See Wigmore (1892) i, pp. 75, 78, 85.

[4] Escarra (1936), p. 453.

L'exécution forcée n'est pas dans les mœurs parce qu'elle est contraire aux habitudes bien connues de rechercher toujours l'arrangement, le compromis, la 'voie moyenne'. De même que le sentiment du commandement impératif de la loi n'est pas nettement perçu par une mentalité chinoise, de même qu'une décision de justice tranchant rigoureusement de prétentions contraires n'est pas regardée comme un idéal, ainsi l'exécution forcée n'est pas en honneur. Exécuter un débiteur, c'est lui faire perdre la face, c'est contraire aux rites de la modération. Il faut que, de lui-même, le débiteur accepte son sort et prenne les mesures nécessaires. Or, le débiteur appartient nécessairement à un groupe: famille, clan, guilde, etc., qui a, lui, le souci de maintenir son prestige. Le créancier le sait, qui peut être débiteur demain. Il n'enverra pas l'huissier chez son débiteur. Il fera approcher un membre influent du groupe et celui-ci veillera à ce qu'il obtienne satisfaction sans heurts et sans qu'il puisse subsister de rancunes. . . .

The last proviso suggests that satisfaction in full was unlikely!

Righteousness, the 'ought-ness' of the situation (*i*), also had a place in the Chinese ethical system but did not displace *ho*; harmony was a good of the entire universe, while righteousness applied only to human conduct and is therefore subsumed in *ho*. Propriety and righteousness seem sometimes to be commended (by Wang Hui-tsu, for example), as a *means* of achieving *ho*. For the human being, *ho* consisted in conducting one's human relationships harmoniously, that is, being at one with one's immediate environment, since that was where frictions might develop. On the plane of ideas, then, great stress was laid on agreement and harmony.

In practical matters such as adding to one's holding of land, being able to borrow in time of stress, or arranging favourable marriages, for example, to be a respected member of one's group was an important asset. Progress towards prosperity would be impossible unless one had the support of relatives, neighbours and fellow-traders. Nor could the successful afford to deprive themselves of this support lest they be attacked by enemies or 'bandits' with impunity. Not to stand well in the opinion of one's fellows would cause more certain discomfort than to incur the displeasure of an official in the *hsien* city. These considerations gave force to group judgments and sanctions, as well as to less formal mediation—and rendered them more effective supports of social norms than the official legal machinery would have been, if invoked.

It seems relevant here to point out that the sanction employed to enforce group judgments was frequently one which, as well as penalizing the offender and reminding him and others of the rule he had broken, served also to re-integrate the whole group by joint participation in an enjoyable activity. By making the wrong-doer provide a feast or entertainment for the group, they gave him the chance to compensate for his recent loss of reputation. Not only was he accepted back into the group after estrangement, but he was restored to general favour by playing the honourable role of host to the whole membership or, if not the whole membership, at least to their official representatives. Harmony was thus restored and group strength preserved.

It was usually urban guilds that awarded their members the punishment of providing a feast for fellow-guildsmen. In the settlement of village disputes, the milieu in which mediation often took place was probably also favourable to reaching compromise and re-integration. 'The market town tea-house is a place where many community disputes and neighbourhood quarrels are settled by drinking the so-called "mediating tea".'[1] The urbane good manners associated with tea-drinking were likely to dissipate anger and dissension.

Informal mediation might in practice begin by one of the parties to a dispute calling on a third person, either in virtue of friendship or other personal relationship *or* because he had served as middleman or witness in the transaction which had given rise to the difficulty, to try to persuade the other party to fulfil his obligations. Or, a third person, knowing of an incipient quarrel, might offer his services as mediator, in the hope of winning some return for his help, or because he felt some duty to keep kinsman or friend out of trouble. More specifically, relatives within degrees for which mourning was prescribed, the *wu fu*, 'were not only obliged to attend each other's family rites . . . but also act as negotiators and arbitrators in disputes arising in and between the individual *chia*. At the division of property particularly the elders in the circle of mourning relatives make decisions and witness the transaction. . . .'[2] hence they would be a natural choice for arbitrators. If neither of these methods had achieved results, the dispute might be discussed openly by the two parties and a number of other members of the group, co-ordinate in status with them; they would offer suggestions for solving the matter but had no power to force acceptance on the parties except moral suasion, which the disputants might choose to ignore if they felt that they could count on support in other quarters. Or, instead of this group mediation, some more senior or generally respected person—perhaps a senior member of another branch in the *tsu*, or a member of *tsu* or village who held a literary degree,[3] or a retired official living in the neighbourhood—might be called on by one or both of the disputants, or by the bystanders, to offer an opinion as to who was in the right. The prestige of such an arbiter would give him slightly more authority[4]: general respect paid him by the group would assure its support for his pronouncement, and to ignore his advice would be to flout public opinion, even if expressed through an informal channel; cf.:

[1] Yang (1945), p. 196.
[2] See Hu (1948), p. 17.
[3] cf. Chang Chung-li (1955), p. 63.
[4] In describing the behaviour of Singapore Chinese, Dr Freedman has used the term 'prestige-arbitration' for this technique of settling disputes. See Freedman (1952), p. 122.

. . . so soon as two people lose control of themselves in a quarrel, a mediator, usually an older person, will appear at once and separate the two and argue with them until they stop. To give his words effect he asks each person to stop out of regard for my *mien-tzu* (face). Such an appeal by a person of some standing, made for ego's own good, must not be disregarded.[1]

The next stage would be the formally constituted authority in the group or sub-group, and so on to the leaders of successively more inclusive groups until the *hsien* court was reached. (Lin Yueh-hua's suggestion that disputes moved up the lineage hierarchy step by step until, if they could not be solved at lower levels, they were brought before the *tsu* leaders, may represent an idealized scheme rather than give a realistic picture of what actually went on. If a member of the *tsu* earned a reputation for handling disputes, he might be preferred out of turn to the regular channel of mediation.) The form of intervention ranged from completely private mediation at one end of the scale to public adjudication at the other, the one shading into the other almost imperceptibly as public opinion was felt to be more strongly involved. There was rarely any question of contestants agreeing in advance to accept the decision of an impartial umpire: the process was rather a struggle to exert and resist pressure, *either* between the parties, through an intermediary, *or* between authority backed by growing public opinion and the individual subject to that authority. As suggested in the discussion of 'face',[2] the assertion of standards regarded as right by the community entered into both.

In a discussion of autonomous conflict settlement in contemporary labour relations, Professor Kahn-Freund suggests[3] that the extension of these methods (in this field and in that of international relations) is to be linked with the institutionalizing of the peace obligation. (It can certainly be said that the *obligation* of peace[4] was institutionalized in traditional China—even if peace itself was not always the result.) Professor Kahn-Freund says that the level of dispute is largely irrelevant to the methods of settlement, and distinguishes four forms which represent an ascending scale of participation by outsiders, viz.:

(i) negotiation—in which the parties themselves reach a settlement without outside help;
(ii) mediation or conciliation—in which a third party arranges a compromise without giving his authority to the substance of the agreement;
(iii) arbitration—in which a third party 'hears' the two sides and makes an award, the terms of which are backed by the authority of the arbitrator;
(iv) enquiry—in which a government-appointed body enquires into a particular question and pronounces on its widest issues.

[1] Hu (1944), p. 60.
[2] See above, pp. 99 f., 110.
[3] Kahn-Freund (1954), p. 203.
[4] The reader is reminded of the discussion of harmony and compromise, see above, pp. 114 f.

Leaving aside the fourth method, which had no obvious parallel unless it was the magistrate's court, the Chinese techniques differed slightly in detail—negotiation was rarely direct and mediators were not as a rule completely detached from the substance of the agreement; but a similar progression is noticeable, i.e., the involvement of a wider public in the terms of settlement. In China it is difficult to isolate the stages: negotiation, mediation, arbitration. The Chinese words *wo hsüan* and *t'iao t'ing* are in fact used commonly in association. Theoretically at the point when private bargaining gives place to acceptance of formal group authority we are in the presence of law (on the definition of Roscoe Pound as 'social control through the systematic application of the force of politically organized society'). But as this progression is a continuum along the line of growing public opinion supporting the authority, it would be hard to draw a line at the point where law begins. The same would apply to a distinction based on the application of the sanction. Compare Marrett's definition[1]: 'Law may be defined . . . as the authoritative regulation of social relations and . . . the sanction is the principle on which its authoritativeness depends.'

The leaders of the groups we have been considering might be the first tribunal to inflict a recognized sanction, but withdrawal of general approval and support would operate much earlier, and this would happen regularly enough to justify the description of 'systematic'. Even the third party mediation which takes place privately contains, as I suggested in discussing the role of the middleman, an element of public control in appealing to what will be generally approved and so save face. It seems that through the whole range from informal mediation (which is nevertheless institutionalized, as distinct from private intercession) to court adjudication we are dealing with one comprehensive—if loosely organized—system of social control. On another definition once given by Radcliffe-Brown:

> A 'law' is a rule of behaviour subject to some legal sanction: and a legal sanction is distinguished from other social sanctions by the fact that it involves the interference of some politically organized judicial authority.[2]

It is still difficult to say exactly how much of the judicial machinery we have been considering represents 'the interference of some politically organized judicial authority'. The fact that the authorities referred cases back to *tsu* or guild for decision[3] is evidence that these were officially recognized as judicial authorities by the imperial judicial authority, and K'ang-hsi Emperor's reply quoted above[4] shows that less formal mediation also took place with the approval of the authorities. It seems that, even on the definition quoted, we might be justified in giving the whole complex of institutions of adjudication and mediation the name of legal

[1] Marett (1936), p. 63.
[2] Letter in *Man*, March 1935.
[3] See above, p. 95, f.n. 3. [4] See p. 114.

institutions, and the ordered system of relationships they upheld that of legal order.[1]

If we put this whole system under a critical lens, there seems much to be said for leaving the major control over individuals in the hands of the immediate groups to which they belonged, with appeal from these to the official courts. Matters would first be dealt with by those best able to know both the facts of the case and the local law, and the majority of cases would go no further. This was one way of providing for the great diversity of custom throughout the area of China, whereas to have charged the official courts with the whole burden of applying law would have required much more costly administration and given rise to problems of elaborate codification.

The technique of informal mediation, however, though generally useful, did itself have certain disadvantages. Disputes were sometimes fomented by those who stood to gain, either in prestige or materially, by being asked to mediate. The proportions of the disagreement often increased as more people seized the opportunity to offer their services, all expecting to be rewarded by the unfortunate parties to the original dispute. 'Peace talking' does not seem always to have been an appropriate name for what went on. A. H. Smith described a case of contested inheritance

> which has been in active dispute for a period of twelve days. To adjust the matter 'peace talkers' have been summoned to the number of *thirty-eight*, many of them literary graduates. There have been angry disputes between them and some of the members of the family, and an active fight. The peace talkers were reviled and took revenge by beating the son of number one who was in fault [the person who lodged the claim to the inheritance]. This involved fresh complications which had just been settled by a final feast.
>
> During the course of the intricate controversies the thirty-eight men had by no means omitted to eat and drink (one of the leading functions of 'peace talkers' and for the sake of which many quarrels are purposely stirred up, and many more kept unsettled for long periods). They consumed in all seventy catties of wine, and a hundred more of bread-cakes, and the total cost to number two is about two hundred and thirty strings of cash, one hundred of which are paid by number two to number one's family as 'consolation money'. Yet in this whole matter the financial interest of number two is absolutely nil![2]

Risk of expense was not confined to the official law-courts.

At the opposite extreme, though often with similar consequences, anxiety to put an end to a dispute, and so remove the appearance of conflict which was embarrassing to all, sometimes prevented parties from reaching a real settlement of the differences that divided them. The disagreement was merely driven below the surface and went on simmer-

[1] Students of pre-industrial societies (earlier Europe and North America excluded) seem to be agreed in asking for some flexibility in the application of the terms 'law' and 'legal'—that is, unless we agree to reserve them for (*a*) 'western' and (*b*) modern industrial societies.

[2] Smith (1899), pp. 253–4.

ing, and the situation was ripe for explosion on provocation. The emphasis on finding a compromise which the parties could be persuaded to accept rather than one which was based on the claims of justice gave power to the party able to bring most strength to bear.

Another source of weakness was the ineffectiveness of the 'appeal' procedure—i.e., if plaintiff or defendant, dissatisfied with the treatment of his case by his kinsmen, fellow-villagers or fellow-guildsmen, desired to transfer it to the *yamen* court for adjudication. Firstly, the *yamen* court was a dreaded experience, and secondly the individual who might have felt that the strength of his case entitled him to discount the risks was discouraged by the knowledge that, with his group against him, he would stand little chance of obtaining justice. The magistrate was usually ready to accept the view of the guild or *tsu*, expressed by their influential spokesman, against that of the individual member. That this was an obstacle in the path of justice is indicated by a Presidential Mandate of 1924 that 'gentry were not allowed to influence the court in the names of societies and other bodies'.[1] Group adjudication in fact often meant the domination of weaker by stronger members without much hope of redress.

In theory the *yamen* court provided machinery for dealing with cases arising in the interstices between group jurisdiction. In practice, however, the inefficiency of the official courts left this need unmet. There was no institutionalized mediation between people who were not related by ties of kinship, locality or craft, nor between different large-scale groups—and group solidarity was such that disputes between members of different groups tended soon to become inter-group disputes. This was the reason for trying, if parties to a transaction were not already related, to establish a bond of relationship through an intermediary who did share a relationship with both.

The Chinese system allowed certain solutions of this difficulty. It was possible within the scope of intra-group jurisdiction for the village head to adjudicate between two *tsu* in his village, or for the head of a *tsu* which made up more than one village to adjudicate between two villages.[2] Or, without going to the head of the *tsu*, some members of the same *tsu* but who were not resident in either of the villages concerned might be asked to mediate between them. Instead of calling on the village leader, two *tsu* might call in the leader of a third *tsu* as an impartial judge. In a town, inter-guild disputes were usually argued out by the leaders of the guilds concerned; being removed a little from the details of the quarrel, they could presumably negotiate more dispassionately than the individual parties, besides being better versed in the practices of the trade. An inter-village dispute might be dealt with by a council composed of respected residents of both villages,[3] or it might be submitted to those of

[1] Kotenev (1925) comments (p. 257) that this was customary in the rest of China (i.e., other than in Shanghai).

[2] Kroker (1955), pp. 299–300.

[3] There is an example of this in Hu (1948), p. 123. This contrasts with the

a third village. Where the head of a co-ordinate group is called on to adjudicate an inter-group dispute, the term 'arbitration' would, I think, be appropriate. But these were all ad hoc arrangements, depending on local circumstances, strength of personalities and the influence of the local gentry. The individual guild, *tsu* or village was not formally subsumed in a wider grouping, and only the official court offered institutionalized arbitration between them.

This, in view of the character of the official courts, explains some of the defects in the system as a whole. Those who were prepared to defy their groups could operate fairly freely: for example, the two thieves at Taitou 'did not steal in their own village—they had been caught time and again . . . and punished . . . but the villagers did not bother to do anything about them'.[1] There is an account of 24 villages near Canton banding together because of the increase in crime, the headmen of all consulting together to decide cases or to send them on to the magistrate.[2] So far as I know, this was exceptional; and there are reasons for thinking that relationship by marriage, which, on the face of it, might have facilitated inter-village co-operation, did not always do so. Except perhaps at the level of the gentry, group solidarity normally did not extend outside the village, and where group sanctions were inoperative nothing could be done. This seems also to explain the plight of many ill-treated daughters-in-law. On marriage a girl transferred to another *tsu* and usually also moved to a neighbouring village; both villages nominally shared the same moral ideals and were bound by the same penal law, but the stage between these, that is, customary rights and obligations, might be different in the two villages. In any case, ideals and obligations were not always fulfilled. Institutionalized mediation operated only in its weakest form, i.e., intercession, and there was not normally any inter-group machinery of adjudication to which she could bring a grievance, nor therefore any effective sanction against those who ill-treated her. She would depend on the support of her family of origin, who could call on the match-maker to intercede and remind her new family of their obligations. If that failed, only the physical strength of her relatives could protect her. The *yamen* only intervened when kidnapping or violence was reported, or if, in desperation, the girl committed suicide as her only means of shaming her ill-users.

A good deal has been said of the disincentive to going to law. There were, of course, magistrates who made a reputation for their handling of legal cases, and their arrival at a new post was no doubt greeted with a spate of plaints dealing with differences of long standing. However, in view of the difficulties and risks law cases involved, it can be understood that most magistrates did little to encourage litigants. It appears, how-

situation in Indonesia, where 'inter-communal squabbles and disputes which threaten to lead to war between villages are appealed to the prince, whose decision is accepted' (though 'he is shut out of intro-village affairs'). See ter Haar (trans. 1948), p. 76.

[1] Yang (1945), p. 149.

[2] *Chinese Repository*, vol. iv, p. 414.

ever, that the wrong people were not always discouraged, and it may be well to consider how it was that law cases entered the *yamen* at all.

The complaint that cases involved great expenditure of time and money in travelling to court, and much expense in entertaining the *yamen* staff sent to pursue enquiries, occurs so often in connection with law courts (cf. Appendix 4, §13) that one cannot avoid the inference that the courts must have appeared very differently according to whether one lived near the *hsien* city or in an outlying part of the *hsien*. In the more remote villages, the inhabitants of which would have been the people put to greatest trouble and expense by journeys to court, it would have been difficult to resist *yamen* runners' claims to hospitality or, so far from supervision, their other exactions. These considerations lead to the conclusion that residents of the *hsien* city and villages in its neighbourhood would have run less risk of loss by approaching the courts.

Denunciation by tribunals of *tsu*, guild or village as a sanction of last resort would have brought some cases into court, but, except in the neighbourhood of the *yamen*, it seems unlikely that this was often necessary. The mere threat would probably have brought most offenders into line. We are told of the twenty-four villages which met together in their assembly hall to consider crimes,[1] 'If they agree to present an accusation, the charge with all their names affixed is forwarded direct to the *che heen* [*chih hsien*, i.e., magistrate]. When this happens, seldom does the accused return to his native place again: transportation is the least that will be adjudged to him.'[2]

The courts were brought into action, of course, when cases of violence, kidnapping or arson occurred and could not be 'hushed up', since these were open evidence of failure on the part of the administration and had to be redressed.

> The feeling of blood revenge prevails among the Chinese, and impels many of these weak and unprotected persons to undergo great hardships to obtain legal redress, when the lives of their parents have been unjustly taken by powerful and rich enemies.[3]

To put it another way, filial piety would be a motive for trying to get a malefactor punished. Again,

> Cases of kidnapping . . . not seldom . . . lead to murder and perhaps to wholesale fighting, ending in many deaths, which renders it necessary for a Governor to report the facts to Peking.[4]

If mediation had failed to prevent disagreements from growing to such proportions that they resulted in these major crimes, the courts had to take over when that stage was reached. It appears too that the courts' handling of crimes of violence was more efficient than it was of lesser matters. Giles remarked, à propos self-help in debt-collection:

[1] See above, p. 121.
[2] *Chinese Repository*, vol. iv, p. 414.
[3] Williams (1900), p. 433.
[4] Unsigned article (1890).

Were manual violence resorted to, the interference of the local officials would be absolutely necessary; and in all cases where personal injuries are an element, their action is not characterized by the same tyranny and corruption as when only property is at stake. The chances are that the aggressor would come off worst.[1]

If disturbances occurred in any area on a scale large enough to bring criticism by the Censors on the head of the magistrate in charge of it, and an official enquiry was held into his failures, this might for a time create an atmosphere in which those who had long nourished legitimate grievances without hope of ever obtaining redress might feel sufficiently confident to claim justice in the official court.

It seems, however, that among the most frequent motives for an action being brought into court were mischief or malice on the part of those who had little to lose—either to damage an enemy or to pay off an old score. To involve someone in a lawsuit was a way of ruining him; when feelings ran high, it might be worth the trouble.[2] This operated, of course, to confirm magistrates' harshness towards those who went to law, and made the individual more than ever dependent on his group for support in his defence. The threat of denunciation for fictitious crimes was regularly used by blackmailers to extort money from the rich, and magistrates had to be on their guard against trumped-up charges.[3]

. . . there is no lack of law cases and it is by no means always justice that is sought when appeal is made to officials. It is more often a desire to gratify the passion for intrigue and to make use of rank and money to remove out of the way obstacles in the path of ambition.[4]

There are even suggestions[5] that magistrates—no doubt an exceptional minority—themselves resorted to stirring up trouble, in the hope of reaping a harvest in official fees, as a way of building up official and personal reserves. That the system as a whole achieved its purpose at all seems to have been largely due to the effective control of the groups I have been discussing over their members, and it will be seen that the purpose served was the maintenance of order rather than the protection of the citizen. Neither official courts nor subordinate tribunals provided any check against oppression, the former being administered by the same power as was responsible for the oppression,[6] the latter being tools in the hands of the stronger members.

[1] Giles (1876), p. 47.

[2] See Appendix 4, nos. 15 and 20; also the passage already quoted from Hu (1948), see above, p. 84. The Chinese language is much richer than English in expressions meaning to implicate someone in a crime.

[3] See Appendix 4, nos. 19 and 20.

[4] 'Lex' (1873), p. 239.

[5] See Jernigan (1905), p. 190; also Staunton (1810), p. 433, fifth para.; Boulais (1924), p. 711.

[6] A point which is brought out many times by Justice Feetham in the course of his Report.

10

The Content and Sources of Law and its Effectiveness as a Support for the Social Order

TO sum up the evidence of the last four chapters: much of the ordinary business of life was not catered for by the official courts, and as the latter in any case had little to recommend themselves to ordinary people, much of what in our western type of society has come to be the function of lawyers and courts was performed in China by other agencies. Both by default and with positive official encouragement, large areas of life, which in other societies are dealt with by specialized legal institutions, fell under the diffused jurisdiction of individual units of non-administrative social organization or were dealt with by still more informal techniques of mediation. Rules for the conduct of everyday life were formulated by the different small communities or associations to which a person belonged and were enforced by whoever exercised authority in these. In addition, a large volume of transactions was regulated by a body of unwritten customs, varying in different parts of China but well known to the inhabitants of any given locality. And there were formal or informal agencies ready to punish lapses from the accepted standards or to adjudicate, in case of dispute, as to which of two individuals (or groups) had right on his side according to the rules or customs.

The question arises: 'What was it that the complex of legal institutions taken as a whole enforced?' An examination of the substance of laws and decisions reveals several different ingredients. First, in both official and non-official codes, there were prohibitions against crimes which were regarded as threatening the continued existence of society. As in other societies, these included such actions as homicide, robbery and treason. The Chinese world-view, however, saw a threat to society in any lapse from moral perfection—unless amends were made; so law included a command to obey the dictates of the highest morality (as distinct from customary morality). This accounts for the penal form of all codified law (except the administrative statutes), the symbolically harsh punishments, and the different treatment of persons according to status and relationship: moral lapses, if discovered, had to be punished, and the degree of guilt varied with status and circumstances.

A second element in the content of law was what we may call administrative requirements. In this category are included both statutes which laid down what the government required of its subjects (like collection of taxes, and enrolment of population), and the rules of other organizations which represented their requirements from their members: the collection of guild dues and the performance of duties assigned by the village or the *tsu*.

Thirdly, customary law—for example that regarding inheritance, land tenure and trade—as enforced by the lower tribunes (but, as has been emphasized before, backed by the official courts), contained customary standards for the conduct of routine transactions and allocation of rights between persons. Customary law provided practical sanctions for the enforcement of these standards, and is to be distinguished from mere custom by its more objective statement and the provision of criteria for decision. It should be noted that while officially administered sanctions were provided in the Penal Code for breaches of laws containing commands to comply with the requirements of the administration, in practice, by the delegation of authority and responsibility, enforcement of these laws was left to the lower agencies and their practical sanctions. Similarly by allowing analogical application, all customary law was covered by some section of the penal code, but this was not the power that enforced it. The identification of law with morality in the official code made it virtually certain that part of the law would be disobeyed and that disobedience would not always be punished. This does not mean that all law was disobeyed: where it was based on custom or recognized administrative necessity (the knowledge that a minimum of government was essential to maintain irrigation-works, for example), fulfilment was probable, but the official machinery was not itself the power than enforced the laws. It is perhaps worth stressing that, though the substance of the laws included administrative requirements, there did not exist in China administrative law in the sense of a 'body of law controlling the exercise of governmental power outside of traditional civil and criminal justice'[1]—except in so far as this power vested in the Censorate, in accordance with the Administrative Code, *Ta Ch'ing Hui Tien*. This was in any case internal to the administration and only incidentally of help to the public against the administration.

The juxtaposition of morality and harsh punishments in the official code has puzzled many observers. It appears to go back to Han times when the Confucianists, though committed to the principle of governing men by *li* (morality), adopted something of the outlook of their rivals, the *Fa Chia* (see Chapter 2 for the controversy between the two schools), admitting the need for punishments to deal with the uncultured people who could not be controlled by *li*. The problem occurs in studies of other dynasties, and some illuminating suggestions are made by Professor Balazs in his study of Sui laws.[2] He suggests that Confucianists' dislike of written law—and consequent unwillingness to extend its scope to

[1] See Freund (1930). [2] Balazs (1954), pp. 13–14.

customary law or to rationalize the whole system—arose from a desire to throw a veil of mystification over the privileges they enjoyed as a class, and that this attitude explains much of the continuity in Chinese law.

The contrast between the high morality on which the official code was based and the practical nature of customary law may perhaps be compared with the existence side by side in mediaeval Europe of feudal law and canon law, of which Vinogradoff wrote that the dualism was necessary because of the extreme one-sidedness of both, the one providing no theory of justice or crime, the other having no system of land law or of status.[1]

A slightly different case of dualism of two complementary systems occurred in Roman law before the Empire, where the *jus civile*, national customary law, was considered as valuable as the *Leges*. In both mediaeval Europe and in the Roman law of that period, according to Ehrlich,[2] the two systems were available to be appealed to, neither possessing exclusive validity.

> It is only when the state has grown extremely powerful and has begun to tend towards an absolute form . . . [that the idea arises] of making the state the authoritative, and in course of time the sole, source of law.

In China a theoretical absolutism created what appeared on the surface as a unified system, but as it permitted autonomy at the lower levels, the reality beneath the surface remained a plurality. However, as the relationship was one in which the subordinate elements were permitted to exist by authority of the higher, they did not conflict on equal terms, which, if it had happened, might have resulted in juristic advance. Max Weber has pointed out that codification is not always synonymous with rationalization (and in China did not signify the end of pluralism):

> A good many collections of laws and regulations created at the behest of patrimonial monarchs and appearing externally as codes, as for instance the official Chinese compilation, have little to do with real codification [which he identifies with systematic revision of the substance of law]; they are nothing but mechanical arrangements.[3]

Now that the character and extent of Chinese legal institutions have been examined and the content of law analysed, it should be possible to face the difficult question of the sources of law in China.

All law, I have suggested, was enforced by command of the Emperor, if only by much delegated authority. The position of Emperor was thought of as being mediate between mankind and heaven, and on this account one might suppose him to be above the law. But this view is not tenable, since the reigning Emperor could himself be criticized and the mandate to govern could be withdrawn from him if his administration did not maintain harmony in the human part of the universe.

[1] See Vinogradoff (1920), vol. i, pp. 158–9.
[2] Ehrlich (trans. 1936), p. 14.
[3] Weber (trans. 1954), p. 271.

It has been suggested that the administration would not have been so unwise as to enforce laws which would meet with resistance from ordinary people. For example, Hsieh writes[1]:

The law-making power, we should here recollect, was an imperial power, possessed and exercised by the Emperor, and by him alone. Not infrequently, however, was a law proposed by a minister and sanctioned by his imperial master; in fact the great majority of the laws were initiated by ministers, and a fairly good law proposed by a minister stood a very good chance of being adopted, though the final deciding power belonged unconditionally to the monarch. Whenever a new law was enacted, explanatory edicts as to the reason and necessity of its enactment prefaced the announcement of the law. In most cases, it was first put into trial, then given a prohibitionary [*sic*] term, and perpetuated only after successful experiments. Scarcely ever was a law contrary to the wishes of the people given permanent operation. The absolute power of the Emperor in repealing or annulling laws came in very handily to remove laws objected to by his 'children people'.

It might appear from this that law derived from the combination of Emperor's command and people's consent. The words 'resignation' and 'acceptance' might better describe the attitude of the ordinary Chinese towards officialdom, but even so, much of their lives was governed by custom, which, when it was publicly enforcible, we are justified, I think, in calling customary law, though it was never officially promulgated. As Vinogradoff has written[2]:

It is not conflicts that initiate rules of legal observance, but the practices of everyday directed by the give and take considerations of reasonable intercourse and social co-operation. Neither succession, nor property, nor possession, nor contract started from direct legislation or from direct conflict. Succession has its roots in the necessary arrangements of the household on the death of its manager, property began with occupation, possession is reducible to *de facto* detention, the origins of contract go back to the customs of barter. Disputes as to right in primitive society are pre-eminently disputes as to the application of non-litigious custom.

While all these are, I think, to be counted subsidiary sources, the ultimate source of law is traceable to the belief shared by all sections of society—or at least never openly challenged—that there was an overriding obligation to preserve the harmony of the universe, under pain of evil consequences for all, if the natural order were disturbed. It was this belief and this fear that led Emperor, officials and people to accept theoretically the necessity for the enforcement of morality, administrative requirements and legal custom.

It remains to consider the contribution made by legal institutions (in the inclusive sense in which I have used the term) in preserving social order, in relation to that made by other institutions.

It has been suggested above that the effectiveness of the legal system

[1] Hsieh (1925), p. 216. [2] Vinogradoff (1920), i, pp. 368–9.

taken as a whole lay mainly in the control exercised by its inferior tribunals; if they failed to control their members, little control could be exercised, and where their machinery was inadequate to judge between the claims of individuals, the latter had little hope of asserting them. It would seem that by constant recourse to the techniques of mediation which I have described, the danger foreseen by the K'ang-hsi Emperor —that half the Empire would be occupied settling the quarrels of the other half—may not have been avoided. However, the system possessed two advantages. Firstly, it was cheap, in that lay judges did not have to be paid and presumably those who could best spare time bore the 'opportunity cost' of the service. Secondly, it must have served as a sort of discussion-group technique in spreading knowledge of what the social norms were. And the ease with which mediation agencies were brought into operation promoted social cohesion and prevented waste of energy in inter-personal friction to some extent. As the machinery did not always get to the root of legitimate grievances, however, and disputants were left with no effective legal remedy for their dissastisfaction, they were frequently driven to violence. At this stage, the official courts came into action and dealt with matters as crimes of violence, a criminal aspect thus being given to what were in essence civil disputes. Many cases of homicide reported in the *Hsing An Hui Lan*, for example, prove on examination to have arisen out of failure to get satisfaction in trivial inter-personal disputes.

At the highest levels (the administrative sector) almost entirely, and further down (the unit tribunals) to a very considerable extent, the legal system was a system of control (though there were gaps in this), and the distribution of rights was only secondary and incidental. Max Weber observed that 'the Chinese administration of justice represents a type of patriarchal obliteration of the line between justice and administration'.[1] As noted above, it provided no check against official oppression: when the administration was most oppressive, the actual operation of the legal system was at its worst. Nor did it offer protection to the weak against domination by stronger members of groups.[2] Deprived of all legitimate expression, opposition was driven into secret societies.

While freedom was not a value on which great store was set in China, ownership of property was, but this was no more effectively safeguarded, and security, except in the short run for the strong, was unknown. The well-known institution of banditry, which existed particularly in the mountainous districts on the borders of different local authorities' areas,

[1] Weber (trans. 1954), pp. 264–5.

[2] Nor of weak groups by strong groups. Dr Freedman quotes evidence of a weak lineage's dependence on a stronger lineage to which they paid a proportion of their crop for protection. Without this they would have had no guarantee for their personal safety and no guarantee for their property, which might be encroached upon or plundered. See Freedman (1958), p. 112.

testifies to the incompleteness of the group-control system. Instead of expecting the law to protect their property, people adopted measures of preventive self-help, as for example the style of architecture and the employment of watchmen. The houses (of the better off, at least) were built round inner court-yards, and presented a blank wall to the roadway; if there were any windows on that side, they would be well above eye-level. Many towns and villages were surrounded by a wall with gates which were closed at night, and, though it was not impossible to penetrate, any but the most determined intruder would be diverted to easier targets. In the villages crop-watchers were regularly employed to guard ripening crops, and, as a precaution against theft in towns, valuables were lodged with a pawn-shop which had facilities for their safe keeping. Perhaps one can say that the practical capacity of the Chinese for overcoming difficulties by utilizing the means that lay to hand allowed them to evade the problem of creating a system of law that would have inspired confidence and given security.

The courts were not a vehicle for the expression of aspirations, nor an engine of social change. The restriction of efficacy—in practice—to the lowest tribunals and the failure to develop a satisfactory judicial umbrella over all was a barrier to social development. Reliance on personal relationship and the need to appeal to a group which included both defendant and plaintiff, instead of having Johnsonian confidence in impersonal recourse to the law, limited the scale of economic activities and hampered expansion.[1] Stability was what the system promoted and, if development did occur, it was not assisted by law. This aspect of Chinese law is in contrast with our own but was not inconsistent with the values of Chinese society, in which (until the second half of the nineteenth century) the past was seen as a golden age and all change was regarded, at least in theory, as change for the worse.

A society's legal system is only one among many institutional complexes —morality, custom, convention, education and others—which support the social order, each with its own practices, rules and sanctions, and it is difficult to estimate what each contributes to maintaining the social order. As has been pointed out by Ehrlich, Malinowski and others, while the sanction draws attention to the rule, behaviour in conformity with norms is equally part of the machinery by which they are maintained.

In China the share taken by legal institutions in fulfilling these functions was probably small in relation to that of other supporting institutions and smaller than that taken by law in other societies. There was marked uniformity in the content of the different sets of norms. As Von Rosthorn has

[1] Considering the pre-requisites of industrialization in China one writer has said, '. . . the entire credit and banking structure has rested upon personal rather than institutional relationships. There has been an unwillingness to entrust funds to a corporation where the relationship between the investor and the management is quite impersonal. . . .' See Orchard (1937), p. 41.

put it,[1] Confucianism, which infused the laws, may as a world-view have been limited to the educated class, but the ethic which it incorporated reached down to all classes and was the living ethic of the kinship group.[2] While Buddhism and Taoism may have displaced it in popularity as a religion, the Confucian ethic had exclusive influence in practical affairs and provided the norms by which social and economic life were regulated. (A slight overstatement, perhaps, of a generally valid observation).

The consensus of norms may mislead us on the question of the effectiveness of legal institutions, which on balance may in fact have done as much to undermine the social order as to uphold it. I have quoted cases where the victims of injustice had to fall back on the faith that supernatural power would help them or punish their ill-users where human agencies had failed to do so.[3] Such failures could only have strengthened irrational tendencies which were at variance with the commonsense humanism of Confucianism. In a society dominated by the belief that harmony was the highest value and righteousness the way it was to be attained, a legal system which, by failing to provide effective remedies, conduced to violence and actually operated in part as an instrument in the hands of norm-breakers, weakened at these points the social values it would be expected to sustain.

If there was social cohesion nevertheless, these disruptive tendencies must have been counteracted either by other aspects of the legal system—in particular the effectiveness of mediation in the majority of cases—or by institutions supporting other sets of norms. Perhaps it should be attributed to the educational and religious institutions which inculcated morality, or to government policies which, because they promoted welfare, commanded loyalty. But to pursue these further is beyond the scope of the present study.

[1] Von Rosthorn (1923) ii, p. 228.

[2] Liu (1959)[2] suggests (pp. 90, 94) that *tsu* rules adapted Confucianism to the concrete situations of everyday life and the needs of uneducated people, but she also notices divergencies.

[3] See above, p. 25, fn. 4, pp. 73 f.

APPENDIX I

Ta Ch'ing Lü Li (Penal Code)

A SPECIMEN PAGE, TO SHOW LAY-OUT, AND THE SUMMARIZED CONTENTS OF ONE SECTION

Each page is divided into horizontal layers, each printed in vertical columns, thus:

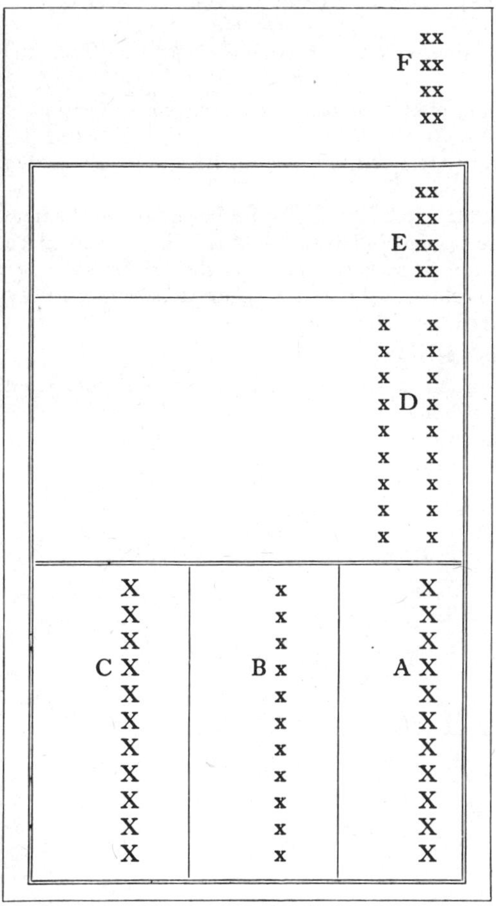

Right-hand page

(Upper margin)

F More specific details of how *lü* and *li* are to be applied.

E References to other relevant articles in the code.

D Commentary — Explanation of intention of law, detailed procedure, particular malpractices to be guarded against.

A Sets out general law (*lü*).

B (in smaller type) gives explanation.

C Extensions and modifications of general law (*li*).

Summary of contents of section 76
(1824 edition used)

People to be registered in categories.[1]

A. People should be registered in categories of military, peasant, artisan, salt dealers, medical men, musicians, etc.

Then follow punishments for falsification, omission, impersonation, and equivalent punishment for the magistrate who allows it. Those who falsely register as military to evade corvée are to get extra punishment.

Registers should be corrected and duties performed.

B. Explanation says that corvée should be entered against each family and carried out by successive generations. Falsely to register as military results in evasion of responsibility under both heads.

C. [Two examples out of many]

(1) Land sold without proper documents or of which the size is misrepresented is to be forfeited to the government.

(2) States conditions on which slaves of Manchus might buy freedom.

D. Commentary:

(1) Wherever there are households there must be corvée, so evasion is irregular.

(2) If registers are arbitrarily falsified, officials must be to blame, hence the punishment for officials.

(3) A case of removal to a place 500 *li* away should be entered in the new district. Notice should be sent in advance. Officials in the new place are allowed three months to make the entry in their records.

(4) A case was reported by the Censors of a magistrate accepting bribes to enter families under the wrong heading.

E. Various references to other sections of the code.

F. Instructions for registering: those who have purchased rank, remarried widows, divorced wives, adopted children, adopted children who have returned to their original family.

[1] See Staunton (1810), p. 82.

APPENDIX 2

Examples of Deeds of Sale, Mortgage and Loan

DEED OF SALE[1]

A sale in perpetuity of a shop, houses and land. The Seller, Chen Shih-yen, and his three younger Brothers, being the owners of a certain plot of land with houses thereon which was purchased by their father and left to them by him, being in need of money, are willing to sell the same, and their relations [names] after being duly requested having declined to purchase, they have now agreed through the intervention of middlemen to sell in perpetuity to Kwei Shih-chih all that plot of land [description] for the sum of 300 Taels, which sum they hereby acknowledge to have received in hand, the wine money on signature and cost of offerings to the gods in token of divestiture being included. From the date of this sale the purchaser shall have entire liberty to repair, build, let or himself live in the houses. This is a genuine sale for money now received, both parties acting of their own free will; it is no pretence, nor a set-off against an old debt. There will be no claim hereafter of additional purchase money on the one hand, nor of a right of redemption on the other. This and the old deeds, five in number, are now delivered to the purchaser and will be evidence of Title to his sons and grandsons for ever.

Signed by: [Middlemen, six in number]
,, [Sellers, four brothers]

Official Annex or Deed-tail

The proprietor Kwei Shih-chih of —— Hsien —— chia has bought from Chen Shih-yen of —— (x) acres land and (y) houses situated in ——. The price of the land is 300 taels, and in accordance with the law he has now paid duty at 3%, viz. 9 taels.

This deed-annex No. 14447 is issued to Kwei Shih-chih, Tao-kuang 12.5.16. [14 June 1832].

FORM OF NOTE WHEN PROPERTY PLEDGED AS SECURITY[2]

—— being in need of money pledges the following piece of land [description giving location, size, boundaries, character] by the agreement of the two parties and the middleman to —— of —— village for the sum of $—— with interest at the rate of — per cent a month. On [date] the principal and interest will be paid. Oral agreements cannot be depended upon, therefore this written contract is signed.

________ Middleman ________ Borrower

[1] Quoted after Jamieson (1921).

[2] Gamble (1954), p. 257.

FORM OF NOTE FOR LOAN WITHOUT SECURITY[1]

——, being in need of money borrows from —— of —— village with —— a middleman, as witness, the sum of —— dollars principal and interest. This amount is to be repaid on [date]. Oral agreements cannot be depended upon, therefore this written contract is signed.

____________	____________
Middleman	Borrower

[1] From Gamble (1954), p. 256.

APPENDIX 3

Proverbial Sayings

The following sayings[1] indicate popular attitudes to court trials.

1. *On avoiding legal actions*

Don't eat anything poisonous, and don't break the law. (p. 88)

Though you are very angry do not go to law; though you are very hungry do not be a thief. (p. 235)

Let householders avoid litigation; for once go to law and there is nothing but trouble. (p. 334)

2. *On the disadvantages*

Win your lawsuit and lose your money. (p. 334)

Official underlings see money as a fly sees blood. (p. 343)

You pour wine and put meat into the leather bag but the suit is still before the court, i.e., *yamen*-runners must be fed. (p. 344)

The magistrates may go but the officers [*yamen* clerks] remain: the officers may go but the law-case remains. (p. 335)

3. *On indictments*

An indictment cannot be got up without lies. (p. 333)

Wishing to incriminate, no difficulty will be met in finding a pretext. (p. 334)

Inform against a man once and three generations of his family will become your enemies. (p. 333)

The bite of a thief goes three inches into the bone. [Said to refer to false statements made by prisoners, charging others with complicity in their offences.] (p. 333)

4. *On the Magistrate's judgment*

One word may decide for life or death; therefore be careful how the pen is used. (p. 332)

A man once dead cannot be brought back to life; punishment once inflicted cannot be taken back. (p. 332)

No punishment on the Bench, no law below it. (p. 332)

Though the steel knife is sharp, it does not behead the innocent man. (p. 332)

Of ten reasons by which a magistrate may decide a case, nine are unknown to the public. (p. 335)

[1] Selected from Scarborough-Allen, *A Collection of Chinese Proverbs* (the page numbers refer to this), which gives the Chinese version.

5. *Arbitration is to be preferred*

Even an upright magistrate has difficulty in deciding family disputes. (p. 54)

Disputes and lawsuits cannot be settled except in accordance with propriety (*li*[1]). (p. 336)

Nine lawsuits out of ten are settled by arbitration. (p. 334)

[1] For discussion of this concept, see above, pp. 30 ff.

APPENDIX 4

Extracts from the *Tso-chih yao-yen*

Precepts for local administrative officials by Wang Hui-tsu

The material that follows is translated from the *Tso-chih yao-yen*—Precepts for local administrative officials—by Wang Hui-tsu (1731–1807).

Wang Hui-tsu was a native of Hsiao-shan in Chekiang and the son of a prison warder; he was forced by the death of his father to support his family from an early age. He spent more than thirty years working in the capacity of *mu k'e* or *mu yu*—magistrate's secretary, having obtained his first post in 1752 by being taken on as secretary by his father-in-law. Later he trained under a secretary who specialized in judicial cases, and took up this work himself, because it was the best-paid work open to a *yamen* secretary. During these years he resigned posts several times to sit for the official examinations, taking the *chin-shih* degree at the age of 46 (Chinese age) after three unsuccessful attempts. He continued to work in the capacity of legal secretary even after this success, as he was not appointed as a magistrate until eleven years later. In all he worked for sixteen different magistrates at places in Chekiang and Kiangsu (provinces with a reputation as forcing-houses for officials).[1]

The fruits of his experience he put into two works which were regarded as indispensable guides to local officials until the 1911 revolution.[2] The *Tso-chih yao-yen* (first printed 1785) consists of forty passages each of which contains a homily on some aspects of the work or career of a legal secretary. The passages that follow (which I have numbered for ease of reference) have been selected for the light they throw on the handling of law cases in the *yamen*. They represent (in length) slightly more than half of the work; the remaining precepts have to do with the secretary's own conduct, counselling frankness and independence in dealing with his master, hard work, and carefulness in money matters so that he can avoid taking favours, maintain his personal integrity and always be in a position to resign in case of disagreement—all with a view to establishing a good professional reputation which would ensure steady employment. The work is accessible in the *Ts'ung-shu chi-ch'eng* collection, no. 895. There is a continuation which I have not translated.

It is of interest that Hu Hsien-chin has cited three of Wang's court cases[3]; also, significantly, a case in his own *tsu* on which his advice was sought without taking it to court. These are all quoted from his autobiography (first printed 1796 but supplemented by the author until 1806).

[1] Zi (1894), p. 221, gives the provincial origin of all candidates who obtained the first three places in the *chin-shih* examination from 1646 to 1894. 190 out of 324 were candidates from either Kiangsu or Chekiang.

[2] Tu Lien-che in Hummel (1943), ii, 825.

[3] Hu (1948), pp. 103–5.

12. CONTROL OF YAMEN CLERKS (*Chien tien shu li*)

Every *yamen* has clerks in its six offices, among which the law office is under the control of the law secretary, and the revenue department is under the control of the financial and census secretary. The reason why the magistrate relies on these secretaries alone is not because there are no other experienced staff, but because their particular skill is what helps him in controlling the clerks. The saying goes: an honest and uncorrupt magistrate has difficulty in escaping from the hands of unscrupulous clerks. For the magistrate has under him a crowd of clerks, all of whom spare no effort to conspire to take advantage of his weakness. Since the matters dealt with by the magistrate are so manifold that it is impossible for him to examine every one in detail, only by having secretaries who can concentrate on their special duties can he control the corrupt practices of his clerks. Since clerks do not get a salary but rely for a living on their incorrect yet normally-accepted practices, it might not seem necessary to clean these out ruthlessly, but where corruption is concerned and trouble is caused to other people, this must be stopped at its source. In general, secretaries and clerks differ greatly in their methods: the clerks delight in disturbances among the people, taking advantage of these for their private profit; whereas the secretary takes pleasure in the existence of harmony[1] among the people, so that he may have peace if there is no trouble among them. Sometimes quite unexpectedly the clerks offer a suggestion, or a trick, which appears beneficial to the people, and in many cases may be theoretically quite correct, but, if this is acted on rashly at first hearing and without thorough consideration, it may cause endless trouble for the people. So the most important of the secretary's tasks is to keep the clerks under control.

13. KEEP CASES TO THEIR LOWEST PROPORTIONS (*Sheng shih*)

There is a saying that if the six doors of the *yamen* are open wide, those who have right on their side but have no money will not enter. This is not to say that all magistrates are necessarily avaricious or that the staff under them are always greedy. Once a petition has been admitted for hearing, official messengers arrive at the homes of the litigants, and there will be the expense of entertaining them and giving them gifts. Or, if people have to go to town for enquiries, there will be travelling expenses. When the hearing is fixed for a certain date, petition-writers and witnesses, also friends and relatives concerned, come forward one after another, and everyone claims from those who bring the appeal. Or perhaps the date of the hearing is altered: then the expense will be incurred a second time. And besides, there are many different kinds of exactions by messengers and office staff. There is a saying that if you live by a mountain, you must get your living from the mountain, while you must get it from a stream, if you live beside a stream. This is something that cannot be stopped by law. (Then one has to pay all those normal expenses), let alone bribes extorted by threats. I said before that secretaries should always watch with extra attention cases of serious crimes involving the punishments of beheading, strangling, banishment and penal servitude (to avoid summoning innocent people). Often, litigation

[1] *ho*: see p. 114.

is the origin of people's troubles and burdens. Take for example village people owning 10 *mu* of land, where the husband cultivates and his wife weaves: they can thus (barely) support a small number of people. The burden of one lawsuit can amount to three thousand cash. They must borrow on interest in order to manage, and in less than two years they are forced to sell land; if they sell one *mu*, they get income from one *mu* less, and so a spiral starts of borrowing and selling, and in about seven or eight years they have nothing to live on. This poverty occurs after seven or eight years, but the cause that brought about this poverty really began with the court's acceptance of the lawsuit. So, unless the matter is urgent, it is better to reply advising the people concerned to behave, rather than send out for evidence and issue a summons. As the number of witnesses is not of great consequence, the secretary should at all times use his own discretion to release the innocent, and should not dash off a warrant to involve more people. If there are many defendants, why should he not select only a few to be called for attendance at court? With thousands of pieces of evidence before him, he naturally will be able to select and eliminate the irrelevant. If he brings one person less into court, then one person less is involved in the proceedings. There is a saying: one red ink mark in court means a thousand drops of red blood among the people. If in using your brush you take a little extra thought, this will already amount to immeasurable benefit for the disputants. It follows therefore that what secretaries need to keep in mind most is the aim of reducing matters to their lowest proportions.

14. LEGAL CASES SHOULD BE SETTLED SPEEDILY (*Tz'u sung su chieh*)

The hearing of legal cases is the job of a magistrate and is not something that a secretary can deal with on his own, but to estimate the relative urgency of cases and plan the journeys to be travelled, sending out messengers and convening the court—these are all the responsibility of the secretary. Most careful consideration should be given to the announcement of the date of the hearing, taking into account the magistrate's capacity and allowing him ample time, so that he does not reach a stage where he fears difficulties and despairs. When the date of a hearing has been announced and the two parties have already assembled, it should certainly not at that moment be postponed. If, by chance, at the appointed time some other business should crop up, as soon as the other matter is finished, settle this case straight away, letting people all know clearly the reason for the postponement. If an alteration is made without any reason, the two parties will wait about the whole day, thus spending an extra day's expenses, wasting money and being absent from their work, and people's resentment will be aroused. Rather than accept a case and then not proceed with the hearing, it is better to be more careful at the time of admitting it for hearing, and rather than announce a date which is subsequently changed, it would be better to be more careful when first announcing the date. There was once a woman offender who had been condemned to the lingering death[1] and had been kept in prison a long time. She asked the gaoler: 'Why haven't I been hacked to death yet? Once I have been hacked to pieces, I would like to go back and tend my silk-worms.' Although this is a rather horrible jest, it does emphasize that delay is worse than being cut to pieces. So among the

[1] *ling ch'ih*. See above, p. 62.

things that help the people, there is nothing better than hearing cases and bringing them to a conclusion promptly.

15. LAWSUITS WITHDRAWN (*Hsi sung*)

Those lawsuits that ought to be given a hearing amount to less than four or five out of ten. Wrangling between neighbours or trifling affairs between hostile kinsmen are only momentary quarrels and they are brought into court on impulse or else because some worthless character has stirred up trouble between them. If you can make them reason and calm down their feelings and sincerely make them see things clearly, people of this kind can be made to feel ashamed and the troubles all disappear in due course. When, as sometimes happens, after a petition has been accepted, relatives or neighbours mediate and appeal to them to drop the case, and the two parties become reconciled, the court should show compassion and recognize that they are now in agreement. If it is possible to stay the proceedings, to do so is one way of bringing about peace among the people, and it would be quite wrong to be obstinate and force them to continue with the case and shatter the harmony of the neighbourhood in order to satisfy the greedy desires of the *yamen* staff.

16. SEEK TO PRESERVE LIFE (*Ch'iu sheng*)

The words 'seeking to preserve life' indicate respect for justice and a benevolent disposition—this verse has been handed down from the brush of Ouyang Hsiu.[1] This has in fact always been the secret of those who specialize in law. True enough, if anyone commits a crime for which he must be put to death by law—and in any country there must be some invariable punishments—in such a case, the secretary should not find a roundabout way to dismiss it. However, some cases can be regarded as something between trivial and serious, or possibly either way, and the point at issue is focussed at no more than a single sentence, the interpretation of which concerns a life-and-death matter. In such cases you have to put yourself in the other's place to search with sincerity for a way of forgiveness. If you sincerely search for it again and again, then there must be one thread that can be made use of to save life. I acted as assistant in administering punishments for twenty-six years altogether. In that time I entered the names of only six people for capital sentences. There was Mrs Mo in Jen-ho who, because of her adultery, had plotted and murdered her husband. There was a person named Cheng in Ch'ien-t'ang who had plotted and murdered a whole family, and unlawfully caused two innocent deaths; in this murder there were also the two persons who had conceived of the idea, taken part in the plot and helped to bring it into effect. At P'ing-hu there was a person named Mao, who had committed theft and deliberately killed his wife, and a person named T'ang who committed larceny and robbery and, in offering resistance (i.e. unintentionally) killed the master. In other cases, which I did not enter as 'proven',[2] always at the time of making my first report, I examined them, repeatedly, and with caution, with my superior. This is how it came about that after the Autumn Assizes[3] my requests for leniency and mitigation of punishment were always successful. From this we know that the preservation of life is something that sometimes can be sought.

[1] Lived 1007–72. [2] See no. 18 in this appendix. [3] See above, p. 68.

17. CAUTION IN MAKING A FIRST REPORT (*Shen ch'u pao*)

As one pays most attention to the first evidence in a trial, so *hsien* magistrates' first reports are the most vital. The complications arising from criminal investigations are a burden to both magistrate and people, and the cause of this is always lack of care in the original report. In making your first report, make conciseness your first object; all evidence which has no bearing on the crime and any testimony which has no relation to the issue involved should be scrutinized and cut out. The more evidence is adduced, the more suspicious the case will appear: the more testimony is entered, the more involved the matter becomes. How could it be right not to exercise caution? As regards the method of treating the case, it is not only in deciding to allow a charge that caution is needed; to decide to dismiss a charge is by no means simple. For if a man deserves to atone for misdeeds against another, and you deliberately dismiss the charge against him, then the dead man will have been wronged. I once heard that in the triennial examination hall, ghosts occasionally cling to the candidates' seats, and whenever I want to dismiss the charge against someone, I make a point of going over the case again and again, supposing in imagination that the dead man is confronting me from his seat; only when I have a satisfactory answer to give him do I put down my brush and decide on my report, otherwise I would not dare to write heedlessly. For the past twenty years and more, the determination to be able to face the ghost has remained as fresh as if it had only been made yesterday.

18. IN CASES INVOLVING LOSS OF LIFE, EXAMINE INTO THE CIRCUMSTANCES (*Ming an ch'a ch'ing hsing*)

The outcome of cases involving loss of life depends wholly on the circumstances, by which is meant both the cause in which the conflict originated and the nature of the actual violent encounter. The rights and wrongs at the origin of the conflict will determine, at the time of the Autumn Assizes, into which category cases are put: 'Proven', [i.e. sentence to be executed immediately], 'Sentence suspended pending reconsideration of the case', or 'Pardoned'.[1] Details of the encounter—the instrument held at the time and the position of the injury—provide a means of distinguishing between intentional and unintentional actions. If intentional, the crime is to be considered as wilful murder,[2] which will result in its being put in the first category above; if unintentional, it is to be considered as accidental homicide in the course of a fight[3] and can be assigned to the category 'Sentence suspended'. Moreover, if the nature of the encounter is not made clear, the facts of the case can easily be distorted at the trial. This is the key-point of the whole issue. When you are conducting your enquiry, you must make

[1] See above, p. 68. The Chinese expressions for the three categories are: *ch'ing shih* (facts verified); *huan chüeh* (delay sentence); and *k'o chin* (to be treated with clemency). (See character index.)

[2] *Ku sha* ('killing with intent to kill' in Staunton's translations). See Staunton (1810), p. 311; Alabaster (1899), p. lviv.

[3] *Tou sha* (Staunton's 'killing in the course of an affray' in the same section).

both the coroner[1] and the suspected murderer give evidence, weighing one against the other, and the detailed evidence in their statements should produce a clear picture of the struggle before your eyes. Only then will you be without anxiety lest your recommendation be set aside or reversed.

19. IN CASES OF ROBBERY, BE CAUTIOUS ABOUT THOSE WHO HAVE BEEN IMPLICATED (*Tao an shen chu lei*)

On the evidence of stolen goods, robbery can be corroborated; the same is the case with theft. As regards the chief robber and the chief thief, their crime should not be leniently regarded, but those about whom you have to be particularly careful are the other people who are implicated and those who have bought these stolen goods. Very often someone will choose rich persons to harm, and make a pretext to involve them. People who have been implicated must of course give evidence and be cross-examined, but those against whom the charges are not substantiated at all should be singled out to be released. As for those who unwittingly purchased stolen property, according to the code itself their action is not a crime; but statements have to be taken from them and produced for examination in court. In such a case, I used not to send *yamen* runners with a summons, but left it to the local headman[2] to transmit the official orders. In the warrant it was explained that, if stolen goods were found, they should give them up to the headman, and there was no need for them to appear before the court; if not, this should be reported back, and no further investigation in the court should be allowed. I have never summoned them simply because the stolen goods were hidden and not surrendered by them. This is also a way of protecting people of good character, for once you send a summons, not only will they be put to a lot of expense, but besides this, as the thieves and robbers have implicated these people in their crimes, it is likely that they will be looked down on by their neighbours. To bring good people who have committed no crime face to face in court[3] with robbers is a thing that a good official has no heart to do.

20. STRICTLY CONTROL VILLAGE BULLIES (*Yen chih ti kun*)

The administration should have the protection of good citizens as its chief object, and, if good citizens are to be protected, it is most important to eliminate intimidation. If there are bullies[4] in a village, then the households are insecure because of this. If they are denied when they try to raise loans on false pretences, they may trump up some charge and in extreme

[1] The *wu tso*, usually translated as 'coroner', was the member of the magistrate's staff who conducted an elaborate examination of the corpse at the inquest in the presence of the magistrate. It involved boiling the body, if it had decayed, and rubbing the bones clean so that wounds would show up. See Hutson (1921), p. 106.

[2] The *ti-pao*. See above, pp. 46 f.

[3] To make plaintiff and defendant confront one another in court and watch their behaviour was, for some types of case, one of the accepted techniques of investigation.

[4] The characters are *ti* (place, local) and *kun* (stick, cudgel; in compounds, ruffian). To a Chinese reader the expression has the rather more specific meaning of a man who lived by stirring up lawsuits. *Sung* (lawsuit) *kun* is used with the same meaning.

cases even accuse someone of promoting gambling or prostitution. Even though there is no basis of fact, such a bully may seek to destroy a family against whom he has a long-standing grievance by a whole network of lies. No matter whether the injustice is cleared or not, the mere carrying out of an investigation into the false charges will lead to the ruin of the family and the exhaustion of its means of livelihood. If you confine yourself to dealing with the plaint at its origin, without bringing the person against whom these charges are made into court, then decent people will at least have some security. The only difficulty is that the village bullies rely on the petty clerks in the *yamen* as their weapons and the latter count on them as completely reliable accomplices. Thus, had the wrongly accused not been the ones in whom the upright and worthy magistrate has had a trust of long years standing, it would be as hard for them to prove their innocence as it is to pull a boat against the stream, even with a hawser of bamboo.[1]

21. STUDY THE LAWS (*Tu lü*)

For magistrates' secretaries and assistants everything depends on their understanding of the legal code.[2] In considering the text of the code[3] every clause[4] has its special meaning. The extreme of humaneness and the utmost of duty are not easily comprehended, so unless one has thoroughly digested and mastered the similarities and differences between the various sections, one is likely to miss the point completely, missing it at a certain point by an inch which leads one to depart from it by a thousand miles. The magistrate's secretary should deal with the code in exactly the same way as a candidate for the *hsiu ts'ai* degree deals with the books of the four philosophers. Whereas, however, a candidate's mistake in the interpretation of the books of the four philosophers will not result in greater harm than a low place in the examination list, if you make a mistake in interpreting the text of the code, the harm will affect living beings.

I have a friend who was dealing once with a case of 'abduction for the purpose of rape'. He was of the opinion that the man concerned ought to be acquitted, saying that this adulteress had re-married after her flight and had certainly not been kidnapped for the purpose of rape. Later on, since the woman was thought to have been unfaithful to her husband and re-married of her own accord, the crime was to result in the punishment of death by strangulation. The judicial enquiry and cross-examination to reverse the case have, with all the complications, cost a tremendous amount of trouble. Thus, the desire to reduce the adulterer's punishment to banishment amounted almost to condemning the raped woman to death. This is to reach a conclusion without having considered all aspects of the case. Therefore it can be said that comprehension of the meaning of the code consists in being able to avoid the use of some sections, and not merely in quoting any section. If all you were able to do was to quote a section of the code, then such a simple task as picking out one clause of that section and attaching a person's crime to it would be one for which an underling who executes the punishment order would be quite adequate—and what then would be the point of relying on a professional law secretary at all?

[1] *pai chang*. I am grateful to Dr G. N. D. Malmqvist for elucidating this expression. [2] *lü li*. [3] *lü*. [4] *t'iao*.

[*Note*

In order to make sense of the anecdote above, it is necessary to bear in mind the penalties prescribed in different sections of the code:

For adultery with mutual consent (according to the circumstances) 80 or 100 blows

For attempted rape of a married woman (on evidence of force having been used) 100 blows and perpetual banishment to 3,000 *li*

For actual rape (on evidence of force) death by strangulation

For a wife who deserted her husband against his will, absconded, and contracted a second marriage death by strangulation.

The first three are to be found in the section on incest and adultery, among the criminal laws (Department of Punishments section). The last is in the *lü* on divorce, which is in the part of the code dealing with enrolment of population, marriage etc. (Revenue Department section).

Presumably the case entered the *yamen* as a charge of abduction and rape, brought by the first husband against the second. The magistrate's secretary saw that there were grounds for reducing the degree of the defendant's guilt in the matter—hence his suggestion to treat the case as one of attempted rape, but he overlooked the fact that the particular grounds that he invoked exposed the wife to a charge as serious as the original.]

22. ALSO STUDY GOOD BOOKS (*Tu shu*)

To study ancient classics and to enter the royal school (for classics)—these are not things to be exacted from secretaries. On the other hand, for the secretary who is assisting the magistrate to administer the law, it is his duty to discuss and deliberate with his master, and sometimes, when cases of doubt and difficulty arise, it is necessary to quote from the canonical books in order to give a decision—which would be impossible if one had not studied them.

Once while I was at Hsiu-shui,[1] there was a certain Mr T'ao[2] who,

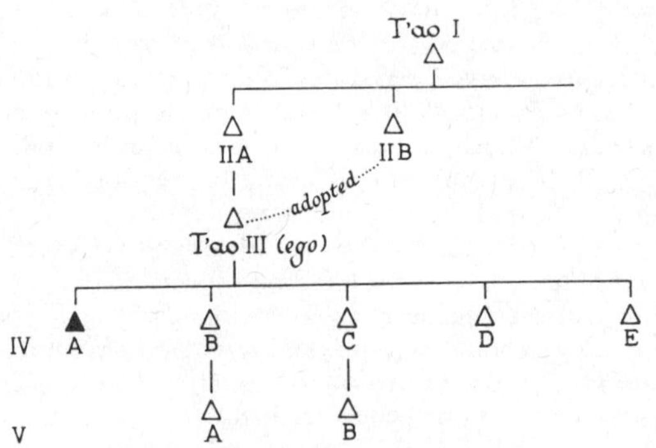

Diagram to show succession in the T'ao lineage described in no. 22

[1] A *hsien* in Chekiang which, together with Chia-hsing hsien, formed the prefectural city of Chia-hsing-fu.

[2] Tao III (=ego throughout). See diagram to which numbers in brackets refer.

although he was the only son of an eldest son, was adopted as heir by his father's younger brother [IIB]. To him were born five sons, the eldest of whom died without an heir. According to the rules, the succession should have been regarded as continuing through the son of his second son, but T'ao's third son [IVC] schemed to make his own son [VB] heir to his eldest brother [IVA], and, availing himself of the occasion of the death of his father [T'ao III], he forged a will ordering the second son [IVB] to revert to being heir to the only son's own father [IIA]. The supporters of the second son argued that it would not be in accordance with the rules of rites for him to revert to the original line of succession, as he would then have to perform for his grandfather the rite due to a father; while the supporters of the third son [IVC] maintained that for the main line [i.e. Mr T'ao's own father, IIA] to have had a son but to have no descendants was contrary to natural feelings, and that it would be not improper to carry out the proposal [for IVB] to revert to the succession in the original line. The Confucian scholars were as much divided in their opinions about this as parties in a law-case, and the higher authorities sent orders that the question be considered by the *hsien* magistrate. I was unable to find an equitable solution; through the long night I searched for an answer, when suddenly I remembered the text in the canonical books[1] in which it says that anyone who died young or who had no heirs should share in the sacrifice made to his grandfather.[2] I therefore helped the magistrate to frame a recommendation saying that the idea of performing on behalf of his grandfather the rite due to a father was definitely improper. Since this man T'ao had been adopted as heir by his father's younger brother [IIB], it was quite impossible for a son of his to revert to the succession in the original line. However, the fact that Mr T'ao's own father [IIA]—an eldest son—should have had a son and yet this line should be cut off without descendants made people feel uneasy. So T'ao's own father's tablet should be placed with that of T'ao's grandfather [I], and then T'ao's descendants would automatically carry out the sacrifices. This solution was greatly praised by our superiors.

Later when I was at Wu-ch'ang,[3] there was a case of a Mr Feng's heir. As there was no one in his own lineage to succeed him, he himself adopted as his heir the grandson of his paternal aunt. Then he died and a man named Feng, who had the same surname but different ancestry, lodged a claim to the inheritance and the Prefect was satisfied with this. I helped the magistrate frame a recommendation based on the theory of the Sung Confucian scholar, Ch'en Ch'un, that to be of the same family-name but of different ancestry was equivalent to having different family-

[1] Li Chi xiii (i): *Shang yü wu hou che tsung tsu fu shih . . .*, translated: 'Lorsque quelqu'un mourait avant l'âge de vingt ans ou sans postérité, sa tablette était placée dans la salle de l'un de ses aïeux et il participait aux offrandes présentées à ce dernier', in Couvreur (1913) vol. i, part ii, p. 747.

[2] The word *tsu* (pronounced in the third tone, as distinct from *tsu* in the second tone which means lineage, etc.) can mean 'grandfather' or 'ancestors from grandfather back'. There is no real confusion here since the distinction being made is that between the initial ceremony of setting up a tablet for one's deceased father and the sacrifices to the line of ancestors regularly performed by succeeding generations.

[3] With Kuei-an, formed the prefectural city of Huchou-fu in Chekiang.

names—which is in his *Pei Ch'i Tzu I*—and this settled the dispute.[1]

If in the past I had not had these books to turn to, what difficulties should I not have been in? Whenever *yamen* secretaries have time to spare from their duties, often they drink or play chess, sometimes they chat to pass the time or perhaps they amuse themselves with novels and romances—these things are indeed without profit for body or mind, or any relevance to the affairs of the world. How much better would it be to put all these aside and read useful books, the benefit from which would be by no means inconsiderable in the discharge of their duties.

23. WOMEN SHOULD NOT BE SUMMONED TO COURT WITHOUT GOOD REASON (*Fu nü pu k'o ch'ing huan*)

There is no question but that great care must be taken in summoning people for trial, but special care must be exercised in a case involving a woman. She should on no account be called in lightly for interrogation: do so only if you have absolutely no alternative. If a woman has committed any crime, then you should let a man, her husband, replace her at the trial. Or again, if a petition is to be presented on her behalf, a form of proxy should be used. When we consider how inexorable and strict is the spirit of the code, and yet at the same time how compassionate, we can see that quiet and refined women keep their good name and preserve their modest demeanour, while women who might otherwise become fierce and violent are kept within the bounds of decency and prevented from becoming troublesome, and showing fits of temper.

My teacher, Mr Sun Ching-ch'i (his other name being Eh-chou), told me once that while he was in charge at Wu-ch'ao[2] the man whom he invited to be his law secretary was a certain Mr Yeh, a man of great ability. One evening, just as he was drinking some wine, he fell prostrate on the ground foaming at the mouth and choking for breath. Four hours passed before he got up. The next day he fasted, made ablutions and shut the doors. He wrote down a statement on special note-paper. Then he went in person to the temple of the guardian deity of the town to worship and burn the paper. After he returned to the *yamen*, he resumed eating and sleeping normally. Six days later he again fell prostrate as before and only got up again after a

[1] See Appendix 5 in which the relevant passage from *Pei Ch'i Tzu I* is translated. It is quite typical of Chinese procedures that an argument for deciding a disputed inheritance in the eighteenth century should be grounded on the views of a twelfth-century moralist, who himself relied on events that are supposed to have occurred 1,500 years earlier.

Nevertheless, Ch'en Ch'un would not seem to be a very good authority to quote in support of a claim to inherit through the female line, since his statement that identity of family-name is not in itself proof of eligibility to succeed is followed by an explicit criticism of the practice of adopting heirs descended through females. The alternative possibilities seem to be *either* that the whole passage was felt to justify a scale of priority in rights—descent through males taking precedence over descent through females, though any degree of blood-relationship gave rights as against claimants who had none—*or* that Wang Hui-tsu was using his wide knowledge of earlier literature to quote selectively in support of a decision which he felt to be justified on other grounds.

[2] A *hsien* in Ho-chien fu, in modern Hopei.

long while. Then he asked if he might remove his lodging and live outside the *yamen*. When he was asked his reason, he told this story:

> Eight years ago when I was working at Kuan-t'ao in Shan-tung I had to deal with a case of a scholar who accused a depraved young man of trying to seduce his wife. As I went through the papers my view was that the magistrate should deal only with the young man's offence; it would be unnecessary to interrogate the woman. My friend Hsieh, however, said, 'This woman must be beautiful. Why not have a look at her? In my opinion it would be in accordance with law to bring her into court.' So I summoned the woman to appear, and thereupon she hanged herself. The depraved young man also died, condemned to death by the court. Now he has appealed[1] in the underworld, saying that if the woman had not died, he would not have received a sentence of death, while the real cause of the woman's death lay in my action as law secretary in summoning her to appear in court. The city god of Kuan-t'ao sent for me to state my case. So the next day I wrote a letter giving a full explanation, saying that this woman, who had been seduced by a youth of bad character, had been brought before the magistrate in accordance with the law; moreover, that it was Mr Hsieh's idea to summon the woman to appear in person. The god promised to communicate his answer later. That was why I was happily free from trouble for several days. Then I was sent another summons. The god now said that after the woman had been enticed, the husband had already brought the matter to official notice, so originally she had not had any intention of committing suicide. It was only when the magistrate had summoned her to appear for interrogation that her indignation had first been aroused and she had ended her life. And the idea of having her interrogated had originated in a desire to look at her beauty and not with the motive of righting the wrong she had suffered. Now although this idea had occurred originally to Hsieh, it was Yeh who was actually holding the pen. 'Hsieh has already been arrested here', he concluded, 'so it would not be permissible to exonerate Yeh', and I shall not escape the consequences.

Thus he was helped to move out of the *yamen* and he died the next evening. Now in this case, though it was in accordance with the law to interrogate the woman, yet, the reason for doing so being a corrupt one, there was no escape from retribution in the underworld. How much more would this apply if the interrogation were not permitted by the law?

24. CONSTABLES' REPORTS OF RESISTANCE TO ARREST SHOULD NOT BE TAKEN AT FACE VALUE (*Ch'a ping chü pu i ch'a*)

Where my family[2] live in the remote countryside, whenever we saw the local headman bring the magistrate's messengers to take someone away to attend an enquiry or give evidence in connection with a crime, they always had a most ferocious air. Even the educated people dared not contradict them; when they came on helpless and timid peasants, they were all the more harsh in making demands, and if their requests were not met, they would shout abuse at them. Sometimes they would destroy the warrant

[1] The word used is '*k'ung*', which means to appeal to a higher court.

[2] The word actually used is *tsu*, lineage.

themselves (making it appear the peasant's doing) and apply for further enquiry on grounds of resistance to arrest, so people were all terrified of seeing them and none would risk clashing with them openly. There might occasionally, of course, be cases of hardened robbers, who had committed many crimes and knew that they would be put to death, who would resist arrest; but in trivial disputes, such as those that arise over marriage settlements or claims on land in repayment of debts, none of the contestants, if they are of the common people, would dare to destroy the warrant in order to resist arrest. Reports of arrest being resisted usually arise out of unsuccessful threats and demands, but if you once start an investigation and summons on the basis of the reported resistance to arrest, life will be unendurable for people, even though the enquiry proves it to have been unfounded.

During the time that I acted as law secretary, whenever I came across a case like this, I would immediately dismiss the charge of destroying the warrant and send a different constable to carry on with the case, dealing only with the original charge, while the question of finding out whether the report of resisted arrest was true or not remained for the magistrate to deal with by confidential enquiries; moreover in the warrant sent by the new messenger, nothing would be said about resistance to arrest, thus avoiding further mischief, and investigation always proved the report to be unfounded. So if the constables report resistance to arrest, you should never accept it without hearing the other side of the story.

25. ONE MUST GIVE THE ACCUSED SOME CONSIDERATION (*Hsü wei fan jen chu hsiang*)

It is the duty of officials in the *yamen*, whose work brings them into close touch with the people, to be in sympathy with the people. How much more so then should we be, who merely assist officials to govern the people and are ourselves of the ordinary people!

I once came across a *yamen* secretary who assumed too high a status and presumptuously classed himself with the magistrate. Eating delicious food and wearing luxurious light silk, he had gradually forgotten the sufferings among the ordinary people. When he came to deal with some matter, he could not avoid making arbitrary decisions according to his whim. On some occasions, though his argument was not sound, he would twist phrases to justify himself and, against his own judgment, his master would follow his advice; it is to be feared that there were many evil results from this.

When I was a *yamen* secretary assisting in dealing with legal cases, whether the case was important or not, I would always sit quietly awhile and reflect; I would try to put myself in the place of the accused and deliberate, and then I would think out the whole affair from the point of view of his parents and family. At first I might feel angry, then I would become calmer and finally I would realize that the accused was to be pitied. Then I would consult with my master and make careful investigations: I never applied torture light-heartedly, and yet the true state of affairs emerged naturally, and that is why cases of mine which had resulted in confession rarely required a different verdict later on. By the use of this method my master often won favour of his superiors while I was able, also thanks to this means, not to expose my incompetence and was never out of employment.

To sum up: for those who assist in administration the most important things to avoid are hasty emotions, easily provoked anger and obstinate adherence to prejudice.

26. DO NOT QUOTE PRECEDENT TOO READILY (*Wu ch'ing yin ch'eng an*)

Precedents[1] are like traces of writing in ink: they indicate only a pattern and outline, and that is all. If you insist on quoting one as a standard to be followed, this is like making a mark on a moving ship to show where to recover a sword which has been dropped over its side into the river. There is rarely one which exactly matches. For under the one heading of robbery and theft, the ways in which the robbers ganged together and conducted their robberies, and various other aspects, are different from one case to another; and under the one heading of fighting and violence, the circumstances in which the fight started are different from one case to another. By the same analogy, all other categories of crime each have their individual cases. Human nature is infinitely varied and there never is a case which is exactly the same as one that has been decided before. If only to a small degree there are differences, this means that you will have to ponder them at length. In doing this lies the way of saving life: in failing to do so lies equally the reason for sending in a mistaken report. If you omit giving careful consideration to this and insist on adducing precedents, the least that will happen will be that witnesses will later retract their testimony and at worst you may even make a completely wrong judgment. One has to be very careful about this.

27. CAUTION MUST BE EXERCISED IN INSTITUTING PRIVATE ENQUIRIES ABOUT LEGAL CASES (*Fang an i shen*)

A magistrate who prides himself on his ability likes to use private individuals as his eyes and ears. In making private enquiries about legal cases, however, the people to whom he entrusts this responsibility may be moved by thoughts of their own advantage or they may be deceitful about the information they give and cannot by any means be considered any too trustworthy. If the magistrate believes what he is told by people who are not really reliable, everything depends on the law secretary doing the right thing without flinching and without bowing to the magistrate. If the magistrate goes by what his private informants say in making his first entry and then the legal secretary accepts idle gossip as reliable evidence, cases will always be wrongly dealt with. Therefore, whatever matters the magistrate is called on to adjudicate, the best method is for him to stand aside from the matter, so that he can judge with an open mind. For as soon as one adopts a policy of making private enquiries, one becomes too much involved in the situation and frequently one's hands are tied. Therefore, in making private enquiries into a case, be cautious, and do not undertake them heedlessly.

[1] The Chinese term '*ch'eng an*', completed legal cases, has an overtone of 'successfully completed cases'—from the official point of view—which might be a guide as to how a similar case should be correctly treated. There is no suggestion of the law having been extended by the previous case, or a principle established which can now be appealed to.

28. CONSCIENTIOUSNESS (*Ch'in shih*)

In performing the duties of secretary to a magistrate, the most important thing is to work steadily. When a case has entered the *yamen*, there will be quite a number of people waiting to hear the result, and the longer you delay it, the longer they will have to wait. Take for instance country people who come into the town to make enquiries: if they get news before midday, they can easily get home, but if they are kept until afternoon, they will have to look for somewhere in the town to stay, which involves not only spending money but also losing a day's work; and for ordinary people who rely on their own efforts for their livelihood, to waste one working day means being short of one day's food. As for those being kept in custody, the sufferings caused by delay would be even more unendurable. How could you not be mindful of things like these? Moreover, if cases are dealt with immediately they come in, the details are clear and it is easy to investigate them, but if they get into arrears, the more they accumulate the more difficult will it become to settle them. Then you will be forced by circumstances into slipshod and careless performance of your duties, and, what with those who live by framing petitions and unscrupulous *yamen* clerks, all sorts of corrupt practices will flourish, and the widespread misery thus arising will be beyond description. It is like what happens with boats which sail on a river to the town: those coming up and those going down both travel freely and there is no stoppage, but once one boat gets held up, tens and hundreds of boats following one another also get obstructed, and the river-way is completely congested the whole day long. The moral is to keep working conscientiously—then those who assist you will also get some free time in the end, and, when free, will have an easy mind. If you don't work conscientiously, then those assistants will be busy, and, being busy, they will never be free from anxiety.

35. YOU MUST RESPECT LOCAL CUSTOMS (*Hsü t'i su ch'ing*)

The primary study for a legal secretary is to know the code,[1] but skill in its application depends still more on being in sympathy with the ways of the people. Now as customs often vary from place to place, it is essential to find out all about them, without preconceptions, and make it your chief concern to abide by them. If you never act on a penal law or an edict without first seeing that it does not conflict with what local custom values, then there will be harmony between *yamen* and people, the magistrate's fame will spread, and his secretary's prestige will increase accordingly, whereas applying the law rigidly on every occasion would probably give rise to much dissatisfaction and complaint. There is an old saying: only by common consent can you promote good and dispel evil. This has stood the test of experience and should be borne in mind.

36. AVOID GOING TO EXTREMES (*Chieh i shen*)

During the time I was with Mr Hu, when I was only beginning my study of law and my anxiety was lest I should not be capable of practising as a legal secretary, a friend, Lo Ping-wen, an upright and experienced person whom I treated with particular respect, said to me one day: 'With your

[1] *lü*.

talents and knowledge, becoming a magistrate's secretary is like a Confucian scholar becoming a doctor, or a fresh cabbage being made into a coarse salted vegetable: there is no danger of your not being able to do it, but what is to be feared is that your ability may be too much for it.' I asked him the reason and he answered: 'In official matters, if you are able to deal with something, then deal with it and have done with it. You should never seek too deeply into matters to which no great significance is attached. Often if you insist on going into everything minutely, not allowing any shred of evidence to pass unnoticed, unforeseen ramifications will arise and cause endless trouble. This is what is called going to extremes—which is something the sages warned against.' I understood this and never allowed myself to forget it. In the years since then I have come to realize the great advantage to be derived from this counsel.

APPENDIX 5

Extract from *Pei Ch'i Tzu I*

The *Pei Ch'i Tzu I* is a book of moralizing essays, on such topics as 'The Will', 'The Desires' and so on, by the Neo-Confucian philosopher, Ch'en Ch'un (1153–1217). It is in two *chüan* and is included in the *Hsi Yin Hsien Ts'ung-shu*. It seems that the passage referred to in Appendix 4, no. 22, is part of the essay on spirits (on pp. 29a-30a of the second *chüan*), which is translated below. It illustrates the way relationship to the spirits of deceased relatives was used to organize relationships among the living:

SPIRITS

The spirits do not accept sacrifices from persons who have no blood-relationship to them,[1] while men do not worship those who are not of their own descent group.[2] The ancients established as the principle of succession that where there is no direct descendant, a son from within the descent group should be selected to succeed. The reason for this is that as they are of the same blood, they can communicate with one another; therefore they can succeed each other and the continuing line will have no break. This is indeed a fair and justified act which the sages would not condemn. In later periods people have forgotten righteous principles. Some families do not like it to be known that they have no heir, so they are not willing openly to adopt a son from within their own lineage[3]: instead, it often happens that they will secretly raise a child of a completely different surname and pretend that the line continues normally, when in reality the blood-relationship has already come to an end. Thus in Ch'un Ch'iu times Tseng-tzu took as his heir the son of the Duke of Chü; therefore the Sage [i.e. Confucius] wrote, 'The people of Chü extinguished the Tseng.' The fact is not that the people of Chü extinguished them, but only that someone of a different family-name was taken to conduct the sacrifice. This is indeed a way to extinction.[4] The Ch'in dynasty came to an end because of Lü and Cheng,[5]

[1] The opening sentence echoes a passage in the *Tso Chuan*. See Legge (1895), vol. vii, p. 218. (Chinese text, line 13.) [2] *tsu*. [3] *t'ung tsung*.

[4] Chü and Tseng were small feudal states in (modern) Shantung. Ch'en Ch'un quotes four characters from the Spring and Autumn Annals, '*Chü jen mieh Tseng*', for which, as he introduces the quotation à propos of discontinuity in blood-relationship in a line of descent, he rejects the *Tso Chuan* interpretation (followed by Legge (1895), vol. viii, p. 428) in favour of that given in the Kung Yang commentary—which is based on the fact that Tseng took as heir the son of a daughter married into the house of Chü (vol. 5, ch. 19, pp. 4b and 6a of SPPY edition).

[5] Prince Cheng, who succeeded as king of Ch'in in 246 B.C. and later unified China, was said to be the natural son of the merchant-statesman, Lü Pu-wei. Han dynasty Confucian scholars spread the story in order to defame the Emperor they loathed and to link the downfall of the hated Ch'in dynasty with neglect of Confucian virtues. See Bodde (1940) pp. 4–5, 18.

and the Chin because of Niu and Jen[1]; these are examples of the same kind.

Tung Chung-shu[2] has related in the *Ch'un Ch'iu Fan Lu* a story of Han times which goes like this. There was a family paying sacrifice to its ancestors, praying for the spirits to descend. After the whole ceremony was finished, the chief celebrant told the others: 'What I saw just now was very strange. There was an official dressed in official robes, wanting to go forward and yet hesitating—he dared not proceed. There was also at the same time a ghost, with untidy hair and exposed arm,[3] holding a butcher's knife, who bravely marched forward and accepted the sacrifices. What sort of spirit was this?' he asked. He himself was not able to explain the reason for this, but there was an old man who said that in this family some time before, as there had been no heir, a son from a butcher's family with a different surname had been taken as heir; that was why the man conducting the sacrifices could only recall ancestors of the butcher's family to come forward, while he had no means of communicating and making contact with ancestors in the line he was supposed to be continuing, as he was not of their blood.

If we are to speak of the present time—to set up as heir someone of the same lineage is still not a complete guarantee. The reason for this is that while in origin family-names were created by the sages precisely as a means of distinguishing those who were related by blood from those who were not, in later times there have been cases of bestowing family-names on people,[4] thus concealing the original family-name, so that family-names have become altogether confused and muddled. Therefore, in those cases in which an heir is being set up with a view to the continuance of the lineage, it is not right to rely on identity of family-name as being in itself complete evidence of acceptability. It is necessary to examine and select from among those who are closely related and for whom there are distinct records of origin, and to set up such a person. Then the blood relationship will take effect, so that father and grandfather will not lose the offerings of descendants.

Nowadays there are quite a lot of people who take as heir a boy related through the female line. They consider that, although the family-name is different, there is a close blood-relationship, and that therefore such persons should prevail against the claims of those who, besides being of different family-name, are unrelated[5] (by blood). However, when in Chin times Chia Ch'ung took as his heir Han Pi, a grandson through the female line, Ch'in Hsiu, who was Erudit of the Court of Imperial Sacrifices at the time, criticized him for violating the rules.[6] In this example, although the blood-relationship was close, the family-name was in fact not the same. So we see that this idea is certainly not one that it would be right to follow.

[1] This may refer to Niu, who was the illegitimate son of Shu-sun Pao. His story is told in Legge (1895), vol. viii, pp. 594, 598–9.

[2] See above, p. 33, note 3. [3] To a Chinese this signifies complete déshabille.

[4] For example, it was not uncommon in the T'ang dynasty for the Emperor to confer the surname of the imperial house, Li, on persons he wished to distinguish.

[5] The text has *shu su*, literally 'distantly related', but the context here seems to require 'unrelated'.

[6] Ch'in Hsiu's criticism of Chia Ch'ung (who was incidentally the official in charge of codifying the laws of the Chin dynasty) is included in his official biography (*Chin shu*, ch. 50), and in it are quoted the same four characters from Ch'un Ch'iu about Chü extinguishing Tseng. (See above, p. 152, note 4, in this Appendix.)

Bibliography

ALABASTER, E., 1899. *Notes and Commentaries on Chinese Criminal Law and cognate topics, with special relation to ruling cases, together with a brief excursus on the law of property*. London.

— 1936. 'Dips into an imperial law officer's compendium', *Monumenta Serica*, vol. ii, pp. 426–36.

AMAKAI, K., 1958. A survey of Old Customary Law in China. From a round-table discussion. [In Japanese.] *Tōyō Bunka* No. 25, pp. 50–123.

ARENSBERG, C. M., 1950. *The Irish Countryman, an anthropological study*. New York. [First published, 1937.]

AUBARET, G., 1865. *Code Annamite. Lois et règlements du royaume d'Annam traduits du texte chinois originel*. Paris.

BALAZS, E., 1953. *Le traité économique du 'Souei-chou'*. Etudes sur la société et l'économie de la Chine médiévale, I. Leiden.

— 1954. *Le traité juridique du 'Souei-chou'*. Etudes sur la société et l'économie de la Chine médiévale, II. Leiden.

BALLER, F. W., 1892. *The Sacred Edict, with a translation of the colloquial rendering, notes and vocabulary*. Shanghai.

BARROW, J., 1804. *Travels in China, containing descriptions, observations and comparisons, made and collected in the course of a short residence at the imperial palace of Yuen-min-yuen, and on a subsequent journey through the country from Pekin to Canton*. London.

BIOT, E., 1837. 'Mémoire sur les esclaves et des serviteurs gagés en Chine', *Journal Asiatique*, pp. 246–99.

— 1847. *Essai sur l'histoire de l'instruction publique en Chine* Paris.

— 1851. *Le Tchou Li ou Rites des Chou*. 3 vols. Paris.

BIELENSTEIN, H., 1950. 'The Interpretation of the Portents in the *Ts'ien Han Shu*', *Bulletin of the Museum of Far Eastern Antiquities*, No. 20, pp. 127–43.

BODDE, D., 1940. *Statesman, Patriot and General in Ancient China*. New Haven.

— 1938. *China's First Unifier, a study in the Ch'in dynasty as seen in the life of Li Ssu*. Sinica Leidensia, III. Leiden.

(See also FUNG YU-LAN.)

BOULAIS, G., 1924. *Manuel du Code Chinois*. Variétés Sinologiques, No. 55. Shanghai.

BRENAN, B., 1897. 'The Office of District Magistrate in China', *Journal of the North China Branch, Royal Asiatic Society*, vol. xxxii, pp. 36–65.

[BRIDGEMAN, E. C.], 1833. 'Penal Laws of China', *Chinese Repository*, vol. ii, pp. 10–19, 61–73, 97–111. (Unsigned review article so attributed by Cordier.)

BRYAN, R. T., 1925. *An Outline of Chinese Civil Law*. Shanghai.

BÜNGER, K., 1952. 'Religiöse Bindungen in chinesischen Recht', in Bünger, K. and Trimborn, H. (ed.) *Religiöse Bindungen in frühen und in orientalischen Rechten*. Wiesbaden.

CARTER, T. F., 1955. *The Invention of Printing and its spread westwards.* (Revised edition.)

CHANG CHUNG-LI, 1955. *The Chinese Gentry, Studies in their Role in Nineteenth Century Chinese Society.* Seattle.

CHANG YÜ-CHÜAN, 1938. 'The Legal Practitioner in China', *Chinese Social and Political Science Review,* vol. xxii, no. 2, pp. 146–7.

CHENG, F. T., 1956. 'A Sketch of the History, Philosophy, and Reform of Chinese Law', in *Studies in the Law of the Far East and South-East Asia,* published by the Washington Foreign Law Society and George Washington University Law School. Washington.

CHEN HAN-SENG [CH'EN HAN-SHENG], 1936. *Agrarian Problems in Southernmost China.* Shanghai [I.P.R.] (Also under title *Landlord and Peasant in China.* New York.)

CH'EN SHAO-KWAN, 1914. *The System of Taxation in China in the Tsing Dynasty, 1644–1911.* Columbia University Studies in History, Economics and Public Law, vol. lix, No. 2. New York.

CH'EN TUNG-YÜAN, 1937. *Chung-kuo chiao-yü shih* [History of Chinese Education]. (2nd edition.' Shanghai.

CHÜ T'UNG-TSU, 1946. *Chung-kuo fa-lü yü Chung-kuo she-hui* [Chinese law and Chinese Society]. Shanghai.

CORDIER, H., 1904–24 (original edition 1878–95). *Bibliotheca Sinica.* 5 vols. Paris. [Sections on Government and Jurisprudence are specially useful for nineteenth-century western journals.]

COULING, S., 1917. *The Encyclopaedia Sinica.* Shanghai.

COUVREUR, F. S., 1913. *Li Ki [Li Chi], ou Mémoires sur les Bienséances et les Cérémonies.* 2. vols. Hochienfu.

— 1928. *Cérémonial* 'I Li'. Texte et traduction. Sien hsien.

CRESSEY, G. B., 1934. *China's Geographical Foundations.* New York.

— 1955. *Land of the 500 Million: a Geography of China.* New York.

DAY, C. B., 1940. *Chinese Peasant Cults, being a study of Chinese paper gods.* Shanghai.

DOOLITTLE, J., 1868. *Social Life of the Chinese: a daguerrotype of daily life in China.* (Edited and revised by Hood, P.) London.

DUBS, H. H., (trans.), 1938. *History of the Former Han Dynasty by Pan Ku, a Critical Translation with Annotations.* Vol. i. Baltimore.

DUYVENDAK, J. J. L., 1928. *The Book of Lord Shang, a Classic of the Chinese School of Law.* London.

EHRLICH, E., 1936. (Trans. Moll, W. L.) *Fundamental Principles of the Sociology of Law.* Harvard Studies in Jurisprudence, vol. v. (Originally published as *Grundlegung der Soziologie des Rechts,* Munich, 1913.)

EPSTEIN, A. L., 1954. *Juridical Techniques and the Judicial Process: a study in African Customary Law.* Manchester.

ESCARRA, J., 1924. 'Western Methods of Research into Chinese Law' *Chinese Social and Political Science Review,* vol. vii, pp. 227–48.

— 1936. *Le droit chinois.* Peking and Paris. [Bibliography, pp. 465–516.]

FAIRBANK, J. K., 1952. *Ch'ing Documents: an Introductory Syllabus.* Cam bridge, Mass.

— 1953. *Trade and Diplomacy on the China Coast.* 2 vols. Cambridge, Mass.

FAIRBANK, J. K. and TENG, S. Y., 1941. 'On the Ch'ing Tributary System' *Harvard Journal of Asiatic Studies,* vol. vi, pp. 135–246.

FAVRE, B., 1933. *Les sociétés secrètes en Chine, origine, rôle historique, situation actuelle*. Paris.

FEETHAM, R., 1931. [Report on an enquiry into the government of Shanghai] See under Official Compilations etc. at end.

FEI HSIAO-T'UNG, 1939. *Peasant Life in China*. London.

FEI HSIAO-T'UNG and CHANG CHIH-I, 1945. *Earthbound China, a study of rural economy in Yünnan*. Chicago.

FRANKE, O., 1903. *Die Rechstverhältnisse am Grundeigentum in China*. Leipzig.

FREEDMAN, M., 1952. 'Colonial Law and Chinese Society', *Journal of the Royal Anthroplogical Institute*, vol. lxxx [1950 vol. published 1952], pp. 97–126.

— 1957. *Chinese Family and Marriage in Singapore*. Colonial Research Studies No. 20. London. (H.M.S.O.)

— 1958. *Lineage Organization in Southeastern China*. L.S.E. Monographs on Social Anthropology, No. 18. London.

FRIED, M. H., 1953. *The Fabric of Chinese Society*. New York.

FREUND, E., 1930. 'Administrative Law' [article] in *Encyclopaedia of the Social Sciences*.

FUNG YU-LAN, 1948. (Edited by Bodde, D.) *A Short History of Chinese Philosophy*. New York.

— 1953. *A History of Chinese Philosophy* (translated by Bodde, D.). 2 vols. Princeton.

GAMBLE, S., 1921. *Peking: a Social Survey*. London.

— 1954. *Ting Hsien, a North China Rural Community*. New York. (Translated from the Chinese Report published Peking 1933.)

GEN, LEWIS, 1952. 'Some characteristics of the Ancient Chinese Law', *The Asiatic Review*, vol. xlviii, pp. 156–60, 233–40.

GILES, H. A., 1874. 'Hsi Yüan Lu: Instructions to Coroners', *China Review*, vol. iii, pp. 30, 92, 159 ff. Reprinted in *Proceedings of the Royal Society of Medecine*, vol. xvii (1924).

— 1876. *Chinese Sketches*. London.

GINSBURG, N. (ed.), 1958. *The Pattern of Asia*. Englewood Cliffs, New Jersey.

GLUCKMAN, M., 1949. 'Adat Law in Indonesia', *Journal of Comparative Legislation and International Law*, vol. xxxi, parts III and IV, pp. 60–65.

— 1955. *The Judicial Process among the Barotse*. Manchester.

GOUROU, P., 1953. *L'Asie*. Paris.

GRAHAM, D. C., 1937. 'The Customs of the Ch'uan Miao', *Journal of the West China Border Research Society*, vol. ix, pp. 28 ff.

GROOT, J. J. M. DE, 1908. 'Adoption (Chinese)' in Hastings (ed.), *Encyclopaedia of Religion and Ethics*.

GULLICK, J. M., 1958. *Indigenous Political Systems of Western Malaya*. L.S.E. Monographs on Social Anthropology, No. 17. London.

HAAR, B. TER, 1948. *Adat Law in Indonesia*. (Translation edited by Hoebel, E. A. and Schiller, A. A. for I.P.R.) New York. (Originally published Groningen and Batavia, 1939, as *Beginselen en Stelsel van het adatrecht*.)

HOANG, P. 1897. *Notions techniques sur la propriété en Chine avec un choix d'actes et de documents officiels*. Variétés sinologiques no. 11. Shanghai.

— 1915. (2nd edition revised by the author; original edition 1898.) *Le mariage chinois au point de vue légal*. Variétés sinologiques, no. 14. Shanghai.

HOLDSWORTH, W. S., 1928. *Charles Dickens as a legal historian*. New Haven.

HOWELL, E. B., n.d. *The Inconstancy of Madam Chuang and other stories from the Chinese* [Chin ku ch'i kuan 1905 edition]. London.

HSIAO I-SHAN, 1947. *Ch'ing tai shih*. (History of the Ch'ing dynasty.) [*Fu hsing tsung shu, Hsin chung hsüeh wen k'u*.] Shanghai. (First published Ch'ungking and Shanghai, 1945, as *Ch'ing shih ta kang*.)

HSIAO KUNG-CH'UAN, 1953. 'Rural Control in Nineteenth Century China', *Far Eastern Quarterly*, vol. xii, pp. 173–81.

HSIEH PAO-CHAO, 1925. *The Government of China* (1644–1911). Baltimore.

HSÜ, F. L. K., 1940. 'The Problem of Incest Tabu in a North China Village', *American Anthropologist*, vol. 42, pp. 122–35.

— 1948. *Under the Ancestors' Shadow*. New York.

HSÜ, L. SHIH-LIEN, 1932. *The Political Philosophy of Confucianism, an interpretation of the social and political ideas of Confucius, his forerunners and his early disciples*. London.

HU HSIEN-CHIN, 1944. 'The Chinese Concepts of "Face",' *American Anthropologist*, vol. 46, pp. 45–65.

— 1948. *The Common Descent Group in China and its Functions*. Viking Fund Publications in Anthropology, no. 10, New York.

HULSEWÉ, A. F. P., 1955. *Remnants of Han Law*, vol. i. Sinica Leidensia, vol. ix. Leiden.

HUMMEL, A. W., 1948. 'Portrait of a Scholar', in *There is another China: Essays presented to Chang Po-ling of Nankai University*. New York, Columbia University, pp. 131–50.

— (ed.), 1943. *Eminent Chinese of the Ch'ing Period* (1644–1912), 2 vols. (vol. ii, 1944). Washington, D.C.

'An old resident' [HUNTER, W. C.], 1882. *The 'Fan Kwae' at Canton*. London.

— 1885. *Bits of Old China*. London.

[Both published anonymously.]

HUTSON, J., 1921. *Chinese Life in the Tibetan Foothills*. Shanghai. (Serialized in the *New China Review*, vols. i and ii, 1919 and 1920.)

R. I[NGLIS], 1835–6. 'Notices of Modern China', *Chinese Repository*, vol. iv, pp. 17–29, 59–72, 118–35, 214–29, 262–8, 361–92, 415–25, 557–65.

JAMIESON, G. (ed.), 1888. 'The Tenure of Land in China and the Condition of the Rural Population', *Journal of the North China Branch, Royal Asiatic Society*, vol. xxiii, pp. 59–174.

— 1880–2. 'Translation from the *Lü-li*, or General Code of Laws', *China Review*, vol. viii, pp. 1–18, 193–205, 259–76, 357–63; vol. ix, pp. 129–36, 343–50; vol. x, pp. 77–79.

— 1921. *Chinese Family and Commercial Law*. Shanghai.

JERNIGAN, T. R., 1905. *China in Law and Commerce*. New York.

KAHN-FREUND, O., 1954. 'Inter-group Conflicts and their Settlement', *British Journal of Sociology*, vol. v, pp. 193–227.

KATO, SHIGESHI, 1936. 'On the Hang or Association of Merchants in China'. *Memoirs of Tōyō Bunkō* [in English], pp. 60–79.

KEETON, G. W., 1928. The Development of Extraterritoriality in China. 2 vols. London.

KENNEDY, G. A., 1939. *Die Rolle des Geständnisses im chinesischen Gesetz*. Berlin. [Includes glossary of legal terms and bibliography.]

KOTENEV, A. M., 1925. *Shanghai : its Mixed Court and Council*. Shanghai.

KROKER, E. J. M., 1955. Rechtsgewohnheiten in der Provinz Shantung. *Monumenta Serica*, vol. xiv, pp. 215–302.

— 1957. 'Dienst - und Werkverträge im chinesischen Gewohnheitsrecht', *Zeitschrift der Deutschen Morgenländischen Gesellschaft*, Band 107, pp. 130–60.

KULP, D. H., 1925. *Country Life in South China, the Sociology of Familism*, volume i, Phenix Village, Kwangtung, China. New York.

LACOUR-GAYET, J., 1953. *Histoire du commerce; tome III, Le commerce extra-européen jusqu'aux temps modernes*. Paris.

LANG, O., 1946. *Chinese Family and Society*. New Haven.

LAU, D. C., 1953. Theories of Human Nature in Mencius and Shyuntzyy. *Bulletin of the School of Oriental and African Studies*, vol. xv, pp. 541–65.

LAUFER, B., 1919. *Sino-Iranica. Chinese Contributions to the History of Civilisation in Ancient Iran*. Chicago Field Museum of Natural History, Anthropological series, vol. xv, no. 3.

LEGGE, J., 1895. *The Chinese Classics*, 7 vols. (2nd edition). Oxford.

— 1899. *The Texts of Confucianism*. Sacred Books of the East series, vols. iii and xiv, (2nd edition). Oxford.

LEONG, Y. K., and TAO, L. K., 1915. *Village and Town Life in China*. London.

'LEX', 1873. 'The administration of Chinese Law', *China Review*, vol. ii, pp. 230–44.

LIND, A., 1887. *A Chapter of the Chinese Penal Code*. Leiden.

LINGAT, R., 1952. *Les régimes matrimoniaux du sud-est de l'Asie*. 2 vols. Hanoi.

LIN YÜEH-HWA, 1936. 'The Chinese Clan Village: an enquiry from the anthropological point of view.' [In Chinese.] *She hui hsüeh chieh*, no. 9.

— 1948. *The Golden Wing. A sociological study of Chinese Familism*. London.

LIU, HUI-CHEN WANG, 1959. (1) *The Traditional Chinese Clan Rules*. New York.

— 1959. (2) 'An Analysis of Chinese Clan Rules: Confucian Theories in Action', in Nivison, D. S. and Wright, A. F. (editors), *Confucianism in Action*. Stanford.

MCALEAVY. H., 1955. Certain aspects of Chinese customary law in the light of Japanese scholarship, *Bulletin of the School of Oriental and African Studies*, vol. 17, pp. 535-47.

MACGOWAN, D. G., 1886. 'Chinese Guilds or Chambers of Commerce and Trades Unions', *Journal of the North China Branch, Royal Asiatic Society*, vol. xxi, pp. 133–92.

MCHUGH, F. and I., 1958. *The Dream of the Red Chamber : a Chinese novel of the early Ch'ing period*. (Translated from the German version of Kuhn, F.) London and New York.

MAITLAND, F. W., 1936. *The Forms of Action at Common Law*. Cambridge. [Reprinted from *Equity*, Cambridge, 1909.]

MAO TUN (ed.), 1935. *Hung Lou Meng* [Dream of the Red Chamber]. Shanghai.

MARETT, R. R., 1936. 'The Nature of the Sanction in Primitive Law', *Zeitschrift für vergleichende Rechtswissenschaft*, vol. 50, pp. 63–69.

MARTIN, R. M., 1847. See under Official Compilations (at end).
MAYERS, W. F., 1877. *The Chinese Government.* Shanghai.
— 1896. 3rd edition revised by Playfair, G. M. H. Shanghai.
MEADOWS, T. T., 1847. *Desultory Notes on the Government and People of China and on the Chinese Language. . . .* London.
— 1856. *The Chinese and their Rebellions.* London. [Reprinted Stanford, 1955.]
MEIJER, M. J., 1949. *The Introduction of Modern Criminal Law in China.* Batavia.
MILNE, W., 1817. *The Sacred Edict.* London. [Reprinted Shanghai, 1870.]
MÖLLENDORFF, P. G. VON, 1879, 1893. 'The Family Law of the Chinese'. *Journal of the North China Branch, Royal Asiatic Society*, vol. xiii, pp. 99–121, vol. xxvii, pp. 131–90.
— 1895. *Das chinesische Familienrecht.* Shanghai.
[MORRISON, J. R.], 1835. 'The Chinese Government and Constitution', *Chinese Repository*, vol. iv, pp. 11–17, 135–152, 181–9, 276–87. [Unsigned but so attributed by Cordier.]
MORSE, H. B., 1921. *The Trade and Administration of China.* Shanghai. (1st edition 1908).
NEEDHAM, J. (with WANG LING), 1954. *Science and Civilisation in China.* Vol. I, *Introductory, Orientations.* Cambridge.
— 1956. *Vol. II, The History of Scientific Thought.* Cambridge.
NIIDA NOBORU, 1952. *Chukoku Hosei Shi.* [History of Chinese Legal Institutions]. (In Japanese.) Tokyo.
ORCHARD, J. E., 1937. Contrasts in the Progress of Industrialisation in China and Japan. *Political Science Quarterly*, vol. lii, pp. 18–50.
PEAKE, C. H., 1937. 'Recent Studies in Chinese Law', *Political Science Quarterly*, vol. lii, pp. 117–38.
PRESTON, C. F., 1877. 'Constitutional Law of the Chinese Empire', *China Review*, vol. vi, pp. 13–29.
RADCLIFFE-BROWN, A. R., 1933. Law, Primitive, in *Encyclopaedia of the Social Sciences.*
RATCHNEVSKY, P., 1937. *Un code des Yüan.* Paris.
READ, T. T., 1937. 'Chinese Iron—a puzzle', *Harvard Journal of Asiatic Studies*, vol. ii, pp. 398–407.
REDFIELD, R., 1956. *Peasant Society and Culture, an anthropological approach.* Chicago.
ROSTHORN, A. VON, 1923. 'Religion und Wirtschaft in China', in *Hauptprobleme der Soziologie: Erinnerungsgabe für Max Weber*, 2 vols., edited by Palyi, M., Munich.
SANSOM, G. B., 1946. *Japan, a short cultural history.* (Revised edition). London.
SCARBOROUGH, W., 1926. *A Collection of Chinese Proverbs.* (Revised by Allen, C. W.) Shanghai.
SCHERZER, F., 1878. *La puissance paternelle en Chine: étude de droit chinois.* Paris.
SCHURMANN, H. F., 1956. 'Traditional Property Concepts in China', *Far Eastern Quarterly*, vol. 15, pp. 507–16.
SMITH, A. H., 1899. *Village Life in China, a study in Sociology.* New York.
SNOW, E., 1941. *The Battle for Asia.* New York. [Published London also 1941, as *Scorched Earth.*]

SOOTHILL, W. (translator), 1910. *The Analects of Confucius*. London.
— 1937. Republished in The World's Classics, Oxford. (Reprinted 1941.)
STAUNTON, G. T., 1810. *Ta Tsing Leu Lee, being the Fundamental Laws and a selection from the Supplementary Statutes of the Penal Code of China*. London.
STEELE, J., 1917. *The I Li or book of etiquette and ceremonial translated from the Chinese*. London.
TAAM CHEUK-WOON, 1935. *The Development of Chinese Libraries under the Ch'ing Dynasty*, 1644–1911. Shanghai.
TAWNEY, R. H., 1932. *Land and Labour in China*. London.
TENG SSU-YÜ and FAIRBANK, J. K., *China's Response to the West*. Cambridge Mass.
TWITCHETT, D. C., 1959. 'The Fan Clan's Charitable Estate, 1050–1760', in Nivison, D. S. and Wright, A. F. (editors), *Confucianism in Action*. Stanford.
VALK, M. H. VAN DER, 1951. *De Regel Nullem Crimen sine Lege en het Chinese Recht*. Leiden.
— 1956. *Conservatism in Modern Chinese Family Law*. Leiden.
VAN GULIK, R. H., 1949. *Dee Goong An, Three Murder Cases solved by Judge Dee—an ancient Chinese detective story*. Tokyo.
— 1956. *T'ang-yin-pi-shih: Parallel cases from under the Pear-tree, a thirteenth century manual of jurisprudence and detection*. Sinica Leidensia, vol. x. Leiden. [Introduction to the translation has section: 'Court Procedure in Ancient China', pp. 46–64.]
VINOGRADOFF, P., 1920. *Outlines of Historical Jurisprudence*. London.
WALEY, A., 1938. *The Analects of Confucius*. London.
— 1939. *Three Ways of Thought in Ancient China*. London.
— 1956. *Yüan Mei, Eighteenth Century Chinese Poet*. London.
WEBER, M., 1954. (Translated by Shils, E. A. and Rheinstein, M.) *Law in Economy and Society*. 20th Century Legal Philosophy Series, vol. vi. Cambridge, Mass.
WEN CHÜN-T'IEN, 1935. *Chung-kuo Pao-chia Chih-tu*. (The Pao-chia System in China.) Shanghai.
WERNER, E. T. C., 1917. *Law*. (Article in Couling (ed.): *Encyclopaedia Sinica*.)
WIENS, H. J., 1954. *China's March toward the Tropics*. Hamden, Conn.
WIGMORE, J. H. (ed.), 1892. 'Materials for the Study of Private Law in Old Japan', Supplement (in three parts) to *Transactions of the Asiatic Society of Japan*, vol. xx.
WILLIAMS, S. W., 1900. *The Middle Kingdom*. 2 vols. (Revised edition.) New York. [Original edition 1848; published London, 1883.]
WIST, H., 1938. 'Die Yao in Südchina nach Berichte neuer chinesischer Feldforschungen', *Baessler-Archiv Beiträge zur Völkerkunde*, Band XXI, Heft 3, pp. 73–135.
WITTFOGEL, K. A., 1957. *Oriental Despotism*. New Haven.
WOU MON-PENG, 1931. *L'évolution des Corporations ouvrières et commerciales dans la Chine contemporaine*. Paris.
WRIGHT, A. F., 1959. *Buddhism in Chinese History*. Stanford.
WRIGHT, M. C., 1957. *The Last Stand of Chinese Conservatism*. Stanford.
WRIGHT, S. F., 1950. *Hart and the Chinese Customs*. Belfast.

WU CHING-HSÜ, 1958. 'Chinese Legal Philosophy: a brief historical survey', *Chinese Culture*, vol. i, no. 4, pp. 7–48.

YANG, M. C., 1945. *A Chinese Village. Taitou, Shantung Province.* New York. (Published London, 1948.)

YANG LIEN-SHENG, 1946. 'Notes on the Economic History of the Chin Dynasty', *Harvard Journal of Asiatic Studies*, vol. ix, pp. 128–72.

— 1952. *Money and Credit in China, a short history.* Cambridge, Mass.

ZI [SIU], E., 1894. *Pratique des examens littéraires en Chine.* Variétés sinologiques, no. 5. Shanghai.

ZÜRCHER, E., 1959. *The Buddhist Conquest of China.* 2 vols. Sinica Leidensia, vol. xi. Leiden.

UNSIGNED ARTICLE, 1890. 'The Natural History of a Chinese Girl', *Journal of the Royal Anthropological Society of Bombay*, 1890, vol. ii, pp. 224 ff. (condensed from the *N. China Herald*).

OFFICIAL COMPILATIONS AND REPORTS

I. *In Chinese*

1927–8. *Ch'ing Shih Kao*: ch. 149–51, *Hsing fa chih.* [Legal monograph of the Ch'ing dynastic history.]

1952. *Chung-kuo chin-tai-shih tzu-liao ts'ung-k'an, II: T'ai-p'ing T'ien-kuo.* [General outline of materials on modern Chinese history, 2nd series: The T'ai-p'ing Heavenly kingdom.]

1957. *Chung-kuo fa-chih-shih ts'an-k'ao shu-mu chien-chieh.* [Short bibliography of works on the history of Chinese legal institutions.] Peking, Legal Publishing Society. (Fa-lü ch'u-pan shih.)

1834. *Hsing-an hui-lan* [Collection of criminal cases], in 69 chapters, edited by Pao Shu-yün.

1930. *Min shang shih hsi-kuan t'iao-ch'a pao-kao lu.* [Collected reports of an investigation into civil and commercial legal customs.] Nanking.

Ta Ch'ing hui-tien. [Collected statutes of the Ch'ing dynasty.] Editions 1690, 1732, 1764, 1818, 1899. Peking.

Ta Ch'ing lü li. [Penal code of the Ch'ing dynasty.] Peking.

1918. *Ta-li-yüan p'an-li yao-chih hui lan.* [Collection of decisions of the Supreme Court, 1912–18.]

II. *In western languages*

1847. *China; political, commercial and social; in an official report to Her Majesty's Government.* [By Martin, R. M.] London.

1953. *Chinese Law and Custom in Hong Kong: Report of a committee appointed by the Governor.* [Chairman: Strickland, G.] Hong Kong.

1923. *Chinese Supreme Court Decisions (relating to general principles of civil law, obligations and commercial law)*, translated by Cheng, F. T. [from 1918 collection, see above]. Peking. [Commission on Extraterritoriality.]

1924. *Recueil des sommaires de la jurisprudence de la Cour suprême de la République de Chine, en matière civile et commerciale* (1912–18). Pekin. [Fuller than English version, and with introduction by Escarra.]

1931. *Report of the Hon. Richard Feetham, C.M.G. Judge of the Supreme Court of the Union of South Africa to the Shanghai Municipal Council.* 3 vols. Shanghai.

Supplementary Bibliography (1966)

BALAZS, E., 1964. *Chinese Civilization and Bureaucracy*. New Haven and London.

BODDE, D., 1963. 'Basic Concepts of Chinese Law: the Genesis and Evolution of Legal Thought in Traditional China', *Proceedings of the American Philosophical Society*, vol. 107, pp. 375–98.

CHANG CHIN-TSEN, 1960. 'Li and Law', *Chinese Culture*, vol. II, no. 4, pp. 1–16.

CHANG CHUNG-LI, 1962. *The Income of the Chinese Gentry*. Seattle.

CHESNEAUX, J. 1962. *Le mouvement ouvrier Chinois, de 1919 à 1927*. Paris and The Hague.

— 1965. *Les sociétés secrètes en Chine*. Paris.

CH'Ü T'UNG-TSU, 1961. *Law and Society in Traditional China*. Paris and The Hague.

— 1962. *Local Government in China under the Ch'ing*. Harvard.

GAMBLE, S. D. 1963. *North China Villages*. Berkeley and Los Angeles.

HARRISON, J. F. 1964. 'Wrongful Treatment of Prisoners: A Case Study of Ch'ing Legal Practice.' *Journal of Asian Studies*, vol. XXIII, no. 2, pp. 227–44.

HART, H. L. A., 1961. *The Concept of Law*. London.

HO P'ING-TI, 1962. *The Ladder of Success in Imperial China*. New York and London.

— 1954. 'The Salt Merchants of Yang-chou: a study of Commercial Capitalism in Eighteenth Century China', *Harvard Journal of Asiatic Studies*, vol. XVII, pp. 130–68.

HSIAO KUNG-CHUAN, 1960. *Rural China: Imperial Control in the Nineteenth Century*. Seattle.

HUCKER, C. O., 1958. 'Governmental Organization in the Ming Dynasty', *Harvard Journal of Asiatic Studies*, vol. XXI, pp. 1–67.

KROKER, E., 1959. 'The Concept of Property in Chinese Customary Law', *Transactions of the Asiatic Society of Japan*, 3rd ser. vol. VII, pp. 123–46.

MARSH, R. M., 1961. *The Mandarins: the Circulation of Elites in China, 1600–1900*. Glencoe.

PHILASTRE, P. L. F., 1876. *Le Code Annamite*. (2 vols.) Paris.

SAWER, G., 1965. *Law in Society*. Oxford.

SKINNER, G. W., 1964–5. 'Marketing and Social Structure in Rural China', *Journal of Asian Studies*, vol. XXIV, pp. 3–43, 195–228, 363–99.

YANG CH'ING-K'UN (C. K. YANG), 1944. *A North China Local Market Economy* (IPR mimeo). New York.

— 1963. *Religion in Chinese Society*. Berkeley and Los Angeles.

Additional Bibliography (1977)

BODDE, D. and MORRIS, C., 1967. *Law in Imperial China Exemplified by 190 Cases, with Historical, Social and Juridical Commentaries.* Cambridge, Mass.

BUXBAUM, DAVID C., 1966. 'Chinese Family Law in a Common Law Setting', in *Journal of Asian Studies*, vol. XXV, no. 4, pp. 621–44, reprinted 1968 in Buxbaum (ed.) *Family Law and Customary Law in Asia.*

— 1971. 'Some Aspects of Civil Procedure and Practice at the Trial Level in Tanshui and Hsinchu from 1789 to 1895' in *Journal of Asian Studies*, vol. XXX, no. 2, pp. 255–79.

— (ed.) 1967. *Traditional and Modern Legal Institutions in Asia and Africa.* Leiden.

CH'EN FU-MEI CHANG, 1969. 'On Law in Imperial China', *Harvard Journal of Asiatic Studies*, vol. 29, pp. 274–84.

— 1970. 'On Analogy in Ch'ing Law', *Harvard Journal of Asiatic Studies*, vol. 30, pp. 212–24.

— 1969 and 1970 reprinted together as *Harvard Law School Studies in Chinese Law* no. 14.

— 1975. 'Local Control of Convicted Thieves in Eighteenth Century China', in Wakeman, F. and Grant, C. (editors), *Conflict and Control in Late Imperial China*, Berkeley, Los Angeles and London.

COHEN, JEROME ALAN, 1966. 'Chinese Mediation on the Eve of Modernization', *Cal. Law Review* LIX, pp. 1201–26, reprinted in Buxbaum (ed.) 1967 and *Harvard Law School Studies in Chinese Law* no. 3.

COHEN, J. A., EDWARDS, R. R. and CH'EN FU-MEI CHANG, 1978. *China's Legal Tradition.* Princeton U.P.

LUBMAN, S., 1967. 'Mao and Mediation', *Cal. Law Review*, vol. 55, pp. 1284–359.

METZGER, THOS. A., 1973. *The Internal Organization of Ch'ing Bureaucracy: legal, normative and communication aspects*, Harvard Studies in East Asian Law no. 7, Cambridge, Mass.

SHIGA SHUZO, 1967. 'Some Remarks on the Judicial System in China: Historical Development and Characteristics' in Buxbaum (ed.) 1967, pp. 44–53.

— 1974, 1975. 'Criminal Procedure in the Ch'ing Dynasty with Emphasis on its Administrative Character and Some Allusion to its Historical Antecedents' (I) and (II), *Memoirs of Toyo Bunko*, no. 32, pp. 1–45 and no. 33, pp. 115–38.

VAN DER SPRENKEL, S., 1974. 'Chinese Law' in *Encyclopaedia Britannica* (15th edn.), pp. 407–10.

— 1977. 'Urban Social Control' in Skinner, G. W. (ed.) *The city in late imperial China.* Stanford, pp. 609–32.

WATSON, JAMES L., 1970. 'Chattel Slavery in Chinese Peasant Society; A Comparative Analysis', *Ethnology*, vol. XV, no. 4, pp. 361–75.

WATT, JOHN R., 1972. *The district magistrate in late imperial China*, Studies of the East Asian Institute, Columbia. New York and London.

Postscript to Chapter 6 (1977)

Recent work, and particularly an investigation of the legal archive for a district of Taiwan in the Ch'ing period,[1] suggests that some statements made in this chapter need qualification.

In the judicial practice of the period a distinction was made procedurally between civil and criminal cases ; and cases in the recognised civil category (*min sung*)—having to do mainly with marriage, property and inheritance—were entered and accepted for adjudication, and even appeal to higher authority, without any penal implication. The fact that it was normal for such cases to be finally dealt with at provincial level meant that they were rarely included in compilations made by Imperial authority, so they have been less noticed by scholars.

I must admit to having concentrated when writing this chapter on criminal matters and to having thus excluded from view some indications even then available (in the reminiscences of legal secretaries, for example) that this was not quite the whole story.[2] I should, if writing today, express myself more cautiously than I did for example in the second and third paragraphs of page 69.

It has been pointed out also that the method of selecting evidence from nineteenth century accounts—a period when China was beset by special problems within and without—can lead to too great a stress on maladministration and harshness. This criticism deserves consideration, though I would not agree that all nineteenth century observers were predisposed to undervalue Chinese institutions.

[1] See Buxbaum (1971).
[2] See also Watt (1972) ch. 15.

Character Index

Characters for Chinese and Japanese names and expressions

An ch'a shih ssu	按察使司
an lin	按臨
chang (p. 57)	掌
chang (p. 61)	杖
chao hsü	招壻
Cheh-yü-kuei-chien	折獄龜鑑
Cheng (Prince)	政
Cheng k'ao kuan	正考官
Cheng shih	正史
chia (p. 14)	家
chia (p. 47)	甲
chia chang	家長
Chia Ch'ung	賈充
Chieh i shen	戒已甚
chieh-mei	介媒
chieh-shao	介紹
chien t'iao	兼祧
Chien tien shu li	檢點書吏
chih hsien	知縣
Ching pao	京報
Chin (dynasty [A.D.])	晉
Chin ku ch'i kuan	今古奇觀
chin shih	進士
Chin shu	晉書
chou	州

Chou Li	周禮
chuang	莊
Chukoku hosei shi	中國法制史
chung-jen	中人
Chung-kuo chin-tai shih tzu-liao ts'ung-k'an	中國近代史資料叢刊
Chung-kuo chiao-yü shih	中國教育史
Chung-kuo fa-chih shih ts'an-k'ao shu-mu chien-chieh	中國法制史叅考書目簡介
Chung-kuo fa-lü yü Chung-kuo she-hui	中國法律與中國社會
Chung-kuo pao-chia chih-tu	中國保甲制度
chung-pao-jen	中保人
Chung san, tai erh.	中三代二
Chü (feudal state)	莒
chü-jen	舉人
Chü jen mieh Tseng.	莒人滅鄫
Chü T'ung-tsu	瞿同祖
Chün chi ch'u	軍機處
chün-t'ien	均田
Ch'a ping chü pu i ch'ai	差稟拒捕宜察
ch'ang she	常赦
Ch'en Ch'un	陳淳
Ch'en Tung-yüan	陳東原
ch'eng an	成案
ch'eng t'iao	承祧
ch'i	妻
ch'i-yang	乞養
ch'iang-tuo	搶奪
ch'ieh	妾
Ch'ien-ku shih-yeh	錢穀師爺
ch'ih	笞

Ch'in (dynasty [B.C.])	秦
Ch'in shih	勤事
Ch'in Hsiu	秦秀
Ch'ing (dynasty)	清
ch'ing-shih	情實
Ch'ing Shih Kao	清史稿
Ch'ing-tai shih	清代史
Ch'iu Shen	秋審
Ch'u-hsien	滁縣
Ch'uan Miao	川苗
Ch'un Ch'iu Fan Lu	春秋繁露
Cohong [kung-hang]	公行
Dee Goong An [Ti Kung-an]	狄公案
fa	法
Fa-chia	法家
fa-lü	法律
Fa-lü Ch'u-pan She	法律出版社
fan	凡
Fan Nieh Liang Ssu	藩臬兩司
fan tso	反坐
fang (pp. 18, 80)	房
fang (p. 48)	坊
Fang an i shen	訪案宜愼
fang-chang	房長
Fen hsün tao	分巡道
fu	府
fu-mu kuan	父母官
Fu nü pu k'o ch'ing huan	婦女不可輕喚
Han-lin yüan	翰林院

Han Pi	韓謚
hang	行
hang-i	行役
ho	和
hong [hang]	行
hsi	徙
Hsi sung	息訟
Hsi yüan lu	洗寃錄
hsiang	廂
hsiao	孝
Hsiao-shan	蕭山
Hsiao I-shan	蕭一山
hsien	縣
Hsin Chung-hsüeh wen-ku	新中學文庫
Hsing-an hui-lan	刑案匯覽
hsing fa	刑罰
Hsing-fa chih	刑法志
Hsing-ming shih-yeh	刑名師爺
Hsing Pu	刑部
Hsi Yin Hsien Ts'ung-shu	惜陰軒叢書
hsiu ts'ai	秀才
Hsü wen hsien t'ung k'ao	續文獻通考
Hsü t'i su ch'ing	須體俗情
Hsüeh Cheng	學政
Hsün-fu	巡撫
hu	戶
hu fu	護符
hu kuan fu	護官符
Hu Pu	戶部

hu-t'ung	衚衕
huan chüeh	緩決
hui-kuan	會館
Hung Lou Meng	紅樓夢
i	義
I Li (p.34n. and bibliography)	儀禮
i li (p.31)	以禮
I-Yü-Chi	疑獄集
jang	讓
kan-ch'ing	感情
kao feng	誥封
ku sha	故殺
kuan	官
kuan tang	官當
kuo fang	過房
kung-hang	公行
Kung Pu	工部
kung-suo	公所
Kung Yang (commentary)	公羊
Kuo tzu chien	國子監
k'o chin	可矜
k'ung	控
lee [li]	例
leu [lü]	律
li (pp. 31, 125)	禮
li (pp. 18, 47, 62)	里
li (p. 56 ff.)	例
Li Chi	禮記
li-fa	禮法

Li Fan Yüan	理藩院
Li K'uei	李悝
Li Pu (Department of Civil Office)	吏部
Li Pu (Department of Ceremonies)	禮部
liang	良
Liang chien hsiang ou	良賤相毆
Liang Jen-kung	梁任公
Liang tao	糧道
lien	臉
Lin Yüeh-hwa	林耀華
ling	令
ling-ch'ih	凌遲
liu	流
lü	律
lü-li	律例
Lü Pu-wei	呂不韋
Mao Tun	茅盾
mien-tzu	面子
Min shang shih hsi-kuan t'iao-ch'a pao-kao lu	民商事習慣調查報告錄
ming (p. 28)	命
ming (p. 80)	名
Ming an cha ch'ing hsing	命案察情形
ming-ling	螟蛉
mu	畝
Mu-k'e	幕客
Mu-yu	幕友
Nei ko	內閣
Niu [Něw]	牛
nu-pei	奴婢

nu-p'u	奴僕
pa k'ou chih chia	八口之家
pai chang	百丈
pao	保
pao-chia	保甲
pao-chang	保長
pao-jen	保人
Pao Shu-yün	鮑書芸
Pei ch'i tzu-i	北溪字義
Ping Pu	兵部
Po an hsin pien	駁案新編
Pu cheng shih ssu	布政使司
pu ching	不敬
pu tao	不道
pu yao lien	不要臉
pu ying wei	不應爲
p'ai (p. 18)	派
p'ai (p. 47)	牌
p'ai-chang	派長
p'ai ming	派名
San Fa Ssu	三法司
"Shang yu wu hou chih ts'ung tsu fu shih"	殤與無後者從祖祔食
Shao-hsing-fu	紹興府
she-chang	社長
She-hui hsüeh chieh	社會學界
Shen ch'u pao	愼初報
shen shih	紳士
Sheng	省
sheng ch'eng	省城

Sheng shih	省事
Sheng yü	聖諭
sheng-yüan	生員
shichi ire	質入
Shih-chia-chuang	石家莊
shih-li	事例
shou fu	首府
shou hsien	首縣
shu (p. 32)	術
shu (diagram p. 45)	署
shu su	屬疏
Shu-sun Pao	叔孫豹
Souei-chou [Sui shu]	隋書
Sui (dynasty)	隋
Sung Tzu	宋慈
ssu chi	嗣繼
Ssu kang seng	司綱僧
Ta Ch'ing Lü-li	大淸律例
Ta Ch'ing Hui-tien	大淸會典
Ta Ch'ing Hui-tien shih-li	大淸會典事例
Ta Chiu Ch'ing	大九卿
Ta-li-yüan p'an-li yao-che hui-lan	大理院判例要旨匯覽
Ta Li Ssu	大理寺
ta ni	大逆
ta sheh	大赦
Ta Tsing Leu Lee [Ta Ch'ing Lü-li]	大淸律例
tai shu	代署
tao (p. 28)	道
tao (p. 45)	道

Tao an shen chu lei	盜案慎株累
Tao t'ai	道台
Tchou Li [Chou Li]	周禮
te	德
tei tō	抵當
ten	典
ti-pao	地保
tien-mai	典買
tien-tang	典當
ting	鼎
Ting Hsien	定縣
tou sha	鬪殺
Tōyō Bunko	東洋文庫
Tu-ch'a yüan	都察院
Tu lü	讀律
Tu shu	讀書
Tung san sheng	東三省
Tu-fu ssu tao	督撫司道
Tung Chung-shu	董仲舒
T'ai-p'ing	太平
T'ai-p'ing t'ien-kuo	太平天國
T'ai-p'ing t'ien-kuo ts'ung-shu	太平天國叢書
T'ang-yin-pi-shih	棠陰比事
t'iao	條
t'iao-t'ing	調停
t'ien	天
T'ien-ch'ao t'ien-mu chih-tu	天朝田畝制度
t'ing	廳
t'u kuan	土官
t'u ssu	土司

T'ung cheng ssu	通政司
t'ung hsüeh	同學
t'ung tsung	同宗
Tse-li	則例
Tseng-tzu	鄫子
Tso-chih yao-yen	佑治藥言
Tso Chuan	左傳
tsu	族
tsu-chang	族長
tsung-tsu	宗族
tsung-tu	總督
Ts'ien Han Shu[Ch'ien Han Shu]	前漢書
Tzu-p'ai	字派
Tz'u sung su chieh	詞訟速結
Wang Hui-tsu	汪輝祖
Wang Tao	王韜
Wang Yu-p'u	王又樸
wei min	爲民
Wen Chün-t'ien	聞鈞天
Wen-hsien t'ung-k'ao	文獻通考
wo-hsüan	斡旋
Wu ch'ing yin ch'eng an	勿輕引成案
wu fu	五服
wu hsing	五刑
wu-tso	仵作
yamen	衙門
Yao	搖
Yen yün shih ssu	鹽運使司
Yen chih ti kun	嚴治地棍
yung-tien	永佃

General Index